Charles Barnes Upton

Lectures on the Bases of religious Belief

Charles Barnes Upton

Lectures on the Bases of religious Belief

ISBN/EAN: 9783337130947

Printed in Europe, USA, Canada, Australia, Japan

Cover: Foto ©ninafisch / pixelio.de

More available books at **www.hansebooks.com**

THE HIBBERT LECTURES, 1893.

LECTURES

ON THE

BASES OF RELIGIOUS BELIEF.

DELIVERED IN OXFORD AND LONDON

IN APRIL AND MAY, 1893.

BY

CHARLES B. UPTON, B.A., B.Sc.

PROFESSOR OF PHILOSOPHY IN MANCHESTER COLLEGE.

WILLIAMS AND NORGATE,

14, HENRIETTA STREET, COVENT GARDEN, LONDON;
AND 20, SOUTH FREDERICK STREET, EDINBURGH.

1894.

[*All Rights reserved.*]

LONDON:
PRINTED BY C. GREEN AND SON,
178, STRAND.

TO

MY REVERED TEACHER IN PHILOSOPHY,

THE REV. JAMES MARTINEAU,

LL.D., S.T.D., D.D., D.C.L., D.Litt.,

WITH DEEP ADMIRATION FOR HIS EMINENT GENIUS,

AND WARMEST GRATITUDE FOR VERY MANY PROOFS OF HIS EVER-READY PERSONAL KINDNESS.

"Welche Religion ich bekenne ?   Keine von allen,
Die du mir nennst !—Und warum keine ?   Aus Religion."
Schiller.

Ἡ βασιλεία τοῦ θεοῦ ἐντὸς ὑμῶν ἐστίν.
Καὶ οὐκ εἰμὶ μόνος, ὅτι ὁ πατὴρ μετ' ἐμοῦ ἐστί.
Μακάριοι οἱ καθαροὶ τῇ καρδίᾳ, ὅτι αὐτοὶ τὸν θεὸν ὄψονται.
Sayings of Jesus of Nazareth

"The Kingdom of Heaven is within, but we must also make it without."—*Florence Nightingale.*

PREFACE.

These elementary Lectures on the Philosophy of Religion have been delivered and published mainly in the hope that they may prove in some measure helpful to those persons who have ceased to see in an external, miraculously-attested Revelation a satisfactory foundation for Religious Belief, and are seeking a rational basis for faith which shall be in harmony with that general theory of the cosmos to which the soundest science and philosophy of our time appear to lend the strongest support. In this respect, accordingly, the present volume may, perhaps, be found of some service as an introduction to far more elaborate and important works, such as are Dr. Martineau's two treatises, "A Study of Religion," and "The Seat of Authority in Religion."

While recent books on religious philosophy from an "orthodox" standpoint (such as Dr. Fairbairn's erudite and thoughtful treatise on "The Place of Christ in

Modern Theology") represent all that is deepest and most precious in both Ethics and Religion as derived from an abnormal and wholly exceptional disclosure made to humanity through the Incarnation of the Second Person of a tri-une Godhead, the aim in these Lectures is to find a natural and rational ground for Theism in the normal self-consciousness of mankind. Hence, while it is maintained in this volume that the Incarnation or felt Immanence of God in man's rational, ethical and spiritual nature is the only solid foundation of a satisfying theistic faith, the Incarnation here contended for, though, in my view, most completely manifested in the personality and teachings of Jesus of Nazareth, is by no means peculiar to him, but is, in its essence, the intrinsic property and highest privilege of all rational souls. Accordingly, I heartily accept Dr. Lyman Abbott's happy characterization of Jesus as the "greatest religious genius" of our race, but I give to that expression a breadth of meaning, and carry it out to logical issues, which Dr. Abbott, and his *confrères* of the neo-orthodox school, are evidently, at present, quite unprepared to endorse.

The philosophical writers whose works have had the greatest influence on the composition of these Lectures are Dr. James Martineau and the late Prof. Hermann Lotze;

and the position of these two distinguished thinkers on the basal question of the Freedom of the Will is accepted and expounded. On some points, however, of which the more important are, (1) the exact relation of God's direct Causality to physical phenomena, and (2) the question why our Ethical Ideals are felt to carry with them an absolute authority, there will be found some difference, though, I think, of only a superficial character, between Dr. Martineau's views and those set forth in Lectures VI. and VII.; and my treatment of the "problem of evil" deviates in some degree from that sketched in Sections 70—74 of Lotze's *Grundzüge der Religionsphilosophie*. A Lecture has been devoted to the criticism of that form of religious philosophy known as Absolute Idealism, or Hegelianism; and though for the reasons there given I feel myself utterly unable to accept that system as a whole, I am well aware that I owe much to the writings of T. H. Green and of the gifted brothers Caird, as well as to the privilege of personal converse with some of the younger members of this interesting and influential philosophical fraternity. The general theory of the universe, which links together the subjects of the several Lectures, agrees in the main with that which is presented in such fascinating shape in Lotze's *Mikrokosmus*.

I gladly avail myself of these prefatory words to give expression to my grateful sense of twofold indebtedness to the Hibbert Trustees, first, for the great and timely advantages I enjoyed, many years ago, as a Hibbert Scholar and Fellow, and now again for the valued opportunity of offering this small contribution towards the study of a difficult and important subject.

CHARLES B. UPTON.

LITTLEMORE,
    Feb. 27th, 1894.

TABLE OF CONTENTS.

LECTURE I.
	PAGE
INTRODUCTION. THE NATURE OF RELIGIOUS BELIEF	1

LECTURE II.
SPIRITUAL INSIGHT	64

LECTURE III.
AGNOSTICISM	97

LECTURE IV.
CULTURE AND RELIGIOUS BELIEF:
   I. Culture and Dogmatic Religion ... 125

LECTURE V.
CULTURE AND RELIGIOUS BELIEF:
   II. Culture and Rational Religion ... 147

LECTURE VI.
GOD AS GROUND AND CAUSE OF THE COSMOS	194

LECTURE VII.
GOD AS THE SOURCE OF IDEALS	235

LECTURE VIII.

PAGE

ABSOLUTE IDEALISM (including the discussion of the Freedom of the Will) 278

LECTURE IX.

ETHICAL THEISM (including the question of Individual Immortality) 328

Lecture I.

NATURE OF RELIGIOUS BELIEF.

The aim of the previous Lectures which have been delivered under the auspices of the Hibbert Trustees differs in one very important respect from the aim of the present course. Religion has been discussed by my predecessors in this Lectureship mainly as an interesting phase of anthropology; and in their deeply interesting and important descriptions and analyses of the chief forms which religious belief has assumed, they have not been called upon to attempt any settlement of the question whether these beliefs rest upon a permanent basis in human nature, or whether they are merely transient features in the course of man's mental career, which, though incidental to the lower stages of intellectual development, are, as culture advances, discovered to be baseless, and so gradually loosen their hold on reflective minds. Several of the Hibbert Lectures, especially those by Prof. Max Müller, Prof. Kuenen, Dr. Hatch, and Count D'Alviella, do contribute most valuable aids towards an affirmative answer to the philosophical question, but the nature of their specific tasks prevented them from making this the central object of interest. In the present course, on the other hand, the lecturer is called upon to make it his primary business to examine what ground there is for maintaining that these various beliefs contain within them some elements of permanent truth which sound culture in no way tends to undermine and efface, but simply to separate from the accidental and transient concomitants which in the earlier stages of human history, to a large extent, conceal and distort the essential and indestructible factors of religious experience.

It is obvious that the condition of opinion at present predominant in the cultured and critical class is not very favourable to the awakenment of any warm and wide-spread interest in such enterprizes as that in which we are now about to engage. For many reasons, and among others the present engrossing interest in physical and sociological phenomena, metaphysical and theological thinking is for the nonce under a cloud, and there is a widely diffused impression that this is no merely temporary eclipse, but rather the indication of approaching extinction. Religions as *historical* matters, as curious phases in the history of speculative ideas which have once deeply influenced mankind, are no doubt subjects about which even scientific and positivist thinkers delight to hear and to read. The study of the origin and growth of psychological illusions is always fascinating, and it is pleasant to think that our more illumined minds have completely liberated themselves from these hallucinations, which still mislead less enlightened spirits. Around the *post-mortem* dissection of defunct religions a crowd of curious spectators is sure to gather; but he who in the present day still ventures to maintain that religious belief, so far from being either defunct or moribund, is an indestructible and indispensable element in all healthy and progressive social life, must expect at the present time to be passed by as the dull repeater of an outworn tale. Evolution is the key to the solution of all problems, and mental evolution is, in defiance of its etymological meaning, popularly interpreted to mean the mode by which the lowest states of mind, such as sensation, so combine as to become transformed into the highest ideas and emotions. Thus religious beliefs are traced back to no higher sources than human hopes and fears, and to the credulous transformation of gratifying imaginations into objective and solid realities.

A little reflection, however, will, I think, suffice to make this account of the origin of religious belief appear somewhat questionable. Evolution, both etymologically and rationally, means the passage into explicitness of that which was before implicit, and therefore affords not the slightest ground for the alleged conversion of a lower stage of consciousness into one intrinsically higher. If religion really grows out of personal hopes and fears, it can reach no higher level and exercise no higher potency than such as these individual hopes and fears can explain and justify. It cannot, however, be denied that the first impression made on the critical observer by the heterogeneous and often grotesque or repulsive forms of theological belief and practice which the study of comparative religion discloses, is that there is nothing in these religious phenomena which may not be accounted for by the interaction of selfish fears and cravings, and of those fanciful conceptions of the presence and activity of invisible powers which naturally arise in the pre-scientific mind. And this idea, that religion has no loftier source than human passions and human fancies, is apt to be confirmed when it is noticed that religions which in their early stage presented some attractive and ennobling features, often become transformed at a later date into gross and debasing superstitions.

Still even in its corruptions religious faith exercises such a powerful influence over the character and will of its votaries, and calls forth in them at times such emotional fervour and such readiness to sacrifice personal interests, that the conclusion seems inevitable that there must be some deeper spring in human nature than personal hopes and fears, which religion, even in its least rational and beautiful forms, has power to set in action. The superficial aspect of popular religions affords no adequate explanation of the influence which these religions exert. In the present day, for instance, the religious appeals made by earnest Salvationists on the one hand, and by sacerdotal pretensions and ornate ceremonial in ritualistic churches on the other, appear vastly irrational and even childish to a critical and unsympathetic observer; and yet there can be no question that there is awakened in connection with these illogical appeals and with this sensuous imagery a previously latent psychical force, which in many cases kindles in the worshippers a quite new moral enthusiasm, and gives to the character and conduct a decidedly higher and nobler tone. Now the spiritual energy which is thus liberated in the worshippers by the impassioned orthodox preacher or the imposingly apparelled priest, is wholly unaccounted for by either the dogmas of the one or the æsthetic ritualism of the other;

nay, further, these very dogmas and rites generally misdirect in part the energy which they set free, and to no small extent turn it into unlovely and uncharitable channels; nevertheless the power summoned into existence is a very real one, and it is a power which, so far from being a mere compound of personal interests, is the principle of all others which on occasion proves competent to hold in check and even to entirely overcome the most urgent personal claims.

And not only is this natural religious potency in human nature the only adequate explanation of the great influence of theological doctrines and forms which in themselves seem almost beneath the notice of the calm and rational observer, but this same religiosity manifests its indestructible and irrepressible character just as certainly whenever an attempt is made to ignore its existence and to treat human nature as consisting of nothing more than sensations elaborated by association and logical judgment. It is a commonplace remark that the human mind ever tends to rebound from the extreme of materialistic negation to that of over-credulous acceptance of alleged mysteries and miracles; and the passage from the most thoroughgoing secularism to the most unquestioning acceptance of the wonders of spiritualism and theosophy, of which we have in the present day some notable examples, is only a particular illustration of the universal truth that the human mind never remains long satisfied with the information which the mere senses and intellect can supply, but inevitably seeks some form of expression and satisfaction for that consciousness of personal relation with the non-phenomenal and the universal which in some form will assert itself in the mind and heart of man. What, then, is this mysterious element in human nature which finds a strange satisfaction and an access of emotional and moral power in public and private devotions, and in dogmas and rituals which are often intrinsically inconsistent and irrational, and quite powerless to justify themselves in the face of intelligent criticism? Why is it that when, as was the case in this country in the eighteenth century, and in the Illuminism of France and the *Aufklärung* of Germany, common sense and criticism, revolting from ecclesiastical pretensions and theological absurdities, have succeeded in rationalizing everything, and in emptying religious faith of every ingredient which the critical understanding cannot endorse,— why is it, I ask, that this condition of things, in which the spirit of the time confines its attention to physical and psychological phenomena, and rejects all faith which cannot be traced back to this sensational source, is invariably short-lived, and a Wesley in England or a Schleiermacher in Germany soon finds crowds eager to imbibe a fresh and richer supply of that mystical faith in the invisible central Mind and Heart of the universe, apart from which the soul feels a craving which will not for long together leave it at rest?

Why was it, in like manner, that in Rome, when rationalism had so discredited the old religion that, as we are told, a state soothsayer could hardly repress a smile when he met in the street a brother official, Neo-Platonism with its spiritual ecstacies, and Orphic and Chaldaic mysteries with their theurgic rites, flowed into the world's capital to fill the aching void; and why is it now in this country, when one-sided scientific study and philosophical agnosticism have divested a large proportion of thinkers of anything approaching to religious faith, that psychical research, with its eager study of ghost-stories, and clairvoyance, spiritualism and theosophy, indicate the presence of a most eager desire to discover some occult method of getting behind the veil of visible and tangible phenomena, and so attaining living contact with some transcendental spiritual presence? Surely the explanation of this vital connection between atheistic negation and theosophic credulity in both ancient and modern times, is to be found in the fact that human insight and interest cannot be confined to the finite disclosures of the senses, but that there is in the human spirit, in an implicit or explicit condition, an inner sense of relationship to an invisible Presence and Power.

My endeavour in these Lectures will be to indicate what is the rational ground of that first-hand faith in the supersensual, which, though it may be repressed or stifled for a while either by philosophical scepticism or by ecclesiastical formalism, inevitably and speedily begins to re-assert itself in a form which, by reason of the violence of the re-action, is often exaggerated and in part irrational. Is this religious faith an integral and perennial factor in the constitution of human nature, or is it a temporary phase in mental development, which, like the belief in alchemy and astrology, begins to decay and disappear as philosophical and scientific insight broadens and deepens? In other words, we have to inquire whether religious faith is capable of surviving and thriving in the pure atmosphere of clear scientific thinking and philosophical reflection. Our first business, then, will be to form some definite idea of the essential nature of this religious belief, which finds such varied expression both in history and in speculative thought.

It will, however, facilitate our inquiry if, before considering the several definitions which have been given of religion, we inquire whether the scientific and philosophical conception of the cosmos to which our present culture has attained, affords any *primâ-facie* probability in favour of the doctrine that human knowledge and human belief are not essentially confined to the sphere of physical and psychological phenomena, but have to do also with the central ground and cause in which these phenomena have their basis and their unification. The successive stages of human culture are broadly distinguished by the circumstance that some are predominantly analytic and others predominantly synthetic. A generation or two ago the analytic tendency was in the ascendant; to-day, the synthetic rules. The analytic mind fixes on the ultimate individualities which it reaches in the course of analysis as the truly real and the truly important feature of the universe. It is this tendency which gives rise to atomic explanations of the cosmos in science and philosophy, and to extreme individualism in sociology and politics. The synthetic mind, on the other hand, delights to concentrate its interest on the universal principles which are found to be immanent in all the individuals, and to unite the individuals into larger wholes or systems. In science and philosophy, this tendency engenders extreme monistic theories of the universe, either materialistic or idealistic, which treat what are usually called individuals as merely phases in the successive manifestation of one self-subsistent being, and therefore as having no proper independent selfhood or individuality; and in the sphere of politics it seeks to realize that socialistic ideal in which the free initiative of individuals is suppressed and replaced by the dominant pressure of the social whole. The conflict between these two tendencies of thought always leads at length to the conclusion that the truth lies neither in an extreme individualism nor in an all-absorbing universalism, but rather in the constant recognition and re-adjustment of the claims of both. No real existence, be it a physical atom or a rational soul, appears to be capable of intelligible explanation, unless we assume that in its nature individuality and universality inseparably blend.

In the present condition of our knowledge, we can only speculate as to the ultimate constitution of the physical universe; but various considerations render it not altogether improbable that the monads or centres of force into which scientific research resolves the universe, are not merely modes of the being or will of the self-subsistent ground of all things, but have themselves an elementary measure of "selfhood" or individuality. But be this as it may, when we ascend from inorganic to organic being, we find in the lowest forms, and still more in those higher organisms in which we see evidence of feeling and consciousness, an increasing amount of apparently self-initiated activity; and we are led to the conclusion that the end of evolution is the production of beings whose individuality shall be so real that, as in the case of man, they shall not only consciously determine their own action, but shall be able to contrast their own existence with the existence of other finite beings, and thus to attain an increasing insight into the character of the universe of which they appear to form a part. We thus come to regard the universe, with all its modes of matter, force and consciousness, as the form in which the Eternal God calls into existence, by a partial self-sundering, it would seem, of His own essential being, this universe of centres of energy and personal selves, which some philosophers, such as Hegel, designate as the Son of God. But in this self-sundering in which the Supreme Being eternally generates a cosmos in one aspect distinct from Himself, only rational souls possessed of freedom of will are gifted with that high degree of individuality which constitutes them truly "other" than the Eternal, and so capable of standing in moral and spiritual relations to Him.

But it is of the highest importance to observe that no dependent or created existences, whether they be the centres of energy which science investigates, or such high individualities as self-conscious souls, can be regarded as having a separate existence wholly sundered from their supreme source. Even in the case of man, the separation from the Eternal which constitutes his personal individuality is only a partial one; and every moment of our lives our personality depends for its existence and its several activities just as much on that side of our being by which we still remain indivisibly united with the Eternal, as on that other side of our being in which we truly say we have a will of our own. Apart from that theoretical and practical reason which manifests itself in all souls alike as self-consciousness awakens, no knowledge of nature, no interchange of ideas between human minds, no consciousness of moral authority, no possession of the spirit by divine love, would be possible to man. Perpetual unity with Him in whom we live and move and have our being is as essential to all rational thought, to all moral ideals, to all divine affection, as our partial sundering from Him, the separation of our wills from the Divine Will, is essential to all moral freedom and all personal relationship between the soul and God. And as this partial unity with, and partial separation from, the Eternal is the condition of intelligent communion of man with man, and of man with nature, so likewise in the case of physical atoms and physical objects no dynamic relations between them are conceivable, apart from the supposition that every monad or ultimate principle of what we call matter is still on the inner side of its being in continuous union with that Universal and Self-subsistent Being out of whom in part it emerges.

Hermann Lotze argues with great force that the apparent action of atom on atom, and body on body, is wholly unaccountable if we regard the ultimate elements of matter as simply isolated existences existing side by side in space. It is not intelligible, he says, that a change in the inner states of one atom or monad should necessarily be followed by a change in the inner states of contiguous atoms if the several atoms were wholly independent existences. Looked at from the outside, nature, even to the scientific vision, seems to resolve itself into a pluralism of ultimate indestructible existences, and both common sense and science speak of these elements as influencing one another.

Thus things are supposed to exercise what is called a "transeunt" action or causality, whereby the one projects out of itself an intermediate something which effects a change in other things. But it is impossible to form any rational conception of this supposed efficient influence, this intermediate something, which has no independent existence of its own, but which, if it passes from one body to another, must in the transition state be the property of neither. It follows, therefore, that though atoms and bodies appear to be isolated co-existences in space, this complete isolation and seeming independence of each other is only an appearance; for the reciprocal causality by which all these atoms and bodies are linked together, inevitably forces us to the conclusion that, deeper than the apparent spatial distance and division, there is a metaphysical unity, or, in other words, that the self-subsistent creative ground of all finite existence does not wholly separate Himself from any one of the plurality of dependent energies or beings into which He differentiates Himself; and therefore, as every finite atom or finite soul still remains, as regards a part of its nature, in indivisible union with its self-subsistent ground and source, this common relation to the Self-subsistent One affords the true explanation of the metaphysical unity of the cosmos, and also of the possibility of reciprocal action of the monads of nature on each other, and of reciprocal action of the finite mind on nature, and of nature on the mind. Thus the most recent science and philosophy appear to assert at once a real pluralism or individualism in the world of finite beings, but at the same time a deeper monism. The Eternal who differentiates His own self-subsistent energy into the infinite variety of finite existences is still immanent and living in every one of these dependent modes of being; and it is because all finite or created beings are only partially individual, and still remain in vital union with their common ground, that it becomes possible for them through the medium of this common ground to act dynamically on each other; and it is for the same reason that those finite beings such as man, who have attained to self-consciousness, are able to enter into intellectual, moral and spiritual relations both with other rational finite minds and also with the Eternal Being with whom their own existence is in some measure indivisibly conjoined. In support of this conclusion that no satisfactory account can be given either of nature or humanity which does not do justice at once to the individualism or pluralism, the reality of which lends infinite interest to nature and to human history, and also to the divine monistic ground, or God, in which all this variety finds its source, its unification, and its capacity for interaction and mutual understanding, the following passage from Lotze's *Metaphysic*[1] deserves careful consideration:

"In the course of our consideration of the world, we were led at the outset to the notion of a plurality of Things. Their multiplicity seemed to offer the most convenient explanation for the equally great multiplicity of appearances. Then the impulse to become acquainted with the unconditioned Being which must lie at the foundation of this process of the conditioned, was the occasion of our ascribing this unconditioned Being without suspicion to the very multiplicity of elements which we found to exist. If we stopped short of assigning to every reality a pure

[1] § 69.

Being that could dispense with all relations to other beings, yet, even while allowing relations, we did not give up the independence of things as against each other which we assumed to begin with. It was as so many independent unities that we supposed them to enter into such peculiar relations to each other as compelled their self-sufficing natures to act and re-act upon each other. But it was impossible to state in what this transition from a state of isolation to metaphysical combination might consist, and it remained a standing contradiction that Things having no dependence on each other should yet enter into such a relation of dependence as each to concern itself with the other. This prejudice must be given up. There cannot be a multiplicity of independent things, but all elements, if reciprocal action is to be possible between them, must be regarded as parts of a single real Being. The Pluralism with which our view of the world began has to give place to a Monism, through which the 'transeunt' operation, always unintelligible, passes into an 'immanent' operation."

Lotze's theory of the universe is of especial value for our present purpose, seeing that in him, probably in a higher degree than in any other recent thinker, high faculty and achievement in the region of physical science were conjoined with an equally high faculty and culture in the sphere of philosophy. We may then, I think, with some confidence assume that the higher thought of our time discerns that no scientific account of the universe based on the study of particular things and events can be intelligible and adequate, if it does not recognize as immanent in the plurality of atoms and of souls the presence and causality of the Eternal Self-subsistent One. God then, or the ultimate source and ground of dependent existences, is present as the basis and explanation of all mutual dynamic action alike in the inorganic world and in self-conscious spirits; but in the case of self-conscious beings He is also immanent as the necessary pre-condition of all knowledge, of an intelligent inter-communication between mind and mind, and mind and nature. Without the living presence of the universal and the eternal principles of thought and of æsthetic and ethical ideals, neither genuine knowledge, nor genuine morality, nor genuine spiritual love, is possible or conceivable. Unless the universal ground of all beings revealed its universal nature in each self-consciousness, man's nature could not be rational, but would be no more than blind feeling, wholly incapable of recognizing its relation to other beings and to the primal source of all dependent being. The very fact that the self-conscious soul is capable of rising above itself, of comparing itself with other selves, and of passing judgment on its own character, is of itself proof positive that that which is not finite and particular, but is infinite and universal, is immanent within it; and it is this universal element which by its presence kindles that very light of reason in virtue of which the finite soul is enabled to enter into cognitive and sympathetic relations with the other energies and souls which owe their existence to the same primal source.

I have dwelt at, I fear, somewhat tedious length on this question as to what is the general theory of the universe (the *Weltanschauung*, as the Germans term it) which in the present day most recommends itself to cultivated minds. We entered, you will remember, on this inquiry with the object of learning whether what we now see reason to accept as the most satisfactory account of the nature of the cosmos of matter and mind, suggests the possibility, or even the probability, that this religious belief, which we have seen to have been hitherto so influential and irrepressible an element in human nature and human society, has a permanent foundation in the very nature of things, and therefore, amid all the evolution of its changing forms, preserves, and must preserve, its essential character and influence. Now if it be true, as we have seen reason to conclude it is, that the individual man, though in respect to God a finite and dependent being, has yet, immanent in his consciousness, the presence and activity of the universal ground of his own being, and also of all other dependent or created beings, and that it is the presence of this universal principle within him which alone enables him to have dynamic and cognitive relations with the other finite existences in the cosmos, it follows from this very fact that man, as a thinking, a moral and a spiritual being, is conscious of wholly transcending his own finitude, and can discriminate between the action of this universal or higher self, as we term it, and that of his own finite self, that there is a certain self-revelation of the Eternal and Infinite One to the finite soul, and therefore an indestructible basis for religious ideas and religious beliefs as distinguished from what is called scientific knowledge.

Science, in so far as it confines itself to inductions from the deliverances of our senses, does not immediately envisage or apprehend that universal element in our thinking and in our moral and spiritual life with which philosophy and religion are directly and principally concerned. It is true that no science would be possible apart from this immanence in man of the eternal, self-subsistent principles of logical thinking. Were we not enabled by the help of the indwelling God to rise above our finitude and so to see things from a universal point of view, we should, as I before pointed out, be confined to the sphere of blind feeling, and be wholly unable to rise to the level of knowledge, whether of our own existence or of our relations to other beings. But though the activity of the immanent God is necessarily implied in all scientific study, still the attention of the savant is not directed to this inner and immanent condition of all his thought, and he confines himself to investigating the relations which link together the various finite phenomena which his senses report. But while Science deals with the infinite multiplicity and variety of the finite things or energies into which the Eternal One has differentiated His own essential being, Philosophy and Religion are concerned specially and primarily with that monistic side of the cosmos which underlies all the divisions which separate finite individuals from each other; for, as we have seen, it is through the felt presence and activity of this universal ground of all being in the individual consciousness that man becomes at once a philosophizing and a religious being. What constitutes the essential difference between the philosophical and the religious attitude of mind, I will afterwards discuss; but at present I will content myself with having indicated the presence in the consciousness of each finite mind of that immanent universal principle which cannot be said to pertain to or be the property of any individual mind, but belongs to that uncreated and eternal nature of God which lies deeper than all those differences which separate individual minds from each other, and is indeed that incarnation of the Eternal, who, though He is present in every finite thing, and is not only present, but is felt and known to be present, in every rational soul, is still not broken up into individualities, but ever remains one and the same eternal substance, one and the same unifying principle immanently and indivisibly present in every one of that countless plurality of finite individuals into which man's analyzing understanding dissects the cosmos.

If this be so, we are prepared to admit as *primâ-facie* probable that there may exist, as an integral and therefore indestructible factor in human nature, a sense of relationship not only to the finite individualities, which like ourselves are dependent or created beings, but also to that deeper, self-existent ground of unity which is immanent in all finite existences. Now my contention is, that it is the felt relationship in which the finite self-consciousness stands to the immanent and universal ground of all being which constitutes Religion. And in support of this view I will now ask you to examine and compare those definitions of Religion which have recently been given by thinkers who have made religious phenomena their special study.

Among the masters of the science of Comparative Religion, Count D'Alviella will be acknowledged to hold high rank. In the Hibbert Lectures which he delivered two years ago, he defines Religion as "the conception man forms of his relations with the superhuman and mysterious powers on which he believes himself to depend." In another course of Hibbert Lectures, that by Prof. Max Müller on "The Origin and Growth of Religion as illustrated by the Religions of India," we read:

"Religion is a mental faculty which independently, nay, in spite of sense and reason, enables men to apprehend the Infinite under different names and under varying disguises. Without that faculty, no religion, not even the lowest worship of idols and fetishes, would be possible; and if we will but listen attentively, we can hear in all religions a groaning of the spirit, a struggle to conceive the inconceivable, a longing after the Infinite, a love of God."

Some ten years later, in his Gifford Lectures on "Natural Religion," delivered in Glasgow in 1889, Prof. Max Müller admits the justice of the criticisms passed upon his definition of Religion by Prof. Pfleiderer, Dr. A. Réville and others, and proceeds to modify his former statement.

"I had defined Religion," he says, "simply as a 'perception of the Infinite,' without adding the restriction, 'a perception of the Infinite under such manifestations as are able to influence the moral character of man.' The fact was that in my former writings I was chiefly concerned with dogmatic religion. I was anxious to discover the origin of religious concepts, names and theories, and I left the question of their influence on moral actions for further consideration. . . . Still I plead guilty to not having laid sufficient emphasis on the practical side of religion; I admit that mere theories about the Infinite, unless they influence human conduct, have no right to the name of Religion, and I have now tried to remedy that defect by restricting the name of Religion to those perceptions of the Infinite which are able to influence the moral character of man."

Since delivering the Gifford Lectures on "Natural Religion," Prof. Max Müller has delivered and published three other courses of Gifford Lectures, entitled, "Physical Religion," "Anthropological Religion," and "Psychological Religion or Theosophy," this three-fold division of religious phenomena being based on the three different ways in which the Infinite may be conceived, namely, under the forms of Nature, Man, or Self. In Prof. Max Müller's view, Religion is in its "physical" stage when, as in the earlier form of the Vedic religion, there was a recognition of the Infinite in Nature as underlying all that is finite and phenomenal in our cosmic experiences. This apprehended Infinite became named, individualized and personified, till at last it was conceived again as beyond all names. As soon as the human mind succeeds in distinguishing between body and soul, and sees "something infinite, immortal and divine in man," then the stage is reached which Prof. Max Müller terms "anthropological" religion. Kant, when his religious mood was awakened by the admiration and the awe which the sight of the starry firmament suggested, reached Religion, or the apprehension of the Infinite, by the "physical" road; but when, on the other hand, his sense of the Infinite was called forth by awe and reverence in the presence of the moral law within, then his religious feelings sprang from an "anthropological" source. But as Physical Religion grows out of the apprehended presence of the Infinite in nature, while Anthropological Religion supposes the recognition of the Infinite in the human soul, there arises, in Prof. Max Müller's view, a still higher phase of the religious consciousness, which unifies these two seemingly distinct Infinites by recognizing the indissoluble unity of God and the human soul. The two currents of thought which lead respectively to Physical and to Anthropological Religion "always strive to meet, and do meet in the end, in what is called *Theosophy* or *Psychological Religion*, which helps us to the perception of the essential unity of the soul with God. Both this striving to meet and the final union have found, I think, their most perfect expression in Christianity. The striving of the soul to meet God is expressed in the love of God, on which hang all the Laws and the Prophets; the final union is expressed in our being in the true sense of the word the sons of God."[1] Prof. Max Müller's "Theosophy" must not be confounded with the entirely different speculation with which the names of Madame Blavatsky and Mrs. Besant are associated. The Theosophy which Prof. Max Müller appears to regard as the highest form of the religious consciousness is exemplified in various stages of development in the Upanishads of India, the Sufi sect among the Mahommedans, in the Stoic and Neo-Platonic schools of Greek thought, in Alexandrian Christianity with its doctrine of the Logos, and in such Christian mystics and theosophists as Eckhart and Tauler. It may be added, though Prof. Max Müller does not say so, that such religious philosophy as is presented in the Neo-Hegelian writings of T. H. Green, Principal John Caird, and Prof. Edward Caird, is essentially an attempt to give to this Theosophy a rational expression and justification, and to show that religion as so expounded is identical with the presentation of Christianity found in the Pauline Epistles and in the Fourth Gospel.

[1] *Theosophy or Psychological Religion*, p. 542.

Now it must at once be admitted that Prof. Max Müller's account of Religion, as implying a faculty in man to apprehend the Infinite, rightly emphasizes one feature which certainly appears in the religious consciousness when it enters on the more reflective stage. If by the Infinite is meant the self-existent ground of all finite existences, the apprehension of man's relation to such an ultimate Reality could not be wholly absent even from the most elementary religious consciousness; and it is no doubt correct to say that in the order of development of religious ideas this Infinite Ground of all things is first conceived as manifesting Himself rather in the visible external cosmos than in the inner life of the human soul. But even if the consciousness of the Infinite were ever so clear, the apprehension of it alone would by no means be an adequate account of what is implied in Religion. Religion implies the sense of personal relationship between the soul and the object of worship. There is implied a consciousness of dependence upon a Being or Power higher than ourselves; as Count d'Alviella says, there must, to constitute religion, be a felt relation to some superhuman and mysterious power or powers on which the worshipper believes himself to depend. In the early stages of religious thought, it is the superior *power* rather than the *infinity* which is the prominent and influential factor in the idea of God; and that power cannot be conceived as personally related to the worshipping soul, unless it is itself, in some vague fashion at least, regarded as personal. Hence Dr. Martineau fixes upon the essential element in religion when he says: "Religion is belief in an ever-living God, that is, of a

Divine Mind and Will ruling the universe and holding moral relations with mankind." By this description of God as "a Divine Mind and Will" I do not understand Dr. Martineau to mean that God stands in the same relation to our finite minds as these finite minds stand to each other, but only that the words "Mind" and "Will" are our best approximate expressions for a supreme self-consciousness and activity which essentially transcends the limits of human conception. God, as I have before pointed out, appears to be the immanent light of each man's reason, the immanent source of all that is permanent in our ideals and real in our spiritual affections. It may well be, as Lotze maintains, that this Supreme Ground and Source of all finite existence, in whom in a certain real sense all our finite personalities live and move, and on whom we feel ourselves to continually depend both for existence and for our rational and moral insight, is Himself not only most adequately conceived by the human mind under a personal form, but actually is the one sole realization of that absolute and perfect personality of which our finite personalities are but dependent and imperfect reproductions. But admitting this, as I shall afterwards endeavour to give reasons for doing, we must, I venture to think, regard our conception of the Supreme Being as "a Mind and Will," as only the most adequate mode we possess of apprehending a Reality which by the very nature of the case we cannot fully grasp either in imagination or in thought. Be this as it may, there can be no doubt that Dr. Martineau teaches a most important and indeed vital truth when he insists that Religion involves the belief that a personal and ethical relationship exists between the worshipper and his God.

Whenever, as in the Upanishads, the idea of a personal relationship between man and God fades away, and the gods which in the Vedic hymns were invested with personality are replaced by the Pantheistic conception of an impersonal and eternal self, then, though philosophy may thrive vigorously in this atmosphere of speculative thought, religion proper inevitably decays and dies, for it lacks that sense of immediate personal contact with a superior being which is the indispensable condition of its birth and of its life. Hence the definition of religion given by Dr. A. Réville appears to me much more satisfactory than Prof. Max Müller's. "Religion," says Dr. Réville, "is the determination of human life by the sentiment of a bond uniting the human mind to that mysterious Mind whose domination of the world and of itself it recognizes, and to whom it delights in feeling itself united." Elsewhere Dr. Réville writes: "Moreover, we must bear in mind—for this is essential—that the sense of the bond which unites the human mind to the superior spirit (or spirits), whose sovereignity over himself and the world he believes that he recognizes, is the source of secret, though it may be undefinable comfort, of which those only can deny the reality who have never known it."

I conclude, then, with Dr Martineau and Dr. Réville, that it is indispensable to all genuine religious consciousness that it should involve the feeling of relationship with the Being who is reverenced and worshipped. This consciousness of personal union and communion with God is the vital element in the highest form of religion to which the race has attained, and it is equally present and influential in the lowest manifestations of the religious sentiment. But while this feeling of relationship and kinship with a superior Being is the unchangeable essence of religion, the *idea* which is formed of this Object of the religious sentiment—the form, that is, of theological dogma—passes, like the scientific conception of the material world, through successive stages of development corresponding to the gradual evolution of man's scientific knowledge, and more especially to the deepening and broadening of man's consciousness of the immanence of the Universal or the Divine as an inspiring and authoritative element in the soul's individual life.

And it is to be noted that if we would understand what is most essential and permanent in man's idea of God, we must seek it, not in lower manifestations of theological dogma, such as are presented in peoples at a low level of intellectual and moral development, but rather in those conceptions of the Supreme Being which are now found in minds who in the greatest degree combine the deepest personal religious experience with the fullest rational insight into the highest culture of the time. For as religious experience and the accompanying theological ideas are an unfolding or evolving of the capacity of the finite mind to commune with and to rationally apprehend that Uncreated and Universal Being or Divine Self who is immanent in all finite objects, and who is also in varying degrees of fulness revealed in the consciousness of each rational soul, it will naturally be the case with theological evolution, as it is with every evolution, that the true key to the essential nature of the process, and to the relative importance and permanence of each factor in that process, must be sought, not in the embryonic stages, but rather in the most fully developed manifestations of the evolving idea. What is most essential and permanently dominant in human nature will not be discovered by studying the physiology and psychology of the anthropoid apes or even of the most primitive men, and therefore the anthropological question, whether, in the lowest stages of human civilization, the dawning religious sentiment of mankind found its earliest theological expression through the obvious conjecture that the more conspicuous objects and energies of nature were instinct with life and will, or through the notion of immaterial selves or spirits suggested by the experiences of dreams, &c.,—this question, I say, though very interesting, and indeed important from a psychological point of view, has no primary or decisive significance in regard to a true philosophy of religious experience. The elements which are deepest in man's rational, emotional and artistic nature, and which finally clearly reveal themselves in the consciousness as the highest and rightfully dominant ones, are by no means those which first come to the front and find verbal or ceremonial expression in the earlier stages of human evolution.

If, however, I am right in placing the root and essence of religious experience in each finite soul's felt personal relationship to, and continual dependence on, that deeper and uncreated Self who is immanent in all nature and in all souls, and is the eternal Ground and Source of all that is felt to be universal and therefore intrinsically authoritative within us, it follows that this germinal principle of all genuine religion must be in some faint degree operative in the consciousness of even the least cultured of rational beings. But in the early history of mankind, just as in the early years of the individual man, when the perceptive faculties are all active and reflection is as yet at its minimum, the Divine Self with which the soul feels its relationship is naturally regarded as existing and manifesting itself almost exclusively in the outward world of nature; and as natural phenomena do not to the pre-scientific mind bear clear marks of unity of authorship, there was an inevitable tendency to multiply the powers of whose activity the different aspects of nature were regarded as the expression. But even at such low levels of culture as are reached by the Polynesian islanders, there is evidence that, along with the belief in many particular gods in whom the believers feel a more vivid interest, there also exists, more in the background of consciousness, the notion of one supreme Deity who creates and sustains the entire universe of nature and humanity. And when, partly by the experiences in dreams, but in a greater degree, I am inclined to think, by reflection on the fact that the spirit is the motive cause of action and that the body is its instrument, the notion of spirit as capable of existing apart from the body was gained, the idea of God as a Spirit pervading not only nature, but also all human minds, could not fail to arise, as giving a much more satisfying expression to the religious consciousness of personal relation to a higher Being. Thus in one of the Vedic hymns we read:

I. NATURE OF RELIGIOUS BELIEF.

"Whether one walks or stands or conceals himself, whether one lies down or rises up, what two persons sitting together whisper to each other, King Varuna knows it; he is as a third party in their midst. This earth too is King Varuna's, and this wide heaven, together with its distant ends. The two seas (the ocean and heaven) are Varuna's hips, and so also is he contained in each tiny drop of water. If one should fly away to the other side of the heavens, even then he would not run away from our King Varuna."[1]

In this passage we see the transition from the conception of God as another Self, and existing over against the human self, to the more spiritual view of God as the Self immanent, not only in nature, but also in the worshipper's own soul. In the Upanishads, which represent rather a philosophy than a religion, this idea of God as the immanent, all-pervading Self is dwelt upon so exclusively, that the human self tends to lose all true reality and all moral relations to God, and becomes a mere transient phenomenal phase of the life of the Great Self who is the only Reality.

In fact, the Pantheism of India is, like the Pantheism of Spinoza and of Hegel, the inevitable result of treating the relation between the soul and the immanent God as simply an intellectual or rational relation; for the reason alone cannot see any basis for asserting the slightest degree of independent reality or causality in the human self as distinguished from the Absolute or Divine Self, and therefore such systems furnish no foundation for real moral and affectional relations between the soul and God.

---

[1] Prof. O. Pfleiderer's article, *Zur Frage nach Anfang und Entwicklung der Religion*, in the *Jahrbücher für protestantische Theologie*, Vol. I. (1875), p. 101.

Unless the Divine Self who is immanent in the finite soul has by His own act delegated to the finite soul an adequate degree of independent reality and moral freedom, man does not become in any true sense a real *other* than God; and apart from such otherness, there can be no genuine moral responsibility, no justification for that sense of personal relationship and consciousness of dependence which are indispensable factors in all genuine religious experience. I shall have occasion to dwell upon this thought in a later Lecture, when discussing the claims of what is called "Absolute Idealism," or Hegelianism, to represent the truest and highest form of the religious consciousness. Though this idealism is declared by some of its recent advocates to be simply Christianity clearly thought out, I cannot but think that a system of thought which allows of no real dualism of will between man and God is not a religion at all; still less is it identical with Christian Theism; and that as a philosophy it is but a modernized form of the same line of Pantheistic or purely intellectual speculation to which we owe the Indian Upanishads.

The complete conception of Religion is, I believe, not reached till we recognize the fact that the immanent God is apprehended by the religious consciousness, not only as the Light of its reason, but as the Source of its moral imperative and its moral ideal, and is also directly *felt* as in immediate personal relation with the soul. No account of Religion is adequate to cover the facts of religious experience which omits any one element of this three-fold manifestation of the Eternal in the human consciousness. The eternal or divine side of man's self-consciousness manifests itself alike in that *theoretical* reason which enables us to rise above ourselves and to apprehend our relation to other finite and created beings as well as to the infinite whole—in that *practical* reason whereby æsthetic and ethical ideals emerge out of our sensuous experience, and, in virtue of their self-evident universality, carry with them immediate authority to claim our reverence and to dispose of our will—and also in that immediate feeling of dependence on, and sympathetic relation with, that Infinite and Universal Being whose essential nature our highest aspirations are intuitively discerned to reveal. All these aspects of the self-revelation of the immanent Eternal One have the same character, that they raise the soul above the level of its separate individuality and its own personal and finite interests, and reveal the fundamental fact that this rational nature of ours is not a mere finite and limited creation by the Eternal One, but is a real differentiation or reproduction of God's own essential substance; so that in man are potentially present those infinite and divine capacities and faculties whereby he is capable of rising above finite phenomena to unifying thought, above selfish expediency to moral principle, above personal gratification to the ineffable joy and satisfaction of self-forgetful love.

How religious belief becomes mutilated, ineffective and even mischievous, when any one of the three aspects to which I have adverted are overlooked or denied, will become evident by a reference to historical instances. If the revelation of the universal and the divine is recognized in the theoretical reason and in that alone, the inevitable result is a Pantheistic conception of God, man and the universe, in which both nature and humanity come to be regarded merely as transient and illusory appearances, temporal phases of the eternal thought-principle, which thought-principle, as being itself timeless and therefore by us wholly inconceivable, is the only true reality. To such Pantheism the exclusive intellectualism of Hindoo and Neo-Platonic thought inevitably led; and it is this feature which renders the imposing philosophical system of the noble and "God-intoxicated" Spinoza incompetent to adequately explain and justify the soul's ethical experience, and to satisfy its craving for a spiritual and eternal relationship with God. And notwithstanding the fact that Hegel and his Scotch and English disciples eloquently assert that in Absolute Idealism we have the only true and adequate religious philosophy, this system, too, is, as I shall endeavour to show in a future Lecture, essentially Pantheistic, and Pantheistic in the objectionable sense that it, like Spinoza's *Ethica*, makes the human consciousness a mere phase of the Divine consciousness, and, therefore, undermines the feeling of moral responsibility, transforms sin from an ontological reality into an inevitable and therefore salutary phase in the evolution of finite souls, and renders unintelligible that felt personal relationship and communion between God and His rational creatures which is presupposed alike in the ethical and in the religious experience of mankind. In this system the free initiative of the individual will in the formation of human character vanishes; men can no longer, with Tennyson, say to the Eternal, "Our wills are ours to make them Thine;" for at no stage in human life could the will possibly or conceivably be other than it actually is, and therefore the human will and the Divine will are to the consistent Absolute Idealist not two wills, but simply two indivisible aspects of one and the same Absolute Will or Absolute Thought.

And while the exclusive insistence on Reason or Thought, as the only mode in which the finite soul comes into conscious relation with the immanent Universal Principle, or God, thus necessarily leads to a Pantheism which mutilates and paralyzes the ethical and emotional elements in the religious consciousness; so the exclusive insistence on the Feeling of immediate relation to the Universal, which is so eloquently advocated in Schleiermacher's *Reden über die Religion*, though far from presenting so inadequate a *rationale* of the religious consciousness as intellectual Pantheism presents, is nevertheless an imperfect account of the matter, and involves a Mysticism which tends to weaken and destroy all living interest in science and philosophy, as well as in social and political affairs. That the religion of Feeling, or Mysticism, has seized upon and emphasized a real and indispensable factor in the religious consciousness, is evident from the great interest which such preachers as Schleiermacher always awaken, and from the fact that in every stage of historical religion forms of mysticism always assert themselves and exercise a powerful fascination and an elevating influence over some of the choicest spirits. Indeed, wherever we find a form of religion in which the mystical element is wholly absent, where no appeal is made to the soul's immediate consciousness of the Divine presence, and God is treated mainly as a rational *hypothesis* to account for the facts of nature or of man's moral life, there we invariably find a religion which kindles no warmth and enthusiasm, possesses little or no self-propagating power, and which, though in general highly conservative of the recognized moralities, is not favourable to the incoming of new and higher moral and social ideals. At the same time it cannot be denied that Mysticism ignores or neglects some very important elements which are always present in rich and effective religious experience. An admirable description of the merits and defects of the exclusively mystical religionist is furnished in the following quotation from Dr. Charles Beard's Hibbert Lectures on "The Reformation of the Sixteenth Century in its relation to modern Thought and Knowledge."[1]

"The mystic," says Dr. Beard, "is one who claims to be able to see God and divine things with the inner vision of the soul— a direct apprehension, as the bodily eye apprehends colour, as the bodily ear apprehends sound. His method, so far as he has one, is simply contemplative; he does not argue, or generalize, or infer; he reflects, broods, waits for light. He prepares for Divine communion by a process of self-purification: he detaches his spirit from earthly cares and passions: he studies to be quiet, that his still soul may reflect the face of God. He usually sits loose to active duty; for him the felt presence of God dwarfs the world and makes it common: he is so dazzled by the glory of the one great Object of contemplation, that he sees and cares for little else. But the morals of mysticism are almost always sweet and good, even if there be a faint odour of cloister incense about them; though at the same time there are more ways than one from mysticism to immorality, all leading through the Pantheism into which mystics are ever apt to fall. For shall not one who is mystically incorporate with God live in a region

[1] Pp. 14, 15.

above law? And if God be the ground and substance of all things, what justification is there for distinction between good and evil? But these are comparatively rare aberrations, and the essential weakness of mysticism lies in another direction. It much rather consists in the fact that mysticism cannot formulate itself in such a way as to appeal to universal apprehension. It affirms, it does not reason : all the mystic can say to another is, I see, I feel, I know ; and if he speaks to no corresponding faculty, his words fall to the ground. Indeed, the mystic is always more or less indistinct in utterance ; he sees, or thinks he sees, more than he can tell : the realities which he contemplates are too vast, too splendid, too many-sided, to be confined within limits of human words : he looks at them, now in this aspect, now in that, and his reports, while each true to the vision of the moment, have a sound of inconsistency with each other. So mysticism usually fails to propagate and perpetuate itself : the mystic faculty is a gift of God, not an aptitude that can be communicated by man to man. Its appearance in the Church is as that breath of the Spirit which bloweth where it listeth."

The mysticism which Dr. Beard so ably characterizes is rather the mysticism of mediæval times, as exemplified in such views as those of Eckhart and Tauler, than the more sober and rational mysticism which we find in teachers like Schleiermacher and his disciples; and the Pantheism to which, as Dr. Beard truly says, the too exclusively mystical mind is exposed is very different from and far higher and more religious than the intellectual Pantheism which springs out of the attempt to reach God by the sole path of philosophical speculation. Still even such lofty mysticism as that presented in Schleiermacher's school of religious thought does assuredly tend to weaken the soul's interest in the practical and ethical side of life, to undermine the belief in the freedom of the will, and to weaken the faith in personal immortality. The truth for which mysticism stands, but which it too exclusively emphasizes, is the fact that the self-revelation of the Universal Spirit, or the Immanent God, in the finite soul, is not wholly a matter of *inference* from the states of the human consciousness, but is also to a certain degree a matter of immediate feeling, of direct apprehension of the Infinite by the finite spirit. When, for instance, Professor Schurman, of Cornell University, in his very able and acute lectures on "Belief in God," rests this belief solely on the ground that the hypothesis of a God is to be accepted because it alone explains the facts of consciousness, and sums up his reasoning with the words—" It has been shown, I think, that the phenomena both of the universe and of human life require the thinking mind to postulate a Supreme Ground of things which we are entitled to describe as Self-conscious Spirit and loving Father,"—he appears to me to omit that essential element in religious experience on the existence of which mysticism rightly insists. In religious experience there is present as one of its constituent factors what we may describe as the direct feeling or apprehension of a present reality which is not finite or phenomenal, but universal and self-existent, and which the soul feels to be inextricably united with its own immediate consciousness. This primal feeling inevitably blends with, and cannot be wholly separated from, our preconceived ideas of the nature and character of God, and hence it adapts itself to polytheistic or to theistic views. By minds which are pre-occupied with the agnostic or positivist conviction that man's mental apprehension is limited to phenomena, the feeling or God-consciousness I have endeavoured to describe will be regarded as an illusory product of association or imagination. I venture, however, to think that religious belief is to a large extent built upon this immediate feeling of a sympathetic Divine Presence; and that no man, however agnostic or even atheistic his fundamental theory of the universe may be, can wholly divest himself of the consciousness that at certain moments, and especially in those moments when at the call of conscience or of divine love he sets aside private passions and desires, the Eternal is with him as a living presence, and as a source of superhuman support and comfort.

And when the star-lit heaven awakens in the soul the consciousness of the Infinite, or some entrancing loveliness or sublimity of the visible earth or sky calls forth the ideal of beauty in the mind, all souls, I think, feel in some faint form what poets like Wordsworth and Emerson realize with greater vividness—a certain indefinite, but most exhilarating and comforting, sense of communion with what seems to be an all-enveloping, all-embracing personal Presence, an all-pervading higher Self. The same delightful sense of immediate union and communion with the ultimate and universal ground of Being is felt, so it seems to me, in connection with the flashing into consciousness of high and unifying philosophical ideas which reveal to us the presence of a principle of unity underlying all phenomenal differences and varieties. And if it be objected that in the cases I have mentioned I am treating my own subjective fancies as permanent and indestructible elements of human consciousness, I contend that at all events no such allegation can be fairly made by any one who directs unbiassed attention to the feelings which accompany the claim which ethical ideals make upon the individual will. In such cases it is not the bare consciousness of "ought" as a mere subjective factor of our own consciousness that we are immediately conscious of. What we are immediately conscious of is, that the Ultimate Ground of all reality is asserting itself in us, and revealing to us an objective norm of conduct which is felt to possess a universality and an authority such as nothing finite or created could originate.

In a later Lecture I shall endeavour to show that these facts of the moral consciousness rationally demand for their adequate explanation a theistic view of the ultimate ground of Being; but what at present I wish to establish is, that this moral consciousness of ours is attended by the feeling of direct personal relation to the Source of the moral law. If it be said that all we are conscious of is the feeling of obligation, and that we logically *infer* or postulate the existence of a Lawgiver in order to account for the fact, I can only reply that, in the case of the feeling I am referring to, I am not conscious of any such inference. If there be any such inference, it must be one of those *unbewusste Schlüsse* of which German psychologists speak, inferences which the mind cannot help making, and in making which it is not conscious of its own act. My conviction is that we are not, in the case of our senses, so immediately aware of an objective world as in our moral consciousness we are directly aware of the reality of an objective and ultimate source of authority which stands in personal relationship to ourselves. Were it not for this immediate realization, through direct feeling, of the union and communion of our finite spirits with that Ultimate Ground in which our spirits live and move, I cannot see how the most important features of the religious life could possibly be accounted for, seeing that religious experience is often fullest and deepest at the very time when all logical processes of conscious inference are almost suspended. Had we only an hypothetical acquaintance and connection with God, what intelligible explanation could be given of that intense influence on the emotions and on the whole mental life which often accompanies what is called "conversion," and indeed characterizes all the cases in which the finite soul suddenly awakens to a new and deeper sense of its immanent relationship with the Supreme Ground of all reality? The God whose action on the human soul is well described in the following passage from Emerson's profound essay on the Over-soul, must be apprehended directly by the human spirit, and not simply reached by the logical bridges furnished by what are called the proofs of the existence of God.

"We distinguish," says Emerson, "the announcements of the soul, its manifestations of its own nature, by the term *Revelation.* These are always attended by the emotion of the sublime. For this communication is an influx of the Divine mind into our mind. It is an ebb of the individual rivulet before the flowing surges of the sea of life. Every distinct apprehension of this central commandment agitates men with awe and delight. A thrill passes through all men at the reception of new truth, or at the performance of a great action, which comes out of the heart of nature. Every moment when the individual feels himself invaded by it is memorable. By the necessity of our constitution, a certain enthusiasm attends the individual's consciousness of that divine presence. The character and duration of this enthusiasm varies with the state of the individual, from an ecstacy and trance and prophetic inspiration—which is its rarer appearance—to the faintest glow of virtuous emotion, in which form it warms, like our household fires, all the families and associations of men, and makes society possible. A certain tendency to insanity has always attended the opening of the religious sense in men, as if they had been 'blasted with excess of light.' The trances of Socrates, the 'union' of Plotinus, the vision of Porphyry, the conversion of Paul, the aurora of Behmen, the convulsions of George Fox and his Quakers, the illumination of Swedenborg, are of this kind. What was in the case of these remarkable persons a ravishment has, in innumerable instances in common life, been exhibited in a less striking manner. Everywhere the history of religion betrays a tendency to enthusiasm. The rapture of the Moravian and the Quietist; the opening of the internal sense of the Word, in the language of the New Jerusalem Church; the *revival* of the Calvinistic churches; the experiences of the Methodists,—are varying forms of that shudder of awe and delight with which the individual soul always mingles with the universal soul."

I have quoted this passage at length because it seems to me to indicate and emphasize a permanent and essential factor in religious experience, of which much of what is called the philosophy of religion takes little or no account. All the instances referred to by Emerson involve the direct and immediate consciousness in the subjects of these experiences of union and communion with that Universal Ground of all finite being who is immanent alike in nature and in the human consciousness. If it be alleged that these instances of spiritual exaltation are only subjective psychological states, and that the assumed objective action of the Universal on or in the human soul is an intellectual hypothesis which the reason forms in order to account for the emotional excitement, the answer is, that this theory would certainly not be admitted to be an adequate account of the matter by any one who has really enjoyed these religious experiences. The feeling or direct perception of the inter-communion of the finite soul with the Universal Soul is an integral factor of the religious experience itself, a factor in the absence of which no such spiritual phenomena could either arise or persist; and therefore, though the philosopher may justly argue from the existence of such religious experience to the being and immanence of God, he must never lose sight of the truth that it is an essential element or condition of these experiences that to the subjects of them the presence and action of the Universal Soul, or the Father within them, should appear to be revealed by direct and immediate feeling or apprehension, and not by way of argumentation and hypothesis. Nor is this true only in the case of the intense and somewhat exceptional cases of religious experience which Emerson adduces; it holds good also of all the ordinary and tranquil states of the religious consciousness; and it is this immediate feeling of the union and communion of the finite soul with the immanent God in whom all live and move and have their being, which forms the basis of every thrill of religious emotion, and " warms, like our household fires, all the families and associations of men, and makes society possible." In some minds and moods it reaches the higher stages of vividly felt personal relations between the soul and the indwelling Eternal; but in the case of every rational being, this God-consciousness, this immediate sense of the relationship of the dependent soul to the Absolute, of the individual to the Universal, is implicitly, and in some degree explicitly, present; and at any moment may, by some appeal to what is eternal and universal either in our reason, our moral and æsthetic ideals, or our higher unselfish affections, be awakened into vivid realization.

Whoever attempts to ignore this immediate consciousness of the self-revelation of the Eternal in our reason, in our ethical and æsthetic ideals, and in every surrender to self-forgetful affections—and our Anglo-Saxon mind, with its tendency to rest on the deliverances of the senses and the understanding, is far too apt to ignore it—does not penetrate to the inmost core of our religious self-consciousness, and his so-called "proofs" of the Being and Attributes of God will not come home to the mind and heart with conclusive power. We cannot make God an object of thought wholly separate from ourselves who think Him, for it is only in Him and through Him that we can think or reason at all. He is "the Fountain Light of all our day," He is "the Master Light of all our seeing." The most convincing evidence, after all, of the being and nature of God is then, I think, to be found in the direct consciousness that our finite selves are dependent on, and indivisibly united with, a deeper and infinite Self; and that in our higher reason, in our ethical ideals, and in that love which rises above all egoistic interests, we feel ourselves in immediate relationship with elements of absolute and universal worth and authority which inevitably awaken the belief that these are the expression of ultimate Reality, of the self-existent Ground and Source of finite existences. Not, then, in some foreign sphere to which we have access only by the bridge of logical inference, must we seek for the clearest evidence of God's presence and activity, and for the permanent Ground and Source of theological belief, but rather in the immediate deliverance of our consciousness in its highest experiences and moods; and we may say of God what the German poet says of Truth:

> "Es ist nicht drauszen, da sucht es der Thor;
> Es ist in dir, du bringst es ewig hervor."

And if we were right in regarding all finite things and finite minds as differentiations of the essential nature of the Divine Being, in the case of whom God eternally calls into existence partial "others" than himself as objects of his interest and love; and if, as appears evident, He imparts to these projections from Himself varying degrees of selfhood and independence, while still remaining in indivisible union with, and immanent in, each and all,— then surely it is to be expected that there should be an immediate feeling of relationship in our individual minds with the Eternal Mind; for notwithstanding the diversity of persons, all men are ultimately of one substance with the Eternal Father, and in the highest experiences of the human soul man's being and the being of God become in a measure identical. And when we reflect on those rational, moral and spiritual features of the individual consciousness which carry in themselves self-evident marks of universality and eternity, and of absolute worth and authority, and which, though they arise in and illumine our finite existence, find no explanation of their origin there,—is it not, I ask, a rational and justifiable conclusion that these ideas of our theoretical and practical reason, to use Kant's phraseology, are a revelation in us of the true nature and essence of the Eternal Substance, God? And this explains how it comes about that the great founders of religions or of religious revivals have not been men who were wont to attempt any logical demonstration of the being and nature of God. Their method was to give expression and illustration to the deepest secrets of that communion and relationship with God of which they were immediately conscious. Jesus, for instance, speaks of the Father within him as of One whose reality and presence was self-evident, and therefore needed no proof; and when by his glowing words and by magnetic contact with his own divine character he had made the hearers' hearts "burn within them," or, in other words, when he had called out of its latent and dormant condition their sense of relationship with the immanent God, they too needed no other proof, for the Eternal was actually revealing His living presence in their ethical and spiritual consciousness. "Proofs," as we shall afterwards see, are very needful and useful in their way, but it is not by them that the belief in God is first awakened, and it is not in them that the religious mind at length finds repose and satisfaction.

The Mystic, then, that is the thinker who rests religious belief on immediate feeling, stands, I apprehend, on sure ground, in so far as he recognizes a direct consciousness of the presence and activity of God, or the Absolute, in the soul's inner life. Were not the germs of the ideas of self-existence, of infinity, of the absolute worth and validity of our ideals, already given in the very constitution of our self-consciousness, no association or mental manipulation of our sensations could possibly originate and develop them; and with this immediate consciousness of the Universal and the Absolute is indivisibly blended the consciousness of our dependence on, and our intrinsic relationship to, this eternal Reason, this source of Categorical Imperatives, this immanent presence of an all-embracing, all-unifying Love. Of course I do not for a moment mean that this God-consciousness, this immediate inkling of an absolute and eternal life immanent in and inspiring our finite and dependent life, is distinctly and fully recognized till the soul has reached a high stage of thinking and of ethical and spiritual experience; but what I do maintain is, that even in the lowest life that can be called human and rational, the germs of this higher consciousness are present and, to some extent, operative. Though they are at first quite in the background of the moral and religious consciousness, they none the less form an integral and essential factor of that consciousness, and are not wholly without influence on the ethical sentiments and the religious faith of even savage tribes.

All thinkers who recognize an *à-priori* element in human ideas and beliefs will accept the position here assumed, whether they are inclined to what is called mysticism or not. But what is peculiar to the mystic's view is, that he declares that he does not merely *infer* the objective reality of the Supreme Being from the existence in his mind of these *à-priori* elements of thought, but that he immediately feels, in the very having of these ideas and ideals, a direct union and communion with that Absolute Being whose immanence in the individual consciousness is the basis on which all *à-priori* thinking and feeling is founded, and the source whence it arises.

This view of the soul's direct cognitive relation to the Absolute, or the indwelling Father, is, I feel assured, true to the facts of our ethical and religious experience; and therefore I conclude that the supreme Object of religious belief is never entirely an inferred reality, but is even more directly apprehended in the soul's higher life than the external world of nature is directly apprehended in our sentient and perceptional experience. And herein consists, I think, the element of truth in the doctrine so emphatically laid down in Mr. Spencer's "First Principles," that the finite soul has a vague and indefinite, but still most real, immediate consciousness of the Absolute. I shall return to this in a future Lecture.

Having now expressed some degree of sympathy with the mystical emphasis on immediate feeling as a real basis of religious belief, it is necessary that I should briefly note what I regard as erroneous and misleading in all the forms of extreme mysticism. The mystic is apt to forget that though we, as rational and religious beings, have some immediate apprehension of the Divine Presence, and may be said to directly feel the reality of God and our personal relationship to that reality, nevertheless this feeling is not the apprehension of God by some special faculty distinct from our higher reason and our ethical ideals. It is God as immediately revealed *in* these ideas of the reason, *in* these moral imperatives, that we are immediately conscious of, and therefore it is only through our fidelity to truth and our free self-surrender to those ideals which seek and demand realization at our hands, that this immediate feeling of communion with God retains its harmony and its vitality, and passes from the condition of a vague feeling of relationship to the definite and delightful sense of personal co-operation and sympathetic union with that Ultimate and Divine Self on whom we feel our dependence, and whose true nature is revealed to us in those ideals of truth, beauty and goodness, which authoritatively claim to dispose of our will. Hence all mysticism which tends to distract the soul from active interests and endeavours, and aims at a knowledge of God through quiet contemplation alone, is essentially suicidal; for the being and attributes of God are more clearly apprehended in the ethical consciousness, and in the active co-operation of the human will with the Divine, than in any other of our human experiences; and therefore the life in God, and the attendant insight into the nature of God, inevitably loses somewhat of its vitality the moment the interest in the practical realization of ideals droops and fades. The Eternal is immanent alike in our higher reason, in the ideals which invite and command our will, and in the rational affections which overcome all the repulsions of individual self-seeking and create a living sense of universal brotherhood. No account, then, of the nature of religious belief can be sound and adequate which does not find the source and nourishment of that belief in the blended deliverances of our reason, of our ethical insight, and of our self-surrender to the unifying emotion of Divine Love. Reason, Duty, Love, are but different aspects of the one supreme unifying principle, the three modes of the revelation of the Universal and the Eternal in our finite consciousness; and in proportion as any one of these manifestations of the Universal Soul is ignored or neglected, to that extent the finite soul's belief in God either grows fainter and feebler, or else becomes so commingled with narrowness and error as to furnish but a very blurred and distorted image of the immanent Father of our spirits.

And it is to be noted that our ethical experience, which reveals the authoritative presence of the Universal Spirit in our self-consciousness, at the same time as clearly reveals to us that our life and our selfhood is no mere phase of the Eternal thought and life, but that God, in calling into existence our finite souls, provides a *real* and not merely an *apparent* other than Himself as an object of His thought and His affection. For our self-consciousness shows that while God remains in indivisible union with our souls, in our reason, in our ideals, and in our rational affections, He yet withdraws Himself from identity with our *Wills*, and so leaves us in some measure free to determine our degree of essential community with Himself. The recognition or non-recognition of the validity of this deliverance of our moral consciousness constitutes the essential difference between Theism and Pantheism. Hence, as I shall endeavour to show in a future Lecture, this moral nature of ours, which reveals the immanent presence in our finite life of the very life of God, at the same time just as clearly protests against the total absorption of our human personalities in the Divine. Our ethical consciousness bears, I believe, emphatic and unmistakable witness to the real freedom of our will, and to that possibility of a genuine antagonism between our personal wills and the will of the Father within us which almost all extreme mystics, as well as such Pantheistic theologians as Schleiermacher, and such Pantheistic philosophers as Spinoza and Hegel, either silently ignore or explicitly deny.

From the foregoing exposition you will gather that I find the most important basis of religious belief in the fact that man's self-consciousness directly reveals the relation of his finite personality to the Universal and the Eternal. This consciousness of relationship includes the element of Feeling, the element of Thought, and the element of Will, or, rather, these three relationships are really only three aspects of the one relationship of the finite self to the Infinite and Absolute Self; for, as I have before indicated, many considerations appear to lead us necessarily to the conclusion that our finite personalities are the offspring or the individualized differentiations of the Ultimate Ground of all existence. But, as we have seen, this individualism, though in the case of man it extends so far as to admit of a real dualism of will in man and God, and therefore of the existence of true moral responsibility in man, nevertheless is a differentiation which does not mean a complete division; for in all that we call our higher life the identity of the finite soul with the Eternal Ground of its existence still remains.

Unlike what takes place in the case of created beings and their offspring, the bond which unites the life of the Eternal Father with that of His rational children is never wholly severed. In all the higher experiences of the created and dependent soul the essential nature of the Universal Soul is immanent and active. The *à-priori* elements of our thinking, the æsthetic and ethical ideals which with increasing clearness and purity disclose themselves in the course of our experience, and the ineffable thrill of delight which accompanies the victorious dominance of Divine Love in the soul,—all these are but the varying modes or aspects of that eternal life which has its basis and its source in the essential nature of Him from whom we proceed, and in whom we still live and move and have our being. His self-existent, or absolute, life is immanent in our finite and dependent life, and renders us capable at once of philosophic thought, of religious aspiration and devotion, of ethical self-renunciation, and of that highest love which is more fundamental than all individual differences, and as it takes possession of the soul absorbs and so annihilates all private egoistic claims.

I have dwelt at such great length on the immediate feeling of the Divine Presence in the soul as an essential element in religious experience, that it is very possible that my readers may imagine that I myself belong to that mystical school of philosophical speculation, of which the British mind, with its love of precise definition and clear understanding, has an especial distrust. My reason, however, for thus emphasizing this particular feature in religious experience is, that it is precisely the recognition of this feature which appears to me to be lacking in much of the ordinary Theistic philosophy of our time. In religious experience, Feeling, Thought and Will, are simultaneously and, indeed, indivisibly affected. We cannot have the feeling of personal relationship to God without some idea, faint or vivid, of Him as the Soul of our souls, or, as Jesus described it, of the Father within us; nor without the impulse or felt obligation to surrender our will to that higher and Eternal Will which manifests itself in every ideal aspiration.

The Mystic may, as Schleiermacher sometimes does, exclusively insist on the soul's immediate Feeling of the Universal and Divine; the Rational Idealist, on Thought as the ultimate reality; and the Ethical Theist, on the Moral Imperative which commands the Will; but whenever any one of these ignores the other two, he is dealing with an unreal abstraction, and not with the concrete fact of the actual self-revelation of the Eternal to the human soul.

When the Mystic assures us that the immediate apprehension of God in religious feeling constitutes the entire content of our acquaintance with Him, or when Faust exclaims to Margaret—

"Nenn's Glück! Herz! Liebe! Gott!
Ich habe Keinen Namen
Dafür, Gefühl ist alles—"

the objection immediately suggests itself that feeling wholly divorced from thought would be unintelligent and blind, and that therefore in the religious consciousness feeling must be associated with those germinal elements of unifying Thought, which, if developed, lead to that philosophical insight which, however imperfect, is still, we cannot but believe, an approximation to the idea of the universe as it presents itself to the Eternal Mind. But when, on the other hand, the Hegelian Idealist makes Thought the necessary *antecedent* to all religious Feeling, and declares, as Principal Caird does, "that what enters the heart must first be discerned by the intellect to be true,"[1] I cannot but think that he runs directly counter to the facts of experience, and commits in another form the same error which the Hegelian commits elsewhere in making thought the prior condition of bodily sensation; for surely the religious feeling of relationship to God does not wait for its existence upon the successful issue of a course of philosophical thinking. Much more truly does Jesus of Nazareth indicate the true basis of religious belief in the memorable words, "The pure in heart shall see God."

And if neither the Mystic can be allowed to emphasize feeling as the sole constituent of religious insight, nor the Rational Idealist be allowed to make religious feeling a secondary product of intelligent thinking, so, in like manner, those Ethical Theists who, like the early Hebrews, teach that God is known only in the commandment of the moral imperative, though they undoubtedly lay the stress on the most important and influential factor in our apprehension of God and of His relation to our individual minds, yet place an unreal distance between God and the soul; and their view needs to be associated with the doctrine of the felt immanence and inwardness

---

[1] *Introduction to the Philosophy of Religion*, p. 175.

of God's presence in our aspirations after truth, in our æsthetic emotions and in our diviner affections, if it is to at all adequately express the manifold ways in which the Indwelling Father reveals Himself in the reason, the conscience and the heart. That man is of one substance with God is a profound truth which the Hebrew mind, until it came in contact with the philosophic insight of the Greeks, never fully realized.

The chief basis, then, of the belief in God is to be sought, I apprehend, in the fact of self-consciousness—in the fact that the Absolute Being becomes incarnate, so to speak, in those aspects of our feeling, thinking and active personality in which we are intuitively aware that we are in immediate relation with that which is not finite, individual or created, but which is universal and self-existent, and is therefore of absolute worth and validity and of unconditional authority. But of all the ways in which our finite nature feels itself in relation with the Absolute, by far the most important, in an ethical and religious significance, is that consciousness of the Categorical Imperative by which we feel ourselves morally bound to realize as far as we can our highest ideals; for this feature of our self-consciousness not only assures us that God is, but also assures us of close and immediate personal relationship between Him and our finite selves. It is the characteristic of all our ideals that they not only carry with them the feeling or conviction of their absolute worth, but also involve an *imperative*, a sense of obligation to strive after their realization. The philosopher who has experienced the illuminating power of some grand thought feels himself under a moral necessity to develop it and to give expression to it; and if he should, for the sake of avoiding odium or of gaining popularity, keep back the highest truth the immanent Reason has revealed to him, and give utterance instead to conventional doctrines which to him are no longer the whole and the highest truth, he cannot escape the feeling of compunction, the sense of shame, at having proved unfaithful to the light and the summons of the Universal Reason within him; and the penalty for this infidelity to the Higher Self is the painful sense of discord between his individual self and the indwelling Eternal. So also in the case of the artist; he, too, feels the authoritative presence an objective æsthetic Ideal, which he has not originated, but which reveals itself more clearly as he seeks to realize it, and which claims him as its organ of expression; and should he too, like the ignoble philosopher, shirk the divine claims of the Ideal, and at a lowered level of art seek gratification and success for his personal self, the Divine Presence from which he cannot free himself will reproachfully haunt his spirit, and will give him no perfect peace and rest till he becomes true to his genius, and strives to give expression to his highest insight into the eternal principles of Beauty.

The ethical element thus enters into all ideals, for all ideals impose on those whom they inspire the absolute obligation to embody them as far as possible in the work of life. But it is in what are specially called the Ethical Ideals that the consciousness of personal relationship between the finite mind and the Eternal Mind is most vividly realized. The moral imperative which claims to dispose of our life, and is felt to carry with it an intrinsic authority from which there is no appeal, can never be wholly dissociated from a belief, in fainter or more vivid form, in an objective Reality corresponding to this inner divine voice; and when the moral consciousness has reached any high degree of development, the belief in a God or Gods, which previously had been called forth for the most part by the idea of the mighty personal forces from whose activity the phenomena of nature were supposed to proceed, now altogether alters its base, begins to consciously rest on the moral consciousness as its main foundation, and so becomes indissolubly united with the consciousness of Duty and the realization of the progressive ethical ideal.

The evolutionists are certainly in the right in so far as they maintain that the ethical ideal grows or develops, and gradually disengages itself from the mass of prejudices and errors which are always more or less associated with it, and derive from it a factitious authority. Slowly out of experience the higher ideal emerges; and every noble effort to realize this ideal tends to separate the eternal moral Principle from the accidents which conceal and distort it, and also to raise the ideal itself to higher levels of perfection. In all probability it is the frequent intercourse of a nation with other nations which conditions the growth of cosmopolitan interests and affection. But though deeper and wider experience furnishes the necessary condition for the awakenment of higher affections, the theory of evolution in no way explains how it arises that the higher affection no sooner appears than it is felt to have an intrinsic right of supremacy over the lower affection, even though the latter may oftentimes be by far the stronger passion of the two. The recognition of the higher affection as the expression of the character and will of an Absolute Personality revealing His presence in the finite soul, becomes the main source and support of the religious sentiment; and this relation of morality to religion shows itself as soon as the life of mere sensation and perception has passed into the life of reflection, and social conditions have led to the development of higher affections, and hence to the immediate discernment of higher moral obligations.

The lower stages of religious experience do not explicitly exhibit the chief traits which characterize the later and higher forms. The God or Gods of pre-ethical times (or at least of the times when the ethical consciousness was in a very elementary and undeveloped condition) were mainly the product of the imagination or of the primitive understanding in its quest for an adequate cause of particular natural events. Hence the unreflective mind naturally located a personal consciousness and volitional activity in or behind each of the more striking cosmical phenomena. At this stage, too, the Gods were inevitably regarded as persons co-ordinate with human persons, and distinguished from them only by the vastness of their scale of being and the transcendency of their power. It was not till rational reflection on the fact of self-consciousness revealed the presence of a unifying Reason and an absolute Ethical Imperative in man's inner experience, that more thoughtful minds began to realize the idea of the Supreme Being as essentially One— as immanent in nature and in the soul, and as manifesting Himself under the aspects of Thought and Love and Will.

But this highest form of religious belief is only reached when, on the one hand, intellectual culture has disclosed the immanence of God in the human mind as the rational ground and necessary condition of all thinking and all knowledge; and when, on the other hand, the evolution of ethical ideas and sentiments has revealed that same Divine immanence in the felt absolute imperative through which the higher affections of the soul proclaim their intrinsic supremacy, and Divine Love comes to be recognized as the highest spring of human conduct, as the fundamental principle in all ethical ideals, and therefore as pertaining to, or constituting, the very essence of the nature of God.

This culminating ideal of religious faith first bodies itself forth in human history as the result of that supreme synthesis of the Greek recognition of the immanence of God in the Thought or Reason, with the Hebrew recognition of the immanence of God in the Conscience and the Heart, which took shape in Christian Theism, the historical genesis of which is recorded in the New Testament, and the principles of which, though still in the present day largely counteracted by many perverting and paralyzing prejudices and superstitions, constitute the real vitality and power for good of the various sects which lay claim to the Christian name.

The Greek mind emphasized and explicitly expounded the *rational* aspect under which the all-producing and all-unifying Eternal manifests Himself in the human consciousness and in the objects of nature. The Hellene rejoices in external observation, in beautiful forms, in physical and historical science, in the progressive recognition of the underlying Unity of Thought and Reason beneath the infinite multiplicity and variety of cosmical phenomena. The Hebrew mind, on the other hand, fixed upon and emphasized that aspect of the Universal and the Eternal which is revealed in the unconditional imperative of the *Conscience*, in the sense of personal relationship between the soul and God, and in the painful consciousness at times of the reality of Sin—of real antagonism, that is, between the actual dominant desires and will of the individual, and that Higher and Supreme Will which is manifested in the moral consciousness. At first, this Hebrew recognition of God, as revealed in the Ethical Imperative, led to the idea of an insuperable gulf separating the All-perfect Deity from the finite and imperfect creatures whom He has called into existence; but gradually, in the later periods of the development of Jewish religious thought, the feeling of the immanence of God in the soul's higher affections, as well as the growing perception that the utterances of the conscience are no mere injunctions of an external Imperator, but are endorsed by the individual mind itself in virtue of the essential community of essence which still links the rational soul to its Divine Source,—these considerations, I say, gradually bridged over the imaginary chasm between the creature and the Creator.

Hence there is good reason to believe that Jesus only gave fuller and more perfect expression to noble thoughts and sentiments which were fermenting in the consciousness of many of the choicer spirits among his countrymen, when he declared the relation between the soul and God to be of the most inward and intimate character, and accordingly sometimes spoke of God as "Love," and at other times as "the Father within him." The Hebrew mind was so engrossed with these profoundly important *subjective* relations between the soul and the immanent God, that it felt comparatively little interest in the study of the manifestations of the Eternal Thought and Will in the external world; and therefore had not the genius of Greece done justice to the immanence and self-revelation of God in nature, and to the demand of the Reason for the unification of knowledge, Christianity would have been in danger of passing altogether out of touch with Science and Philosophy, and would have been disqualified for becoming, what it now bids fair to become, the final form of religious belief, the world-religion in which lower forms of faith will at length be merged. But, as I shall endeavour to show in future Lectures, the religious belief which will thus survive will assuredly be something very different from any of those complex forms of theological dogma which now claim to be considered orthodox.

While Hebrew thought and sentiment were too exclusively subjective in their recognition of the self-manifestation of God, Greek thought and sentiment were equally one-sided in the other direction; for the Greek, preoccupied with philosophical and æsthetic interests, and eager to discover in all phenomena but the manifold expression of one fundamental unity, paid little attention to that real dualism of the human and the Divine Will to which the conscience bears emphatic witness; and therefore his philosophizing inevitably tended to such

I. NATURE OF RELIGIOUS BELIEF. 59

neglect or denial of the freedom of the human will as we find in Stoicism and in such modern systems as those of Spinoza and Hegel, which are actuated with the Greek spirit, and are content to treat the human mind as simply a necessary mode of manifestation which the Eternal Thought assumes when, as Green says, "it reproduces itself" under the organic conditions of the human frame. I shall return to this subject in a later Lecture.

Here I simply wish to indicate how the different stages of religious belief arise; and my contention is that reflection will justify the conclusion, that when mankind has reached that point of mental and moral development in which the universal and necessary element in the ethical consciousness is clearly recognized, and the main foundation of Theistic belief is seen to lie in that sense of unconditional obligation which accompanies the insight into duty, all further advance in religious insight is determined by the progressive purity and elevation of the recognized ethical ideal. And this position is confirmed by the fact that the founders of religions which claim a universal character, such as Gautama the Buddha, Jesus of Nazareth and Mohammed, have all based their new religious movement on some alleged new insight into man's moral nature and its theological implications. Mohammed saw in the moral consciousness clear evidence of the Unity and Absolute Sovereignty of the Supreme Being; Gautama saw in the purification and elevation of the moral character the only possible way of escape from the inevitable ills of existence into the passionless peace of Nirvana; and Jesus saw in man's moral and spiritual consciousness the revelation that the Author of the ethical imperative is in essence Eternal Love, and that the Eternal Justice or Righteousness on which the earlier Hebrew prophets had insisted as the most essential property or attribute of God's Being was, although a reality, not the most fundamental reality, seeing that Justice is eternal simply because Eternal Justice is an indispensable condition of the self-realization of Eternal Love.

In the foregoing exposition I have laid the chief stress on the self-revelation of the Absolute Being in the *ethical* factor of our consciousness; but I by no means wish to be understood to mean that our moral experience is the sole source out of which Theistic belief can arise, or the sole foundation on which it can find substantial support. A man's faith in the Eternal is doubtless a complex result, in which inklings of the Absolute and Self-existent One, sounding now out of our rational, now out of our ethical, and anon out of our emotional life, all blend; and these different modes of the self-revelation of the Absolute to the finite mind and heart come home with different degrees of convincing force to different persons and to different moods. Among the purely rational grounds for Theistic belief, the most important are the demand of the Reason for an Absolute Being as the Causal Ground of finite and dependent existences, and the parallel rational claim for an adequate cause for the abundant appearances of intelligent purpose which the visible universe presents. I by no means wish to deny a very real cogency to these venerable cosmological and teleological arguments, and I shall in future Lectures discuss their force; but I wish at the outset to express my conviction that no religious faith which ignores or treats lightly the ethical basis of Theism can be a faith competent to satisfy the soul's deepest needs, or to act with great and beneficial effect on the conduct of life.

The chief task of the philosophic student of religion is, I take it, to explicitly disengage and unfold as accurately and fully as he can the contents of what some Germans call our "God-consciousness"—that is, the self-revelation of the Absolute and the Eternal in the highest forms of man's rational, ethical and spiritual experience. But the very immanence of God in our rational nature creates within us an irrepressible longing and demand for harmony and unity in our fundamental ideas concerning God, Nature and Humanity; and therefore the mind and heart of man are always disturbed and dissatisfied, so long as we are unable to unify that conception of the nature and character of God which is mainly based on the consciousness of those highest ethical and spiritual ideals which press for realization in human life, and that conception of the ultimate ground of phenomena which most recommends itself to the students of physical and psychological science. At present, as in similar earlier epochs in the history of thought when science has been enthusiastically studied, and has succeeded in making important new discoveries which lead to a revising and partial recasting of the prevailing theory of the cosmos, a warm conflict has arisen and is proceeding between Theistic thinkers and those savants and philosophers who opine that our present knowledge is incompatible with Theistic belief. Conspicuously is this the case just now, when the scientific doctrines of Evolution and Heredity, and the philosophical doctrine of Agnosticism, appear to many minds to clash fundamentally with the belief that the ground and source of all phenomena is a Being whose essential nature already realizes those ideals and aspirations which progressively assert their presence and authority in man's mind and heart as civilization advances and human knowledge and experience deepens and widens.

In past times, those bitter antagonisms which have arisen between Science and Religious Faith on occasion of the incoming of new scientific views of the cosmos and its history, have after a while lost their virulence, and at length died away; and this return to amicable relations has always been owing, partly to the circumstance that the savants discover and admit that the facts by no means warrant the extreme form in which the new doctrine was presented by its first enthusiastic expounders, and partly to the discovery by the theologians that much which they had formerly supposed to be vital to their Theism is quite unessential and may with advantage be allowed to drop away. Whether such a reconciliation will also supervene upon the present serious discord between influential scientific views and religious faith, remains to be seen. But it is clear that the rational Theist must not be content with establishing his religious belief on the basis of the self-revelation of God in man's higher life; he must also intervene in this conflict between alleged scientific and philosophical truth and the postulates of faith, and see if he can by adequate reasons show that there is no real incompatibility between the facts which scientific research has solidly established and the essential factors of Theistic belief; for it would indeed be a lamentable outlook both for Science and Religion if the permanent result of modern culture should be the conclusion virtually presented by Prof. Huxley in his recent Romanes Lecture, viz., that God, as the source of man's highest ethical ideals and as the cause and ground of cosmical evolution, is hopelessly divided against Himself.

In this introductory discourse I have endeavoured to give an outline of that philosophy of religious belief which I hope to unfold more fully in the succeeding Lectures. In these Lectures I shall examine the agnostic attitude towards religious belief, and then proceed to estimate the value of the cosmological and moral arguments for the being and essential character of God. But as a preliminary to these discussions, it is desirable to consider whether, in addition to those faculties of the human understanding whereby scientific knowledge is reached, man possesses another faculty by which he apprehends, not the finite things and finite phenomena which make up the cosmos as it affects the outer sense, but rather the ultimate ground or central Principle to which finite things and finite selves owe their existence and their intelligible unity. The subject of my next Lecture will, accordingly, be "Spiritual Insight."

Lecture II.
SPIRITUAL INSIGHT.

It will facilitate the clear understanding of the relation between Religious Belief and Science if we first devote some attention to the distinction between Belief and Knowledge. The most appropriate distinction between these two words comes, I think, to very much the same thing as the epoch-making distinction drawn by Kant between the Reason (*Vernunft*) and the Understanding (*Verstand*); and it is, I take it, very probable that many persons in the present day think themselves to be in a sceptical or agnostic frame of mind in regard to Theism, simply because they fail to realize this distinction. Seeing no way of making the existence of God an object of knowledge in the same sense in which the phenomena of nature or the existence of their fellow-men is an object of knowledge, they come to think that all apprehension of the being and influence of an absolute and uncreated World-Soul with whom our finite souls may hold personal communion, is intrinsically beyond the reach of our human faculties.

When I say that Kant's distinction between Reason and Understanding is fundamental and important, I am far from meaning to express my full acceptance of the

II. SPIRITUAL INSIGHT.

results to which Kant was led in his celebrated "Critique of the Pure Reason." You will remember that Coleridge, who imported the distinction into English literature and attached the highest importance to it, interpreted the functions of the Reason in a way very different from Kant's way. Kant applied the term Reason, not only to the ultimate principles of our thinking faculty, but also to the ultimate principle of our ethical insight, marking the difference between these two aspects of the Reason by calling the former aspect the Theoretical Reason, and the latter aspect the Practical Reason. But the questionable feature in Kant's doctrine is, that these two aspects of the Reason, as presented by him, essentially differ from each other in the nature of the insight they afford into the ultimate reality. When we read that Reason is divided into Theoretical and Practical, the natural inference is, that this division simply means that Reason in its theoretical aspect throws light on the ultimate nature of existence as it is; while in its practical aspect it throws light on the ideal end at which the ground of the universe is aiming, and in so doing enjoins on man the ethical principles which ought to govern his conduct. Kant, however, while representing the Practical Reason as a faculty which admits us to objective or absolute truth, will not allow to the Theoretical Reason anything more than a regulative value. In his "Critique of the Pure Reason" he shows that all experience involves two factors—the data of sensation on the one hand, and, on the other hand, the mind's own contributions, i.e. the forms of Space and Time, and the categories of the Understanding, such as Substance,

Causality, &c. The analysis of experience, he maintains, reveals nothing more than these factors; and he also concludes that the forms of Space and Time and the Categories may be only the conditions under which the *human* mind is necessitated to think phenomena, and may not condition the self-consciousness of the Absolute Being. In these forms of the Sensibility and the Categories we see the functions of what Kant calls the Understanding (*Verstand*); but there are, he contends, Ideas in the human mind, viz. the ideas of Self, the Cosmos and God, which cannot be said to be arrived at by the analysis of experience. The forms of Space and Time and the Categories of the Understanding are subjective elements which are only given in connection with the data of sensation; but these Ideas of the Reason (*Vernunft*) have no corresponding association with sensational facts. They appear, in Kant's view, to arise out of a principle in the human consciousness which will not allow man to be content with the apprehension and cognition of finite and conditioned phenomena, and continually prompts him to seek some unconditioned ground of reality. As, then, these ideas have no basis in experience, as Kant defines experience, they are not objects of knowledge, and therefore have no *constitutive* value in a philosopher's world-theory. They have, says Kant, a *regulative* value, and indicate ideal ends which our minds cannot help keeping in view in their attempts to intellectually conceive of Man, the World and God, as unitary realities. While, however, they have no basis in objective experience, and cannot be got at by any analysis of that experience, neither have they, in Kant's view, any absolute value as admitting us to ultimate truth. The Theoretical Reason, then, as expounded by Kant, is in every respect disappointing; it affords no basis either for a philosophy of the universe or for religious belief. Space and Time and the Categories of the Understanding only reveal the conditions to which all human knowledge is necessarily, and therefore universally, subject; but they do not enable us to pass from our human conceptions of reality to reality itself, that is to reality as it presents itself to Absolute Thought. And if we turn to the Ideas of the Reason where the mind appears to transcend finite phenomena and to apprehend the unconditioned ground of phenomena, we are assured by Kant that the unifying Reason is as incapable as the analyzing Understanding of helping us to any insight into the ultimate constitution and drift of the universe.

The metaphysical discussions, then, in the "Critique of the Pure Reason" issue in wholly sceptical conclusions as to the possibility of an ontology, or positive philosophy of Being, and can consequently furnish no ground for Theistic belief. Had Kant written no other work than this, he would, so far as the philosophy of religion is concerned, have proved himself at least as thoroughgoing a sceptic as David Hume. But, as you no doubt are well aware, the Reason which in its *theoretical* aspect is so barren of philosophical and theological results, no sooner presents its *practical* aspect, in the *Kritik der praktischen Vernunft*, than it suddenly and strangely alters its character, and becomes a faculty of positive insight into absolute reality. The Categorical Imperative, with its " Thou oughtest to do this," states a demand which, unlike the relations of the Understanding and the ideas of the Reason in the earlier Critique, has more than subjective validity, and must be accepted as of quite absolute value and authority. Having thus got a firm footing in the realm of the Absolute in virtue of this felt unconditional demand of the Reason in our ethical consciousness, Kant proceeds to establish on this foundation the belief in the Freedom of the Will, in the Immortality of the Soul, and in God.

The chief difference, then, between the view of the basis of religious belief to which I have been led in the first Lecture, and the view of Kant, is, that while I entirely agree with Kant in fixing on the moral consciousness, or the Practical Reason, as the most important and deepest source and ground of religious belief, I do not follow him in his doctrine that the theoretical aspects of the Reason throw no light whatever on what is real in the Absolute Being, and on the relation between His nature and human nature. You will have observed that this faculty of the soul, which Kant calls Reason (*Vernunft*), is precisely the faculty on whose reality and validity I have been insisting all through the previous Lecture: the faculty, that is, whereby the human mind becomes intuitively aware of the presence and operation in its self-consciousness of a Reality which is not felt and thought to be finite and dependent, as the individual soul itself is felt and thought to be, but is felt and thought to be Absolute, Uncreated, and therefore of ultimate and unconditional worth and authority. It is true that it is only through our ethical consciousness that we become at once aware that there is in us a certain community of essence with this Uncreated or Absolute Ground of our finite existence, and also that He has delegated to us a range of moral freedom, a power of free choice between conflicting alternatives, which makes our moral responsibility real, and renders possible a discord between His will and ours. But while this revelation of the Practical Reason is of this momentous significance, it still remains true, I believe, that in the rational and in the affectional features of our self-consciousness we also have authentic insight into the essential nature of the Absolute Reality.

But not only do I think Kant is mistaken when he wholly denies to the Theoretical Reason that ontological vision which he allows in the case of the Practical Reason, but I feel also compelled to dissent entirely from the circuitous way by which he travels from the immediate consciousness of the unconditional ethical imperative to the belief in God. In his view, as all students of philosophy well know, the consciousness of the absolute "Ought" does not immediately and necessarily involve a belief in God as the source of that imperative. His doctrine is, that the human mind is by its constitution compelled to believe that virtue and happiness must somehow and somewhere coincide; and as they manifestly do not always accompany one another in this life, a future life is necessary as a condition of their ultimate coincidence; and the being and the will of God must also be postulated in order to ensure that, either here or hereafter, ethical justice is done. Now, for myself, I am in no way conscious of going through this process of reasoning in passing from my experience of absolute moral obligation to the belief in the reality of God. Indeed, it appears to me that Kant's mode of explanation must be exactly inverted. It is just because we first believe in God and in His eternal justice in virtue of our consciousness of the moral imperative, that we are led to expect that in this or in a future life moral retribution will become a realized fact. But while thus compelled to differ from Kant as to the precise way in which the Practical Reason or Conscience and the Belief in God are related, I can still claim that my insistence on the *ethical* consciousness as the most important source and basis of Theistic belief, is supported by the very high authority of this great philosopher.

Having now given a brief account of the important Kantian doctrine of the *Vernunft*, and of the features in that doctrine which I am unable to accept, I proceed to a brief explanation of the word which in philosophical writings is often placed in antithesis to the Reason, namely, the Understanding (*Verstand*). The Reason is pre-eminently the philosophical and theological faculty; the Understanding, on the other hand, is pre-eminently the scientific faculty. Nevertheless, it is impossible to wholly separate these two modes of cognition. We may say, and rightly, that while the main function of the Reason is to deal with the supersensual, the universal and the ideal aspects of reality, the function of the Understanding is to deal with the finite objects of sense, or the particular events of consciousness; but in point of fact even the exercise of the Understanding involves a certain recognition of, and faith in, supersensual and universal principles; for science could not take a single step in the investigation of phenomena, and in induction and generalization, without faith in the validity of the formal laws of logic. To this extent, then, as also in regard to the acceptance of the so-called necessary truths of mathematics, the operations of the Understanding rest upon a previous exercise of the Reason; and if (as I shall presently urge) it is appropriate to say that the Reason deals with what we *believe*, and the Understanding with what we *know*, it will follow that all knowledge rests ultimately upon belief.

The practical distinction, however, between the Reason and the Understanding is not difficult to discern. When Emerson says, "Give me health and a day, and I will make the pomp of emperors ridiculous. The Dawn shall be my Assyria and unimaginable realms of faerie; broad Noon shall be my England of the Senses and the Understanding; and Night shall be my Germany of Mystic Philosophy and dreams,"—he indicates in poetic phrase what is no doubt to some extent the fact, viz. that while the German mind delights in the exercise of the Reason, that is, investigating the supersensual, the universal, the ontological basis which underlies and unifies all particular facts, the English mind prefers to keep to the region of actually experienced particular sensations, and to that edifice of useful knowledge which, by virtue of the laws of logic and the mathematical sciences, may be legitimately erected upon this sure basis of matter-of-fact perception. Hence when the average English theologian undertakes to discuss the question of the existence of God, he is tempted to deal with the subject solely from the point of view of the Understanding; and the lines of argument on which he professes to rest his religious belief are those which approach the Theistic problem altogether after the scientific fashion—that is, he regards God as an object existing apart from the knowing mind, just as a mountain or a fellow human being is such an object; and he then proceeds to establish the reality of God on the ground that the assumption or hypothesis of such a Being is necessary in order to account for the existence and particular character of the various physical and mental facts. Now the great value of such lines of argument, as furnishing powerful confirmation to a Theistic belief which already exists, cannot be for a moment questioned. If at the core of all reality there is such a rational Ground of all finite existence, and such a Source of our ideals as religious faith accepts, then the world of physical and psychical creatures and phenomena which owe their existence to Him should present features which are in harmony with the essential character of the Being in whom they have their source and ground. And when such arguments as the argument from Design are adduced by the Understanding to show that there really is this harmony between the manifested or created universe and the character which religious belief ascribes to its ontological Ground, such arguments go far to strengthen Theistic faith, and to bring the mind as philosophical and religious, and the mind as scientific, into a condition of inner accord and mental peace.

That such lines of argument, however, do not penetrate to the root of the matter, and therefore cannot of themselves alone establish on a sure foundation a satisfying belief in God, may be safely inferred from the fact that no great religious movement ever has its source in teachers or preachers whose faith in God rests mainly on such considerations as the Understanding alone can furnish; nor is the force of such so-called "proofs of the existence of God" the vital element in the religious faith of any devout mind. The very expression, "proofs of the *existence* of God," is an unconscious admission of the inconclusive character of all such methods of arriving at religious belief by the exercise of the Understanding alone; for the word "existence" strictly means the "standing out" from some fundamental ground, the coming into being as the objects and phenomena of nature and as our dependent minds or individualities come into being; but it is the essential characteristic of the Absolute One that He does not Himself *come into being*, but that He is the Uncreated and Eternal Ground and Cause of all existence, that is, of all finite and dependent realities, whether they be physical or psychical. Of course, I am quite aware that in speaking of the "Existence" of God, the reasoners in question regarded the words "Existence" and "Being" as synonymous; but my point is, that the very fact that this inappropriate word "Existence" has now come to be applied to the Supreme Being, shows that those who initiated that misuse of the term were in the habit of conceiving God as an object of thought quite separate from the thinking mind, and therefore as practically falling into the same mental category as those finite objects and finite individualities to which the term "existence" is rightly applicable. And, in truth, the God which the mind reaches by such arguments as the

Understanding alone supplies is merely an "existent" Being, a Being that is co-ordinate in nature with the human mind, and differing from the human mind only by the immensity of its range. Suppose the presence and action of such an external Mind and Will as these "proofs" by themselves lead us to conceive of were satisfactorily demonstrated, we should not be a step nearer to the Absolute and Uncreated Being; for if He is a Mind and Will in no deeper sense than we are minds and wills (and by the scientific understanding alone no deeper sense is conceivable), then the child's question, "Who made God?" becomes a perfectly legitimate question; for just as we cannot rest in the belief that our own mind and will is uncreate and absolute, so are we just as incapable of resting in the belief that the Infinite Mind and Will as conceived by the Understanding alone is, any more than we are, uncreate and absolute.

The mere Understanding, then, with all its "proofs," is wholly incompetent to afford a satisfying *rationale* of the Ultimate Ground of all existence and of our relation to Him. The God it gives us (even if its arguments be conclusive) is not the God whom the eternal indwelling Reason demands; it is not the God with whom our highest and holiest affections make us intimate; and is, in short, a God who, if he existed, would still need the real God to explain his origin and his relation to the world of matter and mind. The God to which the Understanding alone conducts us (even if he were a real being and not a figment of thought) is at the most a Demiurge, and not the Eternal and Absolute Father who, in His infinite affection, has created His rational children out of His own substance, and still remains in indissoluble union with them as the light of their reason and the basis of their divine ideals and aspirations. That we are justified in thinking of, and indeed are obliged to think of, the elements of the cosmos, physical and mental, as originating in an act of self-differentiation on the part of the Absolute—which act we can only conceive of under the form of Will—is indeed true; but while it is wholly justifiable to reason from the evidences of purpose in nature to the ground and cause of this purpose in the Eternal Reason, it is wholly unjustifiable and theologically misleading to argue, as the Understanding alone must argue, that the cosmos is the product of the activity of a Mind wholly distinct from our minds, and related to human minds as human minds are related to each other. God is the absolute unifying and inter-relating Principle in all minds and all material things, and as such His Being is not inferrible or conceivable by any logical process which the critical Understanding has at its disposal, but is discernible only in virtue of that Eternal Reason which, by its immanence in our consciousness, admits us to an insight into "the deep things of God."

This most profound philosophical and religious truth, that there is in a certain very real sense a true community of essence or substance in God and man, and that what Kant calls the Reason is that faculty in man whereby the immediate presence and operation of the Eternal and the Absolute in our consciousness is discerned, constitutes, I believe, the vital and permanent factor in that Neo-Hegelian philosophy of religion which has been imported into English religious thought by such distinguished writers as the late T. H. Green, of Oxford, and the present Principal of the University of Glasgow; though, as I shall endeavour to show in a later Lecture, these Idealists carry this view of the identity in substance of the human soul and the indwelling Eternal to such an extreme as to leave no possible dualism of will in God and man, and thus entirely remove all rational basis for man's moral responsibility and for the soul's consciousness of sin, the ontological validity of which Kant, with his far deeper and truer reading of man's ethical and spiritual experience, never failed to strenuously maintain.

This distinction between the Understanding and the Reason corresponds to the distinction sometimes drawn between *natural* and *revealed* religion; and in so far as all religious ideas are due to the self-revelation of the Eternal and the Absolute in man's self-consciousness, and cannot be reached by such scientific insight into the particular phenomena of nature as the senses and the understanding of themselves furnish, there is nothing inappropriate in this phraseology. Unfortunately, however, the term "revealed" has been appropriated by those religionists who regard religious ideas and beliefs, not as the outcome of the normal insight of the human mind which has its source in the fact that man is more than a merely finite being, and that in his experience the sense of the finite and the infinite, of the dependent and the absolute, of self and God, are both alike involved, but as entering the soul in an entirely exceptional way through a particular historical channel, and therefore as not discerned by that light of Reason "which lighteth every man coming into the world," but by some other mode of revelation given in a so-called "miraculous" way. It is, as I say, unfortunate that the word "Revelation" has acquired this narrow "orthodox" signification, for it is a word which best expresses a very profound and permanent relation between the individual man and the Father within him, and so cannot well be dispensed with in any thorough exposition of the philosophy of religion. The word "natural," as applied to such religion as the senses and the understanding by themselves can originate, has the same meaning in religious philosophy as it has in our English version of Paul's Epistle to the Corinthians, where, for instance, Paul writes: "Now the natural ($\psi v \chi \iota \kappa \acute{o} s$) man receiveth not the things of the Spirit of God; for they are foolishness unto him; and he cannot know them because they are spiritually judged."

Paul's words naturally suggest the question whether the word "Reason," which I have borrowed from Kant and Coleridge, is the best word to describe this fundamental faculty of spiritual discernment, whereby the individual mind becomes aware of the indwelling presence and operation of the Universal Mind or Spirit. For myself, I am far from being wholly satisfied with the word; for to English ears, at all events, it suggests the idea that the Supreme Being is apprehended mainly by a process of discursive thinking—that is, by the very Understanding which, as we have seen, is of itself incapable of leading to any adequate cognition of the Absolute and the Eternal. And, indeed, in however wide a sense we employ the word "Reason," it will hardly suffice to cover, for instance, that mode of apprehending God by the *heart*, on which Jesus and all deep religious thinkers lay such especial stress.

The Universal and Absolute Being, is revealed to the human spirit through many channels. Even the visible cosmos awakens in the human mind in certain moods, not only the idea of infinitude, but of the personal communion between the finite soul and the Infinite. Such a poet as Coleridge only gives fuller and truer expression to the fainter experience of the average mind when, in speaking of the impression made upon him by the sight of Mont Blanc, he exclaims:

> "O dread and silent mount! I gazed upon Thee
> Till Thou, still present to the bodily sense,
> Did'st vanish from my thought: entranced in prayer,
> I worshipped the Invisible alone."

This deep and comforting sense of relationship to the Eternal which the sweet and solemn aspects of Nature call out, and which for a season lifts the soul above the crowd of petty vexations which harass it, is thus graphically expressed by Mr. Armstrong in his original and valuable treatise on "Man's Knowledge of God:"

> "Has it ever chanced to you in the evening to pass out of the hot room alone under the quiet summer skies? On the lawn or the broad common, with the breeze softly fanning your heated brow, you look up and around. The great stars have come out silently in the darkening sky. The busy hum of day is hushed in the stillness of the night. No footfall strikes upon your ear. You are alone—you and that tumult in your breast. But even as you lift your eyes to the wondrous majesty of the heavens, lo! suddenly a new sense wakens in your spirit. All suddenly

II. SPIRITUAL INSIGHT. 79

the load slips off your heart, and peace steals swiftly, surely on the soul. The discord is solved, and life, just now jarring and discordant, slides into perfect harmony. Alone? No, you know that you are not alone. A Presence that is all love and peace and strength has found you out. It is as though One perfect in strength and goodness spoke in your secret ear and said, 'Behold, I am with you; I care for you and will help you; all is well.'"[1]

This influence of Nature on the mind of man, the reality of which cannot be questioned, is, I apprehend, to be explained as an instance of that fundamental fact to which I have so often adverted, that the human spirit and all the objects of Nature, notwithstanding their seeming total division from each other—an illusion which arises, I think, from the form of space-perception under which the mind must think phenomena—are all rooted essentially in the One Self-existent or Absolute Principle; and therefore any experience which calls forth in the finite mind the often dormant but never wholly absent consciousness of immediate relationship and union with the Eternal and the Infinite, cannot fail to have a certain religious significance, and to awaken in some measure religious feelings and religious faith. In the most religious souls this sense of communion with God awakened by Nature in its grandeur and seeming immensity reaches a most comforting and strengthening vividness, and the New Testament records show that Jesus of Nazareth was wont to seek spiritual refreshment from lonely walks by the moon-lit lake or on the quiet mountain-top. Tranquillizing beyond measure is this vivid

[1] P. 58.

realization of the spirit's union and communion with the Eternal.

But, as I have said, there are many channels through which this immediate sense of the relationship of the dependent soul to the Absolute Soul is, with greater or less intensity, realized. The very feeling of absolute dependence which is inherent in the finite soul, carries with it in man's rational nature the ultimate postulate of, and belief in, the reality of an uncreated Cause and Ground of all that is finite and created; and thus through our reflective reason, as well as through our immediate perception, the visible world of phenomena awakens and sustains faith in the underlying reality of the uncreated Invisible. This, as I shall afterwards endeavour to show, is the real basis of that argument from Causation, or Cosmological Proof of the being of God, which, in conjunction with the argument from Design, has from time immemorial played a conspicuous part in all attempts to furnish a *rationale* of Theistic belief. But not only does this feeling of our essential dependence carry with it, as its inseparable accompaniment, a more or less vivid consciousness of the reality of the Absolute, but all truly philosophical thought—all thought, that is, which penetrates deeper than superficial differences and divisions, and reveals the presence of the Basal Unity beneath and behind all individual varieties—gives a feeling of delight and freedom to the soul; for it, too, awakens the sense of union and communion with the Uncreated and the Absolute.

It is, however, as we have before seen, in connection with the soul's *ethical* and *spiritual* consciousness that the reality of God, and the soul's personal relationship to Him, are most vividly and fully revealed. And therefore it is that the ancient Hebrew mind (whose highest religious experience culminated in the character and faith of Jesus of Nazareth), through its essentially subjective tendency, and its intense realization of the Universal and Eternal One, at first in the character of Justice or Righteousness, and finally in the character of Universal Love, has naturally and inevitably furnished the greatest religious text-book of our race, and that in its imperishable literature the human mind and heart finds a perennial spring of religious inspiration and theistic belief.

I have said that it is in the unconditional or categorical imperative which accompanies the presence of the ethical ideal that the soul most unmistakably realizes the presence of the Absolute Being and its personal relationship to Him. It is necessary, however, here to guard against the possibility of a serious misapprehension. In a later Lecture I shall dwell specially on the moral consciousness as being, in my view, the most important basis of religious belief; but it will be well at this stage of my subject to distinctly state that, in claiming for our sense of duty an unconditional imperative, I am very far from meaning that every line of conduct which presents itself to a man as his duty is absolutely good. It is only too abundantly evident that persons at a low state of intellectual and ethical development often regard as their imperative duty a line of action which other persons who have attained to higher and clearer ethical insight would condemn as being to a large extent wholly wrong. Especially will this be evident when, in a later Lecture, we come to consider the essential difference between Rational Religion and Dogmatic Religion; for the bitter persecutions by means of which dogmatic religionists have in many cases felt it to be their bounden duty to repress, and if possible annihilate, all doubt or disbelief of their fundamental dogmas, are now, by the more enlightened insight of the leading minds even among dogmatic religionists themselves, clearly seen to be based upon a fundamental ethical mistake. How it comes about that theological dogmatism creates in its votaries a factitious ethical ideal, and transfers the seat of ultimate authority from the Reason and the Conscience to the Church, I shall afterwards consider. Apart, however, from this distortion of ethical insight by Dogmatic Religion, there are two normal causes which ensure change and evolution in ethical ideas. In the first place, with the development of social life, higher ideal principles come by degrees into clear consciousness; and in the second place, increased experience discloses more effectual modes of applying and realizing in actual life the fundamental principles of conduct which man's ethical insight discerns. It will be found, I believe, that in all cases where the Ideal appeals with its absolute imperative to any man, there is some true and eternal principle involved; but this principle may be so connected with narrow and erroneous views as to the best mode of giving effect to it, that the line of conduct to which it prompts may in its form be diametrically opposed to the course which a profounder rational and ethical insight would perceive to be the best. Hence it will be evident that, while throughout the whole process of man's historical development there has been an Ideal progressively manifesting its presence in the minds of men, and ever carrying with it, as one aspect of itself, an unconditional imperative, obedience to or neglect of which constituted the ethical nobility or ethical baseness of the individual mind, the particular mode of conduct which the moral imperative has enjoined has been determined by the stage of rational and social development which a person or a nation may have reached. Where this is fully understood, there cannot be any rational collision between the ethical consciousness and culture; for while what I have termed the God-consciousness, that is, the felt presence of the Universal and the Eternal, gives the absolute imperative, it is culture which separates the essential from the accidental in the ethical Ideal, and it is culture which discovers the most effective modes of giving practical effect to the eternal principles which the self-evolving Ideal reveals.

To return now to my main subject. It will be noticed by all who reflect on their own inner life that the Universal and Eternal Being not only reveals Himself in the ideas of the Reason and in the imperative ideals of the Conscience, but He reveals Himself also in our higher Affections. There is a universal and eternal element in Love, as well as in Reason and Duty; and what qualifies Christianity for becoming a world-wide religion is, that it is based on the deepest of all principles, viz. on the principle that only in Divine Love does the soul fully realize its inherent birthright, that birthright which belongs to it in virtue of the presence of the Eternal Father in its self-consciousness, and in virtue of the transcendent truth that God, in calling into existence rational souls, has formed them, not of some foreign material extrinsic to Himself, but in very truth of His own essence and substance, and has therefore to that extent died in order that they may live. What we call Divine Love, though it by degrees emerges in human nature out of the midst of the feelings of family and tribal relationship and widening social sympathies, yet contains, as an essential factor of its very being, a rational and universal element which distinguishes it *toto cœlo* from any mere inheritance or development of gregarious instincts or non-rational sympathy.

If I understand this matter rightly, the great mistake which vitiates that otherwise noble ethical system called "Utilitarianism" is, that it wholly fails to recognize this basal truth, that Love, as the highest ethical principle, is essentially something more than a mere widening of personal sympathies till they attain a cosmopolitan breadth. Enlarge the mere feeling of sympathy to the widest possible extent, and you get no nearer to any genuine sanction for moral conduct, to any real source of moral authority. The revulsion from the absurdities and unsympathetic narrowness of English "orthodox" theology has caused many of our best ethical thinkers, such as J. S. Mill, to turn their faces away from theology, and to seek elsewhere for a rational basis of morality. But it is not possible to place Ethics on any solid and permanent foundation if you leave theology out of account. The teaching of Jesus and of Paul on this question of "Love" as a basis of Ethics still holds good, and will for ever hold good; and their view of the matter is, that men are bound to love their fellow-men simply because God is Love. In other words, such love as Ethics needs for its basis has its origin, not entirely in the finite side of our being, by which we are related to the animals, and out of which Darwin wastes his ingenuity in trying to evolve a moral imperative, but in the universal and eternal side of our nature, where God immediately reveals Himself in our self-consciousness. In all true spiritual love, the God-element, the Universal, manifests its presence and its operation. So far is this Love from being identical with mere sympathetic feeling, that it is capable of entirely ignoring or overpowering all regard for the personal pleasure either of the lover or of the beloved ones; and this clearly shows that its root is not in man as a finite individual, but in that Over-soul, that Absolute Being who is incarnate in the human consciousness, and is at once Eternal Reason, Will and Love. Nothing, it seems to me, can be more pitiable than the shifts to which egoistic thinkers are put, when, in the absence of any admission of the authority of the Universal, or God, in human nature, they endeavour to find a rational ground for real self-sacrificing love. Few men, probably, have felt spiritual love more intensely than J. S. Mill did; but his writings reveal the almost grotesque inadequacy of his sensational and egoistic philosophy to explain and account for his own vivid recognition of the claims which the Indwelling Eternal made on his soul. Rather than worship a deity who had not what we call moral attributes, he would, he says, go to hell, i.e. endure the unending agonies which the creed-books associate with that locality; but the only intelligible explanation that can be given of this statement is, that there was in Mill's self-consciousness, though not in his philosophical system, a quite infinite or incommensurable difference of ethical rank between the cravings for personal pleasure and comfort which he felt as a finite individual, and that demand for absolute rectitude and self-sacrificing love which was the self-revelation of the Eternal and the Infinite within him. It has been conclusively shown by Dr. Martineau[1] that it is utterly impossible for a philosophy which begins with the egoistic maxim, "Each for himself," to find a road that shall lead at last to the universalistic maxim, "Each for all." I contend, then, that the conviction we have that we are unfaithful to the rightful claims of our higher nature whenever we allow selfish desires and ambitions to overrule our interest in the true welfare of others, is only rationally explicable on the supposition, to the truth of which our self-consciousness bears witness, that our nature is not only the seat of private desires and aspirations, but that there is also immanent within us, and apprehended in varying degrees of fulness, the unifying principle of Eternal Love. As our ethical ideal attains greater purity and fuller development, this principle of Love is increasingly recognized as the rightfully dominant spring of action in the soul. If the foregoing exposition is sound, it will follow that religious belief will be called into existence and intensified in proportion as that aspect of our inner experience in which the Eternal reveals Himself is awakened into vivid self-consciousness. We have seen that though the influences of the visible cosmos and the incoming

[1] *Types of Ethical Theory*, Vol. II. p. 331, 2nd ed.

into the mind of loftier unifying ideas at times call forth the God-consciousness in our nature, it is nevertheless through the ethical experience of the moral imperative, and also through the felt supremacy in our nature of the principle of Divine Love, that our sense of personal relationship to the Father within us reveals its deepest significance.

And now let me ask you whether the actual experience of the way in which faith in God arises in the soul does not bear out the above view of the essential nature of man's faculty of religious insight. How, as a matter of fact, do great religious movements originate? Is it by intellectual "proofs of the existence of God;" or is it not rather by some great prophet realizing in his character and in his teachings that universal or ideal side of our consciousness in which we recognize the immanence of God in the soul? Even if we take the case of books as means of awakening faith, is it the books which appeal mainly to the logical understanding that do most to engender belief in God, or is it not rather what are called idealistic utterances, such as form a large portion of Plato's works, which vividly picture an ideal life transcending the actual, or writings which, like the "Imitatio Christi," are written under the vivid sense of daily union and communion with the Indwelling Father? Intellectual proofs are by no means without value, but their value consists, not so much in originating faith, as in refuting by certain lines of thought the sceptical doubts which other lines of thought have engendered. Accordingly, as every generation, owing to change in scientific views and philosophical speculations, has its own special intellectual obstacles in the way of faith, so every generation needs a fresh Theodicy; but the greater part of the plentiful crop of philosophical writings which springs up to meet this demand for the reconciliation of religious faith with contemporary culture, after a few short years lose their interest and take their place along with their predecessors of the same stamp on the undisturbed library shelves; while those books, on the other hand, which grow out of and vividly depict in some fashion or other the felt presence of the Divine and the Universal in human nature, have a perennial charm, and are among the most precious of the treasures which the world will not willingly let die. I need not say that the Hebrew and Greek Scriptures are pre-eminently books of this character; and this fact accounts for their unfading interest, and for the impulse which prompts men to reproduce these writings in countless forms and languages, and scatter the copies broadcast over the wide earth. Superstition, no doubt, has some hand in this Bibliolatry; but superstition alone has not the staying power which this reverence for the Christian Scriptures possesses; and the mainspring of the movement is evidently the instinctive consciousness that this book is the best book for awakening and interpreting that deep feeling of union and communion between the finite and the Infinite, between man and God, which is of all relations in our human life the most momentous, and the one in which man's interest never permanently slackens.

And if in regard to *books* it is chiefly by the writings which directly appeal to the divine and universal side of our consciousness that belief in God is awakened and sustained, so is it in the case of the *personal* influences which are mightiest to banish indifference and doubt, and once more cause God to be felt by the soul as a living Reality. It is the spectacle in actual life, or in biography and history, of moral heroism, of self-devoted love, of high moral principle, and, in short, of every phase of human character in which the finite self shrinks into the background, and the individual man wholly forgets his own personal interests and aims through absorption in some love-inspired cause,—it is, I repeat, the spectacle of the practical realization of the indwelling Universal and Ideal as exhibited in some actual human life, which is ever the most potent agent in kindling the God-consciousness of the spectator, and thus making religious belief a mighty principle of thought and conduct. Not until this vivid realization of the Eternal in a man's nature has come about through contact with this same manifestation of the Eternal, either in the actual flesh or in the records of a divine life, is it of much avail to adduce scientific or philosophical arguments to prove the being of God. Indeed, it would not be a whit more absurd to attempt to give a scientific or philosophical rationale of the physical cosmos to a person who was wholly devoid of the sensations through which the cosmos manifests itself to our minds, than to endeavour to prove and explain the being and attributes of God to those in whom the presence of the Universal in Thought, the absolutely Authoritative in Ethics, and the immanent Divine Love in the heart, had in no way become a fact of immediate consciousness. The essence of the knowledge of God is assuredly the immediate consciousness of God.

Given that awakened consciousness, and we may philosophize about God to some purpose; but the *sine quâ non* of all sound and valuable philosophical and theological speculation is the prior direct recognition of the immediate presence and operation of the Eternal Reality in the soul's higher life.

Hence it is, that as in children it is the *perceptive* faculties that one must develop as a basis for future *reflection* and scientific knowledge, so in the case of the religious training of younger children it would be futile, and indeed mischievous, to attempt elaborate intellectual proofs of the being of God, for these logical proofs can only appeal to the child's Understanding. They must, in order to be intelligible to the child, speak of the Eternal as *another* mind like the child's own mind or the minds of its parents; and therefore the more intelligent the child, the more unanswerable are the doubtful questionings to which this logical presentation of the Absolute as a Being outside of the soul inevitably gives rise; and accordingly the laboured demonstration of God's existence to children is far more likely to sow in the young mind the germs of scepticism than of religious belief. This, efficient religious teachers intuitively discern; and therefore make it their chief business to evoke in the child's mind, by appeal to the beauty and grandeur and beneficence of nature, and more especially to the moral beauty and sublimity exhibited in the noblest human lives, that sense of the reality and authority of the Divine which is implicitly present and always capable of being elicited, in fainter or more vivid fashion, in every child's mind and heart. All effective awakenment or revival of religious faith, whether in the child or in the adult, must be initiated by influences which call forth into clear consciousness the moral imperative and the higher forms of self-sacrificing emotion. Jesus, in his profound saying, "The pure in heart shall see God," penetrated, in virtue of his deep religious experience, to the fundamental principle on which alone a sound and adequate psychology and philosophy of religion can possibly be based.

The faculty of Religious Insight, as distinguished from the powers of the discursive Understanding, is by Aristotle described as a function of the Reason ($νοῦς$), and by Paul as a function of the Spirit ($πνεῦμα$). The Pauline term has in general been accepted by modern theologians as more fully expressive of the range of this power of religious insight than the Aristotelian and Kantian term "Reason;" for the word Spirit includes that most important insight into fundamental religious truth which is involved in the soul's higher or rational *affections;* and it appears that neither Aristotle nor Kant adequately appreciated the influential part which is played by the diviner emotions in the establishment and enrichment of man's religious belief. Spiritual Love, as we have seen, is not, like our lower passions, merely a subjective feeling; it has, like the great unifying ideas of the Reason and the unconditional imperative of the Conscience, an objective or absolute character, and therefore carries with it that consciousness of intrinsic authority which appertains to all those Ideals through which the Universal Mind reveals His presence and His Character in the finite mind.

Intimately connected with this question of the nature

of the faculty of spiritual discernment, is the further question, whether the religious insight gained thereby is more appropriately termed *Knowledge* or *Belief.* Now the mere discussion of such a question as this appears on the surface of it to imply that the Theist holds religious truth by a much lower kind of tenure than that by which the Scientist holds his scientific truth. The scientist positively *knows;* the religious man only *believes.* But this contrasting of knowledge and belief to the disparagement of the latter is really baseless, and rests upon the false idea that the word "belief" has only one definite meaning; whereas the fact is, that this word (and the same probably holds good of the corresponding word in all modern languages) has two distinct and in some respects quite antithetic meanings. In the one sense, Belief signifies something short of Knowledge, an intermediate stage between mere opinion and certain conviction, as when one says, "I *believe* that the apostle John wrote the Fourth Gospel, but I do not feel *sure* of it." But in the other sense, the word "Belief" is employed to express what is often the deepest and firmest of a man's convictions, viz. that complete and perfect trust which religious minds feel in regard to the reality of God and of His personal relationship to the human spirit. As I have before pointed out, it is in one sense true that all Knowledge beyond the mere transient consciousness of our present sensations rests ultimately on Belief. One's knowledge of one's past life rests on trust in the validity of memory; knowledge of the facts and relations of an external world depends in like manner on the belief that such a world beyond our personal consciousness exists; and the whole body of physical and mental science is based upon our confidence in the ultimate validity of those principles of formal logic which are presupposed in all scientific reasonings. But all these assumptions which I have enumerated appear to most persons so self-evident, so incapable of being doubted, that we, in general, extend the term Knowledge till it covers all the conclusions that can be reached by immediate sensations as interpreted in the light of these assumed self-evident principles. The word "Knowledge" is thus extended to include those beliefs which all men, or at least most men, hold in common and in all moods; and we talk of knowing something of what happened on this planet in the Silurian or the Carboniferous stage of its history, of knowing that our fellow-men exist, &c.; and thus in this sense we may, if we believe the teleological argument to be of itself perfectly conclusive, be consistently said to have *Knowledge* of God, for such apprehension of God as this implies is reached by precisely the same logical road by which the knowledge of the existence of our brother mortals is reached; but, as we have seen, no complete and adequate insight into God and His relationship to nature and to man can be attained along this route.

I can now answer the question, why I have described the subject of this course of Lectures as "The Bases of Religious *Belief*," rather than as "The Bases of Religious *Knowledge*." It is certainly not because I regard my assurance of the reality of the Eternal, and of His personal relationship to my spirit, as a weaker assurance than that which I have of the existence of an objective cosmos or of my fellow-men. My reason for preferring the word "Belief" rests upon the distinction, on which I have so often insisted, between the insight of the Understanding on the one hand, and the insight of the Reason or the Spirit on the other. It is characteristic of the Knowledge to which the Understanding of itself gives us access, firstly, that it is based upon sensations and beliefs or forms of thought which men in general have in common and in all their moods, and thus it admits always of sensuous verification; and, secondly, that it does not reach to the root of the matter, and proves wholly incapable of passing behind and beyond the endless variety of finite and particular objects and phenomena, to the fundamental and absolute Principle of unity out of which all these finite individuals arise, and by which they are so inter-related as to form one organic whole. It is characteristic, on the other hand, of Religious Insight—of the insight, that is, of the Reason and the Spirit—that it does, as Kant truly saw, admit us in a measure to the sphere of ultimate reality; for the categorical imperative of the conscience has absolute authority and worth, and the development of the Ideal in our inner life furnishes, I believe, progressive insight into the inmost heart of that Self-existent One who manifests Himself in some measure in the phenomena of nature, but only truly reveals Himself in the self-consciousness of His rational creatures. The Understanding deals with what is less and lower than ourselves; the Spirit, with its ever-developing Ideal of perfection, is the meeting-point of our finite selves with that Eternal Self who is infinitely higher than we. And hence it is that our perception of the reality and authority of these Ideals, which are, as it were, the eyes of our spiritual insight, varies greatly with our moods and with our increasing or decreasing self-surrender to the invitations and injunctions of the Eternal Father within us. This belief in God is not something in regard to which we are merely passively receptive of Divine influence; it is to some extent a matter dependent on our personal volition. The reality and authority of the Ideal do not compel conviction like the truths of mathematics or the laws of thought. We feel its intrinsic beauty and its absolute worth; but we are often conscious at the same time of considerations which make us distrustful of the Divine and the Ideal, and cause us to gravitate downward to that lower level in which for the time we most strongly incline to believe in the finite deliverance of the senses and the scientific understanding alone. Hence we *choose* to some extent our philosophical and religious belief, and in so far we are responsible for it.

For these reasons it seems to me that it is more appropriate to speak of the *Belief* in God than of the *Knowledge* of God, and to reserve the word "Knowledge" for such lower insight into the relations of phenomena as the cultivated scientific understanding is competent to reach. But it must not be forgotten that, though our belief in God may fluctuate in intensity according to the nature of our moods, and the character of the influences which at the time most affect us, this is quite consistent with the fact that in some souls in their choicer moments of experience, and in other souls almost universally, this insight into the reality and character of the Eternal reaches an intensity of assurance which far transcends the degree of certainty to which scientific knowledge can attain. With these remarks I bring to a close this outline-sketch of what I conceive to be the chief basis in human nature of the Belief in God.

The position for which I have contended in this Lecture, viz. that in virtue of the immanence of the Eternal in man's rational, ethical and spiritual consciousness, there is in human nature a capacity, not only for the recognition of the being of God, but also for progressive insight into His character, is called in question at the present time in this country by two influential schools of religious thought; firstly, by the thinkers, of whom Mr. H. Spencer is the acknowledged head, who maintain that though the human mind possesses certainty in regard to the reality of the Absolute, it can yet know nothing of His essential character; and, secondly, by the Positivist school, represented by Mr. F. Harrison, who maintain that insight into either the reality or the character of an Absolute Being is intrinsically inaccessible to man, and that accordingly, in place of the worship of God, the religion of the future will substitute the worship of Humanity. To the consideration of these forms of Agnosticism I will ask your attention in the next Lecture.

LECTURE III.
AGNOSTICISM.

If the conclusion reached in the last Lecture be sound, religious faith is no mere temporary phase in the evolution of mankind, but is based upon a permanent relation between the finite spirit and the Universal Spirit. The view for which I have contended is, that the human soul is not merely the product of the creative energy of the Almighty: it is the real offspring of God; and therefore the self-consciousness of man not only mirrors the multitude of finite and dependent things which constitute the visible manifestation of the Absolute, but contains also the germs of conscious affinity with that Supreme Being out of whose substance it is formed. By the Senses and the Understanding man increasingly learns the relations which link into one organic whole the aggregate of physical and psychical existences, while by the higher Reason or the Spirit he gradually awakens to a clear consciousness of the various modes of his relationship to that Eternal Life out of which his finite personal consciousness is an individual effluence.

This consciousness of relationship between the life of the individual and the self-existent Life which animates and unifies the cosmos, is sometimes faint, sometimes vivid; and the conceptions in which it clothes itself vary with the advancing science and culture of each succeeding age. To the child, or to the adult man who is still in the juvenile stage of mental development, the Gods with whom the soul feels itself to be in conscious and sympathetic relation are the powers to which it assigns the phenomena of nature; but with advancing culture, reflection brings man to the conviction that nature is a unity, and that therefore the God to whom he feels himself related is one God. Thus the *interpretation* of the primary consciousness of man's relationship with the Absolute becomes more complete as the rational and moral life unfolds its deeper resources, till, finally, the earlier conception of God as a Mind, like another human mind, acting on the soul from without through the forces of nature, passes into the profounder and more satisfying conception of the Eternal Spirit, as the immanent life of nature, and the Ground and Source of the universal principles of reason, and of those ethical and spiritual ideals which manifest their presence in man's consciousness, and reveal their divine and ultimate authority by the sense of unconditional obligation and absolute worth which characterizes their presence. In virtue of this deepening interpretation of the religious consciousness, Truth is discerned to be something more than man's individual opinions; Beauty, to be something more than individual tastes; and Goodness, to be a progressive ideal of Perfection which has its source in the essence or will of that Eternal Spirit, out of whose energizing the finite human life emerges, and on whom it feels itself to be ever dependent.

III. AGNOSTICISM.

It cannot be denied, however, that in the present time many thoughtful and religiously disposed minds, on both sides of the Atlantic, are feeling by no means satisfied either that there is any rational unifying Principle as the centre and support of phenomena, or that, supposing there is some absolute reality, man possesses any faculty of insight into its essence and character. Many causes conduce to this distrust. The old Deism rested in part on the evidences of Design in nature, and in part on the supposed manifestation of a Divine Presence and Authority in the moral consciousness; but now an impression widely prevails (though it is much weaker to-day probably than it was five years ago) that the Darwinian view of Evolution has superseded the necessity of postulating a primary Intelligence, and that man's progressive ethical insight and sense of moral obligation may be adequately explained as a gradual development through heredity from the feelings, passions and capacity for sympathy, which already show themselves in the lower strata of animal life. Another cause of the disintegration of religious belief is to be found in the circumstance that careful historical research and criticism, as well as the study of comparative religion, have shown the utter untenableness of the old claim set up by the churches for the wholly exceptional inspiration and infallibility of the Hebrew and Greek Scriptures. And, finally, not the least effective influence in this direction is the supposed proof by Sir William Hamilton, Dean Mansel, Mr. H. Spencer and others, that the human mind is confined by its very constitution to a merely relative apprehension of the Absolute and the Eternal, and is therefore excluded from the possibility of insight into the essential nature and character of God.

It is a significant fact, however, as indicating the deep need in human nature for religion, that among those persons whom the scientific and philosophical influences of the day have placed out of sympathy with Theistic belief, two substitutes for Theism—Agnosticism on the one hand, and the Religion of Humanity on the other— can already count a goodly number of adherents; and the formation of a few societies for "Ethical Culture" is another movement in the same direction. The relation between the Agnostic and the Positivist is very suggestive. Each of these two recent forms of anti-theistic religion denies the principle on which the other most strenuously insists. The followers of Mr. Spencer contend that the recognition of the reality of the Absolute Being is at once a necessity of thought and the basis of religious faith, but deny the possibility of any insight into the real nature of this Being in whose presence the mind is compelled to believe. The sympathizers with Comte or with Mr. Frederick Harrison deny that man has any valid ground for asserting the reality of a unifying Principle behind phenomena, but maintain it to be essential to any effective religious belief that there should be a felt personal relationship between the worshipper and his God. As, then, the Spencerian Agnostic asserts that the belief in the reality of an Absolute Cause and Ground of all finite existence is essential to religion, while the Positivist asserts that an intelligible personal relation between the soul and the Object of its devotion is the indispensable feature, there is surely some reason for presuming that it is in the direction of a Theism which combines the belief in the Absolute God with the sense of man's deep personal relationship to Him, that the final solution of the theological problem of our time will have to be sought.

Mr. Spencer's position is, that the religious sentiments which have grown up around the conception of a personal God, though they must needs be modified when the Theistic conception is changed into the conception of a Power whose essential nature is intrinsically unknowable, are nevertheless not destroyed. He maintains that there would still survive the sentiments of wonder and awe "which are appropriate to the consciousness of a Mystery which cannot be fathomed, and of a Power that is omnipresent."

The incompetency of such emotions as these to constitute a satisfying religion, was admirably shown in the noteworthy controversy between Mr. Spencer and Mr. Harrison in the year 1884. In his article on "The Ghost of Religion,"[1] Mr. Harrison writes:

> "What is religion for? Why do we want it? and What do we expect it to do for us? If it can give us no sure ground for our minds to rest on, nothing to purify the heart, to exalt the sense of sympathy, to deepen our sense of beauty, to strengthen our resolves, to chasten us into resignation, and to kindle a spirit of self-sacrifice—what is the good of it? The Unknowable, *ex hypothesi*, can do none of these things. The object of all religion, in any known variety of religion, has invariably had some quasi-human and sympathetic relation to man and human life..... Whether it was the religion of the lowest savage, of the Polytheist, or of the Hegelian Theist; whether the object of the

---

[1] *Nineteenth Century*, March, 1884.

worship were a River, the Moon, the Sky, Apollo, Thor, God, or First Cause, there has always been some chain of sympathy—influence on the one side, and veneration on the other. However rudimentary, there must be a belief in some Power influencing the believer, and whose influence he repays with awe and gratitude and a desire to conform his life thereto."

The language used by Mr. Spencer in the course of this controversy clearly indicates that he felt to some extent the force of Mr. Harrison's criticism; for in several passages of the articles contributed by him at this date to the *Nineteenth Century*, he, consciously or unconsciously, virtually surrenders to an important extent his own fundamental doctrine that the nature of the Absolute is wholly incognizable by the human mind. To call the Unknowable Absolute a "Power" or "Energy," is surely to bring it in some measure within the sphere of cognition; for these words, which derive all their meaning from man's consciousness of his own personal exertion, at once imply a certain relationship or analogy between human activity and the activity of the Absolute. But Mr. Spencer goes much further than this on the road to Theism. He knows enough about this inscrutable Absolute to be able to say that, if not personal, it is certainly not lower than personal; and that in describing it, our choice lies between the personal and something higher than personality.[1] In his article on "Retrogres-

[1] In answer to Mr. F. Harrison, Mr. H. Spencer writes: "Though the attributes of personality, as we know it, cannot be conceived by us as attributes of the Unknown Cause of things, yet duty requires us neither to affirm nor to deny personality, but to submit ourselves in all humility to the established limits of our intelligence, in the conviction that the choice is not between personality and something lower

sive Religion," written in reply to Mr. Harrison's article from which I quoted above, he declares that this Absolute Reality which Science in the last resort is compelled to recognize, stands towards our general conception of things in substantially the same relation as does the creative Power asserted by Theology. The devoutest mystic could surely find a basis for religion in spiritual communion with this super-personal Presence. And if we are assured of the existence of this identity of function between the Absolute Ground of Nature and Humanity and the God of Theism, we cannot be said to be wholly ignorant of the nature of this so-called inscrutable Being. Further, Mr. Spencer describes the Absolute as a Power which is omnipresent. Nay, he knows enough about the "Unknowable" to call it the Eternal and Infinite Cause, and speaks of the phenomena of nature as its manifestations. If, then, we know that God is the Cause, and that physical and psychical phenomena are the Effects, is it not legitimate, and indeed inevitable, that we should reason from the character of the Effects to the character of the Cause? We know each of our fellow-men only by his manifestations or effects in his actions, gestures, words or writings, and from these manifestations we consider ourselves warranted in inferring the existence of a personal self with a certain character behind these phenomena; and, accordingly, Mr. J. S. Mill wholly, and Dr. Martineau partially,

---

than personality, but *between personality and something higher;* and that the Ultimate Power is no more representable in terms of human consciousness than human consciousness is representable in terms of a plant's functions."—*Nineteenth Century,* July, 1884, p. 7. Compare *First Principles,* sect. 31, and Mr. Spencer's *Essays,* Vol. III. p. 251.

bases the knowledge of God on the study of the phenomena of nature. It is clear, then, that Mr. Spencer, in spite of his so-called Agnosticism, gives evidence of having made very considerable progress in his conception of the nature of the Infinite and Eternal Ground of the universe; and he thus practically verifies, what on à-*priori* principles appears inevitable, that it is impossible to assert a positive knowledge of the reality of the Absolute without in the very act breaking the spell of Agnosticism, and affording a basis for positive theological belief.

Hence there is good foundation for the allegation of inconsistency which Mr. Frederick Harrison makes against this attempt of Mr. Spencer's to find in his philosophy a satisfactory foundation for religious ideas and emotions. In his article on "Agnostic Metaphysics," written in reply to Mr. Spencer, Mr. Harrison thus introduces his argument:

"Ten years ago I warned Mr. Spencer that his Religion of the Unknowable was certain to lead him into strange company. 'To invoke the Unknowable,' I said, 'is to re-open the whole range of Metaphysics; and the entire apparatus of Theology will follow through the breach.' .... We see the result. Mr. Spencer has developed his Unknowable into an 'Infinite and Eternal Energy, by which all things are created and sustained.' He has discovered it to be the Ultimate Cause, the All-Being, the Creative Power, and all the other 'alternative impossibilities of thought,' which he once cast in the teeth of the older theologies. Naturally there is joy over one philosopher that repenteth. The *Christian World* claims this as equivalent to the assertion that God is the Mind and Spirit of the universe; and the *Christian World* says these words might have been used by Butler or Paley. This is, indeed, very true; but it is strange to find the philosophy of one who makes it a point of conscience not to enter a church described as 'the fitting and natural introduction to inspiration (!).'"

These remarks by Mr. Harrison are the prelude to a vigorous attack on Mr. Spencer's incipient theology, which, as Mr. Harrison rightly argues, represents God, after all, as too little personal to satisfy the religious needs of mankind. Mr. Harrison then proceeds to extol the Comtist "Worship of Humanity" as the only religion that is at once in harmony with reason, and at the same time capable of kindling powerful emotion, and therefore of strongly influencing conduct. Now it appears to me very strange that Mr. Harrison does not see that this irresistible drift of Mr. Spencer's philosophy into metaphysics and theology is itself a powerful argument against Mr. Harrison's own religious position. For is not this remarkable outburst of metaphysical, and even theological, ideas from the very heart of the most advanced science of our time, as exhibited in the views of Mr. Spencer to which I have just referred, and still more in the writings of his American disciple, Prof. John Fiske, the very best practical refutation that could be given of the fundamental principle of Positivism? Comte declares that as by degrees all the nations of the earth in their progressive culture reach the positivist stage, metaphysics and theology will receive their quietus, and vanish altogether from off the stage of living and effective thought. The positive stage of conviction towards which all culture is approaching, means, he says, the recognition of the truth that all ontological causes (whether metaphysical or theological) are utterly beyond the scope of man's intellectual insight. His fundamental doctrine is, that "the education of the individual, so far as it is spontaneous, necessarily presents the same phases as that of the race; and in our own days, every man on the level of the age will clearly verify the position in his own case that in childhood he was naturally a theologian, in youth a metaphysician, and in manhood a physicist or positivist. The history of the sciences directly proves that it has been the same with the *ensemble* of the human race."[1] So convinced was Comte that with culture all metaphysical and theological ideas must needs be left behind, that he proceeds to say that the Positivist *régime* will put all retrograde folk aside, by treating any one who still lingers in the theological or metaphysical stage of belief "as disqualified for government by weakness of brain."

So far, however, are the facts of individual life and of history from supporting the theory that all theological and metaphysical interest dies out with the advance of positive knowledge of nature, that observation rather shows that every attempt to establish the principle that nothing exists or is accessible to the human mind save the mere order of phenomena, is invariably succeeded by a re-assertion, first of metaphysical, and then of theological ideas. As I have before mentioned, the revulsion in ancient Rome from Epicurean empiricism to Neo-Platonic mysticism and theurgy, and that in the present day from extreme secularism to spiritualism and theosophy, simply illustrate the universal truth that the self-conscious man, the highest product of cosmical deve-

---

[1] *Vide* Dr. Martineau's *Types of Ethical Theory*, Vol. I p. 440, 2nd ed.

lopment, is never permanently satisfied with the mere observation and classification of the facts and laws which the visible or external side of the stream of evolution exhibits, but is irresistibly impelled by his mental constitution to strive to attain, either by fair or questionable means, some real or fancied acquaintance with the Power or Powers to whose agency he is mentally constrained to assign the successive phenomena of which it is the business of science to take cognizance. Historical facts not only show that it is not true that the Positivist view of the universe is that to which human thought tends and on which it finally rests, but they further show that the prevalence of such a view in any epoch invariably calls forth a counter protest from the theologic or theosophic side. Accordingly, the lesson which the study of the history of scientific and theological thought teaches is, that man is not only related by the senses and the understanding to the world of physical and psychical phenomena, but is also consciously related, in his rational, ethical and spiritual experience, to the Absolute Ground and Cause of these phenomena. Hence metaphysics and theology are not merely transient, but are perennial objects of interest to the human mind; and scientific knowledge and religious faith have each their inalienable and imperishable rights and functions in every stage and form of human culture and mental evolution.

That the present relations of culture and religious belief confirm rather than confute the principle that theological ideas possess permanent interest and validity for the human mind, is abundantly shown by this very incursion of Mr. Spencer's thought into the fields of metaphysics and theology which has subjected him to Mr. Harrison's brilliant charge of inconsistency. That this may be seen more clearly, let me ask you to take a retrospective glance over the course of speculation in this country during the last thirty or forty years. At the beginning of this period, what Comte calls the Positive stage of scientific and philosophical culture appeared to be in a very flourishing condition among us. Mr. J. S. Mill, and later on Prof. Bain, whose philosophy resolved all Causation into merely temporal antecedence and sequence, and all Substance, whether physical or mental, into aggregations of present or potential forms of sensation, were popularly regarded as the great leaders of philosophical thought, and as the inaugurators of quite a new era in mental science—an era in which Comte's ideal should be realized, and in which the retention of metaphysical and theological ideas should be regarded as the sure sign of a weak or retrograde intellect.

In one respect only did our English sensational idealists differ from the great Frenchman whose character Mill so warmly and so justly admired, viz. in the importance they attached to the subjective study of Psychology. Auguste Comte, in his violent reaction against everything metaphysical, had too hastily denied that the mind can make a fruitful study of its own states of consciousness, and had treated psychology somewhat slightingly as if it were merely a branch of biology. The English "psychological school" of thinkers corrected this extravagance, and maintained that the investigation of mental states, and of the laws of association according to which they are connected and "chemically" blended, is a very valuable province of research. Still, while giving to Psychology much greater validity and importance than the founder of Positivism assigned to it, they faithfully adhered to Comte's principle that no metaphysical ideas are to be treated as ultimate, and that all knowledge of the material and the spiritual world is to be resolved into present and remembered sensations associated together in certain discoverable modes. In this way they did what appeared to be good service to Positivism; for while Comte seemed inclined to turn out of strict science all such ideas as Cause and Substance as fanciful and misleading intruders, Mill and his disciples, on the other hand, set themselves diligently to work to explain the genesis of these ideas; and their speculations on this subject are very suggestive. Still the younger members of their own fraternity of thought—among whom the late gifted Professor of Philosophy in University College, London, the lamented G. Croom Robertson, was the leading spirit—candidly admitted that the problem as to the origin of these metaphysical ideas found no adequate solution within the limits of any man's individual experience; and that to account for the presence of such notions in the human mind, the imagination must endeavour to penetrate into the mysterious and almost inaccessible laboratory of Heredity, to which, I need hardly say, it is now the fashion to relegate the genesis of all ideas, rational, moral and spiritual, of which sensational evolutionists are unable to give any satisfactory empirical account.

At the time to which I refer, the doctrine of Heredity was yet in its infancy, and the English admirers of

Comte's principles were sanguine that the secrets of metaphysical and theological thinking could be discovered, and its false pretensions exposed, simply by the careful analysis of the actual facts of man's present consciousness, and without any adventurous expedition into that mist-covered region of life's immemorial past in which the recent impugners of the ultimate validity of all metaphysical and theological ideas find themselves perforce compelled to take refuge. Towards this Positivist goal, the liberation of the human mind from what was regarded as the tyrannous sway of Intuitionalism in philosophy and religion, J. S. Mill and Prof. Alexander Bain worked away with hearty goodwill; and certainly their labours, if unsuccessful in regard to their main purpose, were not without some permanently valuable results. They were full of hope and enthusiasm, and many eager disciples warmly applauded their successive assaults on the Intuitional position. It was supposed that the days in which metaphysics and metaphysical theology had bewildered human thought and narrowed human sympathies were happily nearly at an end. Henceforth physical science and mental science would be placed on the same footing, and both would resolve themselves into the study of the order of man's sensations and appetites, and of the complex processes by which, out of these simple psychical states, all the fundamental ideas of philosophy, ethics and religion, have been gradually elaborated. Now, then, it would seem that the millennium of Positivism was about to dawn: the cultured thought of this country appeared to be bursting the last fetters which bound it to that moribund and effete carcase of intuitional dogmatism which had hitherto prevented the pure spirit of empiricism and positivism from exerting its intrinsic energy, and achieving its legitimate triumphs in the cause of truth and humanity.

But what has been the actual fact? Why, simply this: that just in the very midst of this jubilation of English Phenomenalism or Positivism, Mr. Herbert Spencer, who was in fullest accord with all the scientific tendencies and methods of the English school, and who besides had clear discernment of the significance of Darwinian Evolution and of the possible applications of the principle of Heredity,—Mr. Spencer, I say, began to give to the world of thought a grand theory of the cosmos, based on the most recent scientific discoveries and speculations. And now, as if in utter defiance of Comte's law of the three stages in the evolution of religious thought, our greatest living Evolutionist finds it absolutely necessary to found his scientific and philosophical *rationale* of the universe upon an ultimate intuitive metaphysical belief. All true insight into either nature or man is, he tells us, entirely impossible, unless we recognize the presence in all human thought of some positive consciousness of the Absolute or Self-existing, as the antithesis of all caused and relative existences. Accordingly, we encounter in the present day this most significant fact—a fact which deserves the most serious consideration from all who imagine that man's interest and faith in the Super-sensual is destined to wane and vanish—that it has fallen to the lot of Mr. Spencer, one of the most non-academic and independent thinkers of our time, and certainly one who runs no risk of being charged with "weakness of brain," to once more put upon its legs and to re-invigorate that faith in the possibility of some intuitional insight by man into the very core of cosmical reality—which possibility Hamilton's doctrine of the "Conditioned," and Dean Mansel's "Bampton Lectures," were supposed to have finally extinguished. And not only is the Comtist law practically confuted by Mr. Spencer's writings on the purely intellectual side, but it has received a fatal blow likewise on the emotional and religious side; for the mental development of Comte's chief English admirer, Mr. J. S. Mill, who, in his essay on "Theism," strives with all his might to re-habilitate that very faith in a personal God and in a future life which he had previously treated so slightingly, proves conclusively that, even in the case of men of the greatest mental calibre, experience by no means justifies the conclusion that the theological and metaphysical ideas of childhood and youth naturally give place to Positivism as life advances.

But while the fact of the appearance and influence of such metaphysical views as those of Mr. Spencer proves that no progress in science finally supersedes the need of metaphysical intuition, or permanently weakens human interest in a reality which is not accessible through the senses, it appears to me clear that Positivism itself, the moment it becomes a religious system, inevitably has recourse to those very metaphysical ideas which it claims to have wholly discarded. For what is the Humanity, the *Grand-être*, which is the professed object of the Positivist's worship? Is it the mere aggregate of human individuals, past and present? Surely not: each one of us, apart from our sense of relationship to an immanent

Principle of reason, righteousness and love, is a poor and feeble creature, and no mere collection of such beings could awaken the sentiment of reverence and worship. What the Positivist really worships is the *Ideal* of Humanity—that unifying Divine Principle which finds its highest forms of varied expression in the most gifted and morally noble of our race. Hence this Positivist religious faith is a kind of Platonic Realism; it is the personifying or hypostasizing of the abstract idea of human perfection; and each saint in the Positivist calendar is revered as representing one phase of the life of this unified and personified Humanity.[1] And I feel persuaded that what will always prevent Positivism as a religion from becoming greatly influential is the fact that its implied metaphysics is one-sided and imperfect, and, for want of a principle of unity, leaves Nature and Humanity wholly devoid of any intelligible relation to each other. The Cosmos appears to have

[1] Not only does Comte, in representing Humanity as an object of religious worship, inevitably transform it into a metaphysical Unity, but, as Mr. Spencer has pointed out, he uses language in reference to that Unity which is wholly unmeaning unless it be assumed that Humanity has a corporate consciousness over and above the sum-total of individual consciousnesses. For instance, in his *System of Positive Polity*, Vol. II. p. 45 (Eng. trans.), he writes: "Thus each step of sound training in positive thought awakens feelings of reverence and gratitude which often rise into enthusiastic admiration of the Great Being who is the Author of all these conquests, be they in thought or be they in action." "Feelings of reverence and gratitude" towards a personified abstraction! Surely this is so far from being an escape from metaphysics, that it is, on the contrary, the investment of a mere figment of the imagination with the attributes of a metaphysical reality.

somehow given birth to the *Grand-être*, Humanity; but why Nature, which, in the view of Comte, is either wholly unmoral or positively immoral, should have engendered beings with progressive moral ideals, is left by the Positivists in the form of an insoluble enigma. So far from Positivism being an instance of a religious faith devoid of metaphysics and theology, it really derives what vitality it possesses from a metaphysical conception of a personified Humanity; and the reason of the comparatively small progress which it makes, appears to be chiefly due to the fact that its metaphysics is incomplete and lacks a principle capable of unifying Nature and Mankind.

Whether, then, we look to Mr. Spencer's so-called Agnosticism or to Mr. Harrison's Positivism, the fact forces itself upon our attention that, whenever Religion appears, it inevitably expresses itself in metaphysical language. This language, to be intelligible, must correspond to some fact in man's consciousness. Let me then, in what remains of this Lecture, ask your attention to Mr. Spencer's actual attitude towards theology, and to the question whether the constitution of the human mind presents any real barrier to its advancing farther in the direction of Theism than the point which Mr. Spencer himself has reached. At the time when Mr. Spencer's "First Principles" was published, and reflection began to be turned upon his doctrine that man has an indefinite but yet positive consciousness of the Absolute, it was urged by some religious thinkers that a certain Agnostic attitude towards the Eternal One is common to Mr. Spencer's writings and to some of the grandest and deepest passages in the world's religious literature; and reference was particularly made to such ideas as are put into the mouth of Zophar the Naamathite in the drama of Job: "Canst thou by searching find out God? Canst thou find out the Almighty to perfection? It is high as heaven; what canst thou do? Deeper than Sheol; what canst thou know?" Is there, then, any real affinity between the Agnosticism of the book of Job and the Agnosticism of Mr. Spencer's "First Principles"? If the statements made by Mr. Spencer in the controversy between him and Mr. Harrison represent his well-weighed and permanent thought on this question, there would seem to be some real relationship between the Spencerian and the Biblical doctrine of theological nescience. Mr. Spencer, as I have before mentioned, refers, in that controversy, to the Absolute as the omnipresent Causal Energy or Power of which all phenomena, physical and mental, are the manifestations; and he even contends that this Power must be conceived as certainly not lower than personal. Now, as Dr. Martineau in his great work, "A Study of Religion," has conclusively proved, the notion of Energy or Power can have no conceivable origin save in the consciousness we have that we exert effort, and so produce changes in our own minds or in objects around us. These words, like the word Cause, are simply the interpretation of the phenomena of the macrocosm in terms of the consciousness of man, the microcosm.

The essential feature, however, of Mr. Spencer's Agnosticism is the denial to man of any mental capacity for forming any clear ideas concerning the character of that

Absolute, of which, he says, we have a vague and indefinite consciousness. The Ground of all phenomenal existence must, he contends, be regarded as Infinite and Absolute, and the human mind cannot definitely think it in either of these aspects. But surely the fact that it is Infinite does not disqualify it for becoming an object of our thought. Though we cannot picture or represent in imagination the infinitude of space, yet we can distinctly think it. We clearly distinguish the idea of indefinite space from that of infinite space; the former is qualitatively different from the latter. Indefinite space is that to which I am unable to definitely fix a limit; infinite space is that which I think as having no limit. There is, then, nothing which necessarily baffles the human mind when it attempts to attach the idea of infinity to the being of God. And as to the word "Absolute," this can only mean that the Supreme Being is not dependent on, or conditioned by, any being outside of or other than Himself. But it violates no law of our thinking to regard the Absolute as giving rise, by voluntary self-limitation, to spirits who are reproductions of His own essence, and in favour of whom He in some measure vacates His own causality, in order that the connection between Him and them may no longer be merely that of Ground and manifestation, or of Creator and creature, but may pass into that free spiritual relationship in which man becomes the fitting object of God's approval, and capable of response to God's creative love.

Mr. Spencer himself admits that the human mind cannot escape the conclusion that there is one and the same Absolute Cause both of the phenomena of the external world and of those states of consciousness which constitute our own inner life. He also tells us, as we have seen, that this Absolute Cause is in its essence either personal or higher than personal. Why, then, should the human mind be incompetent to gain some valid idea of the character of this Absolute Cause from the ethical ideals which through its agency arise, and which gradually dominate the consciousness of mankind? Mr. Spencer's reply is, that by reason of the necessary "relativity of our thought," we are wholly excluded from any insight into the real character of the Absolute. This objection might hold good if the Absolute were a Being wholly outside of and apart from ourselves; but its force vanishes the moment it is seen that God is immediately immanent in the soul's higher life, and that consequently the ethical ideals which speak with authority within us are none other than the self-revelation of the Eternal in the consciousness of mankind. And if it be further objected that we can only know of God as He reveals Himself in our rational, moral and spiritual consciousness, and cannot penetrate into the Divine consciousness or super-consciousness itself, this is no doubt true; but it is equally true that we cannot enter directly into the inner life of our fellow-men. And such impossible knowledge of God in His inmost being is in no way necessary for Religion. All the religious man needs to know is, that the Infinite and Eternal One speaks directly to his mind and heart, supports him when he is striving for the right, comforts him in his distress, and invites and enjoins him to rise above his finite animal self, and to realize that higher and diviner self in which his intimate relationship and union with

God consists. Dr. Martineau truly says: "God as related to Nature and Humanity—as embracing and quickening the finite world, as the Source of all Order, Beauty and Good—we are not by Mr. Spencer's hypothesis debarred from knowing, and this knowledge of God is really all that either religion or philosophy demands."[1]

As Mr. Frederick Harrison justly argues, Religion, to be real and effective, must involve the feeling in the worshipper of a personal relationship between him and his God. The question, therefore, whether Mr. Spencer's philosophy really reconciles Science and Religion, practically amounts to this: Is that philosophy compatible with the existence of sympathetic and personal relations between the spirit of man and that Absolute Spirit who manifests Himself in nature and humanity? There is an evident inconsistency in Mr. Spencer's utterances on this matter. If his conclusion be sound, that the vague consciousness of the Absolute which he ascribes to man simply testifies to the reality of the Absolute, but affords no clue to the character of this Ultimate and Self-existent Being, how does it come about that Mr. Spencer feels himself justified in asserting that the Absolute is either personal or super-personal? Again, if the nature of God involves personality, or something higher than personality, where, on Mr. Spencer's theory, does the personal or super-personal life of God find manifestation? Not in relation to other Gods, for in Mr. Spencer's view such Gods do not exist; nor is it in relation to man, for

[1] Article on "Science, Nescience and Faith," in *Essays, Reviews and Addresses*, Vol. III. p. 198.

if man is by his mental constitution precluded from all insight into the true character of the Supreme Being, God and man can have no possible personal communion, and the super-personal life of God becomes wholly isolated and unrelated to the self-conscious life of man. But if the nature of God is such that it excludes all inter-personal relations, it must be regarded, not as *higher* than, but as far *lower* than, the personal life of man; for it is just in the conscious response of soul to soul that the inner experience of man culminates; and it is in a real or supposed conscious relationship and sympathy between the Eternal and the finite soul that man's ethical force and enthusiasm become greatest, and his experience of spiritual satisfaction and blessedness the most complete.

If Mr. Spencer is right (as I believe he is) in maintaining that the consciousness of man is not limited to finite and phenomenal experiences, but involves also an immediate apprehension of the reality and causality of the Absolute; and if he is also right (as I believe he is) in maintaining that the Uncreated Ground of all finite existence is certainly not lower than personal,—then consistency requires that he should not restrict man's apprehension of the Absolute to a vague consciousness of its existence. The universal principles of reason which enable finite minds to communicate with each other and render nature progressively intelligible to human thought; the ethical ideals which emerge out of experience and imperatively indicate the path which human conduct should take; the higher affections which virtually annihilate self-seeking desires and involve Infinity and

Eternity,—all these factors in man's higher life carry with them self-evidence that they are no mere attributes of man as finite and individual, but are the self-revelation in us of features of that Absolute Reality on whom our finite spirits are ever conscious of depending. As human nature becomes more devoted to, and practically identified with, the Ideal, it cannot escape the intuitive conviction that it is attaining to truer and deeper insight into the real nature and character of God.

It is true that this domination of the soul by divine ideas, by high ethical ideals, by self-effacing affections, may not enable us adequately to conceive of that inmost life of the Eternal in which all these ideas and ideals must have their origin and their unification. Still none the less is this apprehension of the character of God, which the human mind in its highest moral and spiritual experience attains, a real, though not an exhaustive, insight into the very essence of the Father within us; and the immense power which this feeling of personal communion and sympathy with the Eternal possesses to comfort the human heart and to stimulate to noble conduct, is presumptive evidence that we have here to deal with no mere illusory fancy, but with the real revelation to the soul of the true nature and aim of that Self-existent One of whose thought and will the cosmos is the visible expression.

We speak, and we cannot but speak, of the Absolute Ground of all existence as Universal Mind and Will; but in so doing we are well aware that these modes of expression may indicate nothing more than the highest conception our minds can form of the self-consciousness and mode of energizing of Him who is felt to be the abiding Ground of our finite existence and the living Source of all that is persistent in our ideals. Yet, as I shall endeavour to show more fully in a later Lecture of this course, man's incompetency to fully realize in thought the self-consciousness of the Eternal Thinker appears to consist, not in the *positive elements* which our idea of personality involves, but rather in the *sense of limitation* which necessarily attaches to all finite consciousness, but which must be regarded as absent from the consciousness of God. While, then, I heartily agree with Mr. Spencer that, if the Absolute Being is not to be conceived as personal, He must be regarded as higher than personal, I at the same time earnestly contend that this "higher than personal" becomes an utterly empty and unmeaning expression, unless it is held to signify that whatever else, of which we can form no conception, the Divine Nature may embrace, it assuredly embraces those positive elements of personality which in the case of man render the experiences of friendship and of love the highest blessedness to which human consciousness can attain.

The lesson, then, which I derive from the comparison of the Agnostic and the Positivist teachings in regard to theology is, that God and man so intimately meet in the rational, ethical and spiritual experiences of the soul, that a measure of real insight into the nature of the Absolute becomes possible to man; and, though all such insight must needs fall short of fathoming the depths of the Self-subsistent Reality, it nevertheless reveals essential features in the eternal character of that immanent God with whom each religious soul is conscious of the most momentous personal relationship. The degree of Agnosticism in regard to the inner life of God, to which by the inherent necessities of our dependent existence we are necessarily subject, is not an Agnosticism which denies satisfaction to the deepest needs and longings of the human mind and heart. This inevitable Agnosticism has no tendency whatever to paralyze philosophical and theological interests and studies, or to discredit and disparage the spiritual insight of the great prophetic teachers of mankind.

All that Religion demands is, that the Supreme Being who is immanent in nature and in man shall know and sympathize with the human spirit's real needs and good exertions, and shall respond to man's aspiration and adoration. Granting this real spiritual relationship between the human and the Divine, Religion would not feel the least alarm or distress if Mr. Spencer or any other thinker should say that the ideas we attach to this word "personal" do not adequately express the deepest reality in the life of the Eternal. Religion neither needs nor expects to attain to an exhaustive knowledge of the nature of God. Books that definitely discuss the psychology of the Eternal, as though He were another mind exactly like our own, and differing from ours only in the vastness of His range, are anything but congenial and helpful to the soul in its more devout moods. It is not improbable that there exists such an essential difference between the consciousness of the Absolute and Eternal One, in whom all finite and dependent souls have their being, and the consciousness of these finite souls themselves, that the latter must be unable to fully

III. AGNOSTICISM. 123

represent to themselves in imagination or in thought the inmost life of the Supreme. Yet as our finite minds bear clear marks of being reproductions or differentiations of the Eternal Substance, there appears to be solid ground for believing, with Lotze, that we are nearer the truth when we say, not that God is *supra*-personal, but rather that man is *infra*-personal, seeing that in the Infinite Being alone is self-subsistence, and therefore perfect personality; and in man only that approximation to perfect personality which is possible under the limiting conditions of dependence and finitude.

I conclude, accordingly, that notwithstanding the arguments which would condemn the human mind to complete theological nescience or agnosticism, there is still a real validity in that faculty of spiritual discernment of which I spoke in the last Lecture, and that consequently the progressive attainment of religious truth, i.e. of insight into the essential character of the Eternal, is intrinsically possible to man, and is actually in differing degrees and aspects realized in the various Sacred Scriptures of Humanity to which the minds and hearts of multitudes have recourse for the bread of spiritual life.

Finally, if we admit that in the different forms of the world's religious literature, and of religious thought and sentiment, there are presented, in various degrees of fulness and purity, phases of religious truth of eternal validity and significance, the question arises, What is the relation of this religious or spiritual truth to that other form of truth which the human mind reaches by the study of nature and of history? If science and historical study throw increasing light on the present relations and past modes of physical and mental phenomena, it would seem that the prophet's direct ethical and spiritual insight into the character of the Ultimate Ground of all finite existence must not contradict the results reached by careful scientific investigation into those cosmical facts through which the Absolute manifests His thought and will under the conditions of space and time. It is evident, however, that the history of theological and of scientific thought discloses frequent instances in which a new access of scientific light, or the dominance of a new and influential idea in general culture, has produced, at all events temporarily, a sharp collision between accepted religious doctrines and the new scientific or philosophical ideas. In the present day, for example, we are experiencing in a somewhat acute form the conflict between the generally accepted modes of Theological Doctrine and the now widely prevalent scientific and philosophical conception of Evolution. In the next two Lectures, accordingly, I will attempt to find some *rationale* of this transient or permanent antagonism between religious faith and progressive culture. This antagonism, however, assumes very different features and a very different degree of importance according as it is an antagonism between Culture and Dogmatic or "Orthodox" Religion, or between Culture and what we may term Rational Religion (*Vernunftglaube*). In the next Lecture I will consider the grounds of the antagonism between advancing Culture and Dogmatic Religion, and in the succeeding Lecture I will call your attention to the far more momentous antagonism between Culture and Rational Religion.

Lecture IV.
CULTURE AND RELIGIOUS BELIEF.

I. Culture and Dogmatic Religion.

The faculty of rational and spiritual insight, which I endeavoured to describe in the second Lecture, reveals to the human soul its relationship with that Self-existent Life which is believed to create, to animate and to unify, the phenomena of nature. To man in an elementary stage of culture, the spirit or spirits with whom he conceives himself to be in sympathetic relation will be the great Powers to whose personal agency he ascribes the natural influences which affect his happiness; but with further and higher culture, the conviction grows that nature is an organic unity, and that therefore it is One Supreme Causality which calls the phenomena of the universe into existence and communes with the human mind. As man's ethical consciousness discloses its range and its authority, the Being whom he worships becomes identified with the source of the idea of Duty, and of those æsthetic and moral ideals which speak with authority in man's inner life. But while the insight of the higher reason and of the conscience is thus awakening in the human mind a belief in its moral and spiritual relation with the Soul of souls, or the creative Spirit of the cosmos, the scientific understanding has been busily engaged with the study of physical phenomena; and on the basis of the uniformities or laws which it has there discovered, it has formed for itself a certain general theory of the order of nature and of what are called the physical causes of phenomena. Hence there arise two theories of the cosmos—two *Weltanschauungen*, as the Germans say— the religious and the scientific; and it is inevitable that the scientific and the religious interpretation and explanation of the world and its Cause should at times come into either apparent or real collision.

The essence of the religious reading of the universe is, that there is a Power behind nature and in close relationship with the human heart and mind, by whose volitional activity the phenomena of nature are called into being. In the lowest as well as in the highest stages of the religious consciousness, the God or Gods are regarded as, in a certain sense, the immediate cause of the changes which take place in the world around. The movements of the heavenly bodies, the succession of the seasons, the new life of spring, the destructive action of the lightning, are all felt by the mind, in its religious mood, to be dependent on the will of the Supreme Object of worship. The mind, however, in its scientific mood, comes to form what appears to be a quite different notion of Causation. Instead of referring the movements of the planets to the direct will of the Deity, it finds an explanation of the phenomena in the previous existence of forces, which, as the solar nebula cooled, passed from a molecular to a molar mode of manifestation; or it brings in the previous existence of electrical energy to explain why the tree or the human being was stricken down by the thunderbolt. Now, as I shall try to show in the Lecture on the Argument from Causation, the collision here between the scientific and the religious conception is only an apparent collision, and arises mainly from an equivocal use of the word "Cause."

But besides such nominal collisions as this, there are, as we are well aware, real collisions between science and the popular religious faith which grow out of something deeper than verbal misunderstandings. In quite modern times, for instance, physical and historical research have completely negatived and exploded certain views of nature and history which were once regarded as forming essential parts of accepted theological dogma. We now see that, as a matter of fact, the sun does not go round the earth, however firmly religious minds may have once believed it to do; humanity in all probability takes its physiological origin, at least, from the anthropoid apes, however dear to many religious minds may be the notion that it is an entirely new and unrelated form of Divine creation; the book of Genesis really is not so valuable from a scientific point of view as are the most recent works on astronomy and geology; the Bible certainly does not bear the impress of being the unique composition of one Holy Spirit, but has all the marks of having been the work of many minds of varying degrees of scientific, philosophical and spiritual insight.

We see, then, that beyond a doubt, not only have there been in the past violent collisions between the scientific and the religious *Weltanschauungen*, but that in all such collisions religious faith appears to have been decidedly on the losing side. The present age is experiencing in an acute form this antagonism between the generally accepted conclusions of Science and what is called Religious Belief; and as one of the objects of these Lectures is to examine into this controversy, and, if possible, to help towards a reconciliation, it is very necessary that we should clearly understand what is essential and what is accidental in these conflicts. The first noticeable feature which strikes us is, that such controversies fall into two quite distinct classes. The science and philosophy of an age may collide with what Kant terms Rational Religious Belief (*Vernunftglaube*), or they may collide with Doctrinal or Dogmatic Belief (*doctrinaler Glaube*), and these two collisions are very different in character and in permanent significance. In the latter case, it almost invariably turns out that Science is in the right; but in the former case, it more generally happens that each party on reflection sees itself to be in some degree in the wrong, and that accordingly, by the removal of misunderstandings and by reasonable mutual concessions, harmony is ultimately re-established.

As a preparation, therefore, for entering into the real merits of this controversy between Culture and Faith, I will now ask your attention while I endeavour to set forth the features in Dogmatic, or, as we may perhaps call it, "Orthodox" Religion, as distinguished from Rational Religion. Positive or established religions inevitably tend to assume the "orthodox" character, that is, to impose on their believers the acceptance of certain dogmas, not on the ground of the agreement of these dogmas with the results arrived at by the scientific understanding in the study of phenomena, or with the ideals which assert themselves with self-evidencing clearness and authority in the moral and spiritual consciousness of mankind, but on the very different ground that they form part of a miraculously revealed system of doctrine and ritual.

How this comes about is not difficult to see. One of the causes is no doubt the temptation which always besets a sacerdotal order, to magnify their own office by making themselves indispensable mediators between God and the individual soul. But there are deeper influences at work than this. If I have rightly explained the origin of great religious movements, they have their source and their divine authority in some new and real insight into the essential nature and relationship with humanity of that Eternal and Absolute Being who reveals His presence in the human consciousness in self-evident and necessary rational ideas, and in those ideal aspirations which, so soon as they are clearly apprehended by the self-conscious soul, are intuitively felt to carry with them an unconditional authority. Jesus, for instance, could not have proved by an appeal to some more self-evident truth, that love of one's neighbour as a spring of action has an intrinsic right to prevail over the counter-claims of personal pleasure; nor did he need to prove it, for as soon as the proposition is distinctly understood, Conscience, or the Practical Reason, which is immanent in man's consciousness, at once declares the principle to be absolutely and eternally true. On the basis of this ethical and religious experience, Jesus proclaims, as the essence of ethics and religion, the profound truth that Divine Love is the supreme spring of action in humanity, and that as such it belongs to the very substance of that Absolute and Self-existent Being on whom every finite soul cannot help believing itself to be dependent alike for its existence and for its ethical ideals. The religious belief of Jesus himself, there is every reason to think, partook in no way of those features which characterize what we call the dogmatic or "orthodox" religions. It rested not at all on external authority; it was in every sense what Kant calls a *Vernunft-glaube*. It was at once rational and revealed. It was *rational*, as being based entirely on that theoretical and practical Reason, that felt immanence of the Universal and the Eternal in our finite nature, which is the ground of all ontological insight, of all firsthand religious belief. It was *revealed*, as being a new and higher stage of man's interpreting insight into the essential character of that indwelling Self-existent One, who is the absolute Ground alike of our power to Reason and of our capacity for spiritual Love.

How, then, does this rational religion in the founder become dogmatic and "orthodox" in the great majority of his future disciples? In this way: whenever a new and vivifying central idea or belief takes possession of a great soul, it immediately tends to modify and partly re-construct the prophet's general theory of the universe. With that new idea as the living principle, the religious reformer constructs, out of the scientific ideas, the recognized social relations and the metaphysical theories which he shares with his contemporaries, the highest and most satisfactory account which he can reach of God, and of His present and future dealings with nature and humanity. The reverent but uncritical disciple recognizes, by virtue of his own moral and spiritual insight, that the reformer is giving utterance to ideas of a most inspiring and elevating character,—ideas which the hearer, though he vividly feels their absolute truth and authority, and their marvellous power to uplift his thoughts, his aspirations and his faith, is at the same time conscious that he could not himself have originated. They seem to him to be, as in truth they are, divinely inspired; but to the disciple, at his far lower level of spiritual awakenment, the inspiration appears to wholly transcend the possibilities of mere humanity. The master thus becomes invested with a certain superhuman character; and hence the disciple comes to ascribe to every feature in the prophet's teaching that absoluteness and infallibility which only legitimately belongs to the vital and essential principle which the immanent Universal, or God, in the master's consciousness has revealed, and which the disciple, in virtue of the same Divine immanence, has felt to be of absolute authority and worth. And this confusion between the essential spirit of the prophet's gospel and its accidental intellectual embodiment is still further extended when, as in the case of Christianity, the same absolute worth is ascribed to the recorded religious utterances of his earliest disciples. The great principle which constituted the life and essence of the reformer's gospel is not, even in the mind of the original founder of the religion himself, seen in all its ethical and social implications. It took, for instance, more than a thousand years' experience for the great body of Christians to distinctly discern that slavery is morally wrong, although its immorality is already implicitly present in the fundamental Christian idea of Divine Fatherhood and human Brotherhood. And even in the present day, the operation in the souls of men of the essential principle of Christian Love, is imparting a moral and obligatory character to certain lines of social and political conduct which have heretofore been commonly regarded even by Christians as morally indifferent.

Thus in all established dogmatic religions, the eternal principles which they enshrine, and which are the source of their mighty power for good, become associated on equal terms with a set of doctrines and ideas which have no universal validity, but belong to a particular stage of scientific knowledge, of social usage and of philosophical speculation; and all alike are represented in the articles of faith of the dogmatic religion as infallible truth, which cannot be called in question save at the risk both of ecclesiastical excommunication and of exclusion from the heaven of God's approving sympathy. For a long time, pious souls, whose moral and spiritual nature has been fed and satisfied by the elements of eternal truth, which, with all its narrowness and error, the dogmatic religion contains, do not clearly realize the essential incompatibility between the vital principles of their religious faith and the stereotyped dogmas by which these principles are repressed and distorted. For a long time they may manage to hold simultaneously the eternal truth that God is Love, and the Church's dogmas of universal depravity, of vicarious atonement, of a personal devil, and the eternal damnation of heretics; but, sooner or later, the implicit contradiction between the eternal principle and the temporary dogma becomes clearly explicit in the consciousness, and an inner struggle sets in which can only issue in the extrusion from the sphere of religious belief of every ecclesiastical dogma which cannot be harmonized with that ethical imperative in which the indwelling Eternal reveals His presence and His will to the finite mind and heart.

But while the higher Reason or Spiritual Insight thus denounces and expels all forms of theological dogma which contravene the highest Ideal through which the immanent God in every age reveals Himself to the finite mind, there is also another powerful protest against the false pretensions of dogmatic religions which proceeds, not from the Practical Reason or the faculty of spiritual discernment, but from the Critical Understanding, the function of which is to study the facts of matter and of mind, and to discover, if possible, the historical development of cosmical phenomena.

In all dogmatic religions, and particularly in dogmatic Christianity, with its infallible Bible, the essential elements of religious belief become associated with certain transient theories of the physical universe which happened to be dominant in the age when the dogmatic religion came into existence. Hence these particular phases in the history of scientific discovery or scientific speculation receive a special consecration in the view of the dogmatic religionist. Therefore, as Science advances, and new conceptions of the universe approve themselves to competent thinkers, a violent conflict ensues between the fresh scientific insight and the established dogma; and, as we well know, even in times so recent as that of the Reformation, the promulgators of the Copernican theory of the cosmos might count themselves fortunate if they escaped with their lives from the clutches of the ecclesiastical dogmatist. Reasonable religious belief is, of all principles in human nature, the most powerful, the most influential for good; but when, as in the case of "orthodox" religions, the rightful absolute authority with which the divine ethical imperative speaks to the individual soul is illegitimately transferred to the dogmas of a Church, the history of religious persecution only too forcibly illustrates the truth of the ancient adage, *Corruptio optimi pessima est.*

And what has been said of Science holds good also of Metaphysical Speculation. We may fittingly take as an illustration of the way in which the particular philosophical views of the period when the dogmatic religion took shape become stereotyped in the Church's creeds, the highest and most influential of the universal Religions, viz. Christianity. At the time when this religion assumed a dogmatic or "orthodox" character, a metaphysical theory of God as being in Himself too exalted to be apprehended by the finite mind, and of the Logos or Word of God as the necessary medium through whom the Eternal manifested or revealed Himself in a way suited to human capacity, happened (and we may say providentially happened) to be the dominant form of religious philosophy among those cultured Greeks in Asia Minor and elsewhere, who were most attracted by the sublime ethical and spiritual features of the religious movement initiated by Jesus of Nazareth. Jesus had ever spoken of God as the Father within him; and though there is good reason to believe that he himself never dreamed that the Eternal was immanent or incarnate in him in any different sense to that in which He is immanent in every rational soul, it is not surprising, when all the circumstances of the case are taken into account, that the world's greatest Prophet and religious Teacher was at length, in the imagination of his enthusiastic disciples, exclusively identified with that Divine Word or Reason which the philosophical believers of that day regarded as the indispensable intermediary between the Eternal God and the human mind and heart. In this way, the son of Mary of Nazareth was removed out of the category of humanity, and conceived of as the Son of God in a quite different sense to that in which, in the view of the rational religionist, all men are sons of God. He was the eternal or *uncreated* Son, while his brethren of mankind are the *created* offspring of the Father. It is foreign to my purpose in these Lectures to trace this dogmatizing process further, and to review the lines of thought by which, out of this dogmatic germ, the full-blown doctrine of the Athanasian Trinity finally grew. As almost always happens with the accepted doctrines of established religions, this figment of the speculative imagination became invested with an infallible character, and thus made an essential part of Christian truth and an essential condition of the soul's salvation. The character of this process, by which the Rational Religion of Jesus became transformed into Dogmatic or "Orthodox" Religion, is thus admirably described by the late Dr. Hatch in his Hibbert Lectures on

"The Influence of Greek Ideas and Usages upon the Christian Church":

"Doctrine came to be thus co-ordinate with character as the basis on which the churches joined together in local or general confederation and accepted each other's certificates. The hierarchical tendency grew with it and out of it. The position of the bishops, which had grown out of the assumed desirability of guarding the tradition of truth, tended to emphasize that tradition. It gave to tradition not only a new importance, but also a new sanction. It rested belief upon living authority. *Men were no longer free to interpret for themselves.*"[1]

I have adduced this case of dogmatic Christianity as being an excellent illustration of the fundamental distinction between Rational and Dogmatic Religion. Rational Religion rests its claim to be received as true on the ground that its principles are endorsed, or may be endorsed, by the direct personal experience of each individual soul; while Dogmatic Religion rests its claim to acceptance on some outward authority altogether extrinsic to the believer's own self-consciousness. Rational Religion, in the person of Jesus, declares that real insight into the nature of God, and into the relationship between Him and the spirit of man, is accessible to every one in proportion to the increasing purity of his conscience and his heart. Dogmatic Christianity, on the other hand, lays down a doctrine of the tri-une nature of God which no purity of heart, however great, has the slightest tendency either to discover or to confirm, and then proceeds to declare the belief in this dogma to be an essential factor of true religion. This identification by the "orthodox" believer

[1] P. 345.

IV. CULTURE AND RELIGIOUS BELIEF.

of a transient phase of metaphysical speculation with the abiding essence of true religion, naturally produces, in the long run, the same evil results which we have seen to follow from a like identification of the essence of religion with a particular phase of scientific conception. Collisions are inevitable between the metaphysical ideas embodied in the orthodox creed and newer philosophical beliefs; and when a thinker like Servetus seeks to divest the religious faith of its obsolete metaphysical dress, and to invest it with a form more in harmony with the thought of modern times, a dogmatist like Calvin thinks that the essence of Christianity is grievously imperilled, and that the only way of securing its integrity is by sending the critical objector to the stake. And it is but a milder form of this same pernicious principle of religious dogmatism which has in recent years passed sentence of ecclesiastical ostracism on men like Channing and Theodore Parker, in whose glowing love for God and for humanity Jesus would have seen the surest marks of true discipleship to himself.

It remains to be noticed further, that all dogmatic religions tend, as we have seen, to take the founder of the religion out of the category of humanity; and thus, by converting him into an entirely exceptional and unique being, ensure perpetual antagonism between dogmatism and progressive scientific and philosophical ideas. The most conspicuous instance of this dehumanizing process applied to the personality of the founders of religion is, of course, to be seen in the popular deification of Jesus of Nazareth; and it is instructive to note how in the present day—when, in the light of free thought and higher ethical ideals, the ungrounded nature of the pretensions to infallibility of Dogmatic Religion is being on all sides more clearly discerned, and thoughtful minds in all sects are passing more and more into the position of rational religionists—this last stronghold of dogmatism, to wit, the wholly exceptional and unique character of the Incarnation of the Eternal in the person of the son of Mary, is being vehemently defended by religious thinkers who appear to have abandoned every other dogmatic entrenchment, but who cannot persuade themselves that the essence of Christianity, as the absolute religion, admits of being dissociated from this particular dogmatic belief also.[1] It appears to me most strange that such able thinkers do not perceive that, in so representing Jesus, they are really undermining the rational ground of the inestimable worth of his character and his teaching, as a revelation and realization of those divine possibilities of spiritual insight and of felt communion with God which are implicit in every rational soul. By those who thus cling to this remnant of dogmatism, and hesitate to fully identify themselves with that Rational Religion which Jesus himself initiated, the following emphatic and important words by Prof. Max

---

[1] *Vide* the Series of Essays termed *Lux Mundi*. The same notion, though in a much more diluted form, appears in the writings of Dr. Lynam Abbott, and of many other advocates of the so called "New Theology." A very lucid and forcible exposure of the inconsistency of this position will be found in a pamphlet by the Rev. R. A. Armstrong on "The New Orthodoxy," and in an article from the same pen on "Thoroughness in Theology," in the *New World* for Dec. 1893.

IV. CULTURE AND RELIGIOUS BELIEF.

Müller in his Gifford Lectures on "Theosophy"[1] deserve the most careful pondering:

"We may make the fullest allowance for those who, from reverence for God and for Christ and from the purest motives, protest against claiming for man the full brotherhood of Christ. But when they say that the difference between Christ and mankind is one of kind, and not of degree, they know not what they do; they nullify the whole of Christ's teaching, and they deny the Incarnation which they pretend to teach. Let the difference of degree be as large as ever it can be between those who belong to the same kind; but to look for one or two passages in the New Testament which may possibly point to a difference in kind is surely useless against the overwhelming weight of the evidence that appeals to us from the very words of Christ. We have lately been told, for instance, that Christ never speaks of *Our* Father when including himself, and that when he taught his disciples to pray, Our Father which art in heaven, he intentionally excluded himself. This might sound plausible in a court of law, but what is it when confronted with the words of Christ: 'Go to my brethren, and say to them, I ascend unto my Father and your Father, and to my God and your God'? Was that also meant to imply that his Father was not the same as their Father, and their God not the same as his God?"

I quote these words with especial pleasure, because they support my conviction that the view of the main basis of religious belief which I am advocating in these Lectures is essentially in harmony with the philosophy of religion implied in the utterances of the Founder of Christianity.

Accordingly, at this point it will be worth while to digress for a moment from the main course of my exposition, to indicate the difference between the doctrine of

[1] P. 537.

the Incarnation, which I regard as the true one and as identical with that implied in the words of Jesus, and the doctrine of the Incarnation as presented in the orthodox creeds. As I have said before, the facts of our ethical and spiritual experience seem to me to clearly show that all rational souls are of the same substance with the Eternal Cause and Ground from whom they arise, and in whom they still have their being. I agree with the late Lord Gifford, the founder of the Gifford Lectureship, who, in his striking essay on Substance, writes: "God must be the very substance and essence of the human soul. The human soul is neither self-derived nor self-subsisting. It would vanish if it had not a substance, and its substance is God." I am far, then, from being disposed to quarrel with the words of the Creed which declare that Jesus is of the same substance as the Father; what I object to in "orthodox" Christianity is, that the creed is too narrow, and confines to the particular case of Jesus a relation with God which holds good of every rational soul. The basal doctrine of Christianity is not a doctrine of a Trinity in Unity, but of a countless plurality of persons in One Divine Substance. This Substance is the Eternal Reason, the Eternal Righteousness, the Eternal Love; and it is just because on one side of our nature we are all alike in indissoluble union with this Absolute and All-embracing Personality, that mutual thought and mutual love become possible, and that no sophistry can wholly stifle the conviction that the omniscient God is an essential party to all our dealings one with another. The Eternal Substance, in which all created things and minds inhere, and by which they are, consciously or unconsciously, related to each other, is, in the words of Jesus, the Father within us. And when the Creeds say that it is heresy to divide the Substance or to confuse the Persons, this, too, is true; but the persons to which it applies are not the three Persons of the Trinity, but the innumerable persons that proceed from, but still remain in living union with, the Indwelling Eternal. Hence, when freed from the unnatural limitations which the articles of orthodoxy impose upon it, the idea of the Incarnation of God in humanity is the profoundest of all truths alike in philosophy and in theology; and no doubt it is this element of truth in the doctrine of the Trinity which has made that doctrine so long-lived, and has enabled it, notwithstanding the errors and the narrow dogmatism with which it has been associated, to be in no small degree helpful to religious minds. But the Trinitarian dogma is not only philosophically false in excluding from participation in the Divine Substance all human beings save one, and in including as a third Person what is merely an abstraction and no concrete reality, but it is also inconsistent and confused from the circumstance that it employs the words, "God the Father," in a double sense; for God the Father is, on the one hand, used to denote the Substance in which the Persons have their unitary ground, but it is also used to indicate one of the Persons in the sacred Trinity. Thus, though this dogma serves to suggest a philosophical theory of the relation of God to man of the highest significance and worth, yet, as it stands in the Creeds, it is too narrow, inconsistent and confused, to be of permanent theological value.

But while the doctrine of the Incarnation, when viewed as limited to Jesus of Nazareth, is a merely transient feature of Dogmatic Religion, which in the present day is being rapidly undermined both by historical criticism and by scientific and philosophical thought, the recognition of the normal Incarnation of God in human nature furnishes, I apprehend, at once the indestructible foundation of Rational Religion, and the true principle of *Authority* in Theology—a principle which in the future will surely replace the spurious Authority on which dogmatic "orthodoxy" rests. The tranference of final appeal in matters theological from an external to an internal court is, as the recent Parliament of Religions at Chicago clearly shows, silently but swiftly advancing in all the great religions of the world; and Dr. Martineau's profound treatise on "The Seat of Authority in Religion" is the work which most consistently and adequately voices this demand of our age for a rational basis of theistic belief. It is one of the most hopeful signs in the religious world of to-day that this work, in conjunction with the same author's "Types of Ethical Theory" and "A Study of Religion," is evidently finding its way into the hands of the more thoughtful and influential members of all religious denominations; and beyond a doubt it will play a most important part in revolutionizing the current conceptions of "Inspiration" and "Revelation," by enabling intelligent believers to discern that the ultimate credentials of a theological dogma can only lie in the power which such dogma possesses to awaken an emphatic response in those rational, ethical and spiritual factors of the individual consciousness through which the Universal Mind progressively reveals Himself in the mind of man. In the Preface of the work to which I refer, Dr. Martineau thus lucidly expounds the central idea to which his book gives complete and eloquent expression:

"I am prepared to hear that, after dispensing with miracles and infallible persons, I have no right to speak of 'authority' at all, the intuitional assurance which I substitute for it being nothing but confidence in my own reason. If to rest on authority is to mean an acceptance of what, as foreign to my faculty, I cannot know, in mere reliance on the testimony of one who can and does, I certainly find no such basis for religion; inasmuch as second-hand belief, assented to at the dictation of an initiated expert, without personal response of thought and reverence in myself, has no more tincture of religion in it than any other lesson learned by rote. The mere resort to testimony for information beyond our province does not fill the meaning of 'authority,' which we never acknowledge till that which speaks to us from another and a higher strikes home and wakes the echoes in ourselves, and is thereby instantly transferred from external attestation to self-evidence. And this response it is which makes the moral intuitions, started by outward appeal, reflected back by inward veneration, more than egoistic phenomena, and turning them into correspondency between the universal and the individual mind invests them with true 'authority.' We trust in them, not with any rationalist arrogance because they are our own, but precisely because they are *not* our own, with awe and aspiration. The *consciousness* of authority is doubtless human, but conditional on the *source* being divine."

On a superficial view it may appear that Dr. Martineau's account of our moral intuitions as being worthy of trust, not because they are our own, but "precisely because they are *not* our own," contravenes the principle which I am seeking to establish in these Lectures, viz. that the authority of the ideal is both human and divine, seeing that God is so truly immanent in the soul that His essential character and will are revealed, not *to*, but *in*, the rational and ethical self-consciousness of man. There may seem, accordingly, to be a fundamental difference between Dr. Martineau's view of the essential nature of the moral imperative and that to which I am led. When, however, Dr. Martineau's doctrine is fully understood, this appearance of difference, I believe, vanishes; for in a most interesting and important section of the "Types of Ethical Theory"[1] Dr. Martineau makes it quite clear that his own doctrine "is in essential accordance" with the late Prof. T. H. Green's statement, that "it is the very essence of moral duty to be imposed by a man upon himself."[2]

Inspiration and Revelation, accordingly, are not accurately described as information or illumination imported into the soul from without, but are rather the emergence into the clear light of self-consciousness of gleams of that eternal Reason, Righteousness and Love which are implicit in humanity in virtue of that essential Sonship which relates the spirit of man to the Father within him. From the basal truth, that all rational souls are of the same substance with the Eternal, it inevitably follows that religious faith, in so far as it is well-grounded, is also rational; that is to say, it finds its justification, not in some external authority, but in the very tissue and ultimate constitution of the human mind itself. All that

---

[1] Vol. II. p. 106, 2nd ed.
[2] *Prolegomena to Ethics*, p. 354.

IV. CULTURE AND RELIGIOUS BELIEF.

Inspiration does, whether it arises from the immediate action of the Universal Mind on the human mind, or whether it be due to kindling contact with some nobler soul or some inspired scripture, is simply to awaken into clearer consciousness that dormant rationality and divinity which God's infinite love has imparted to man in fashioning the soul out of His own eternal essence.

As, then, the seat of final authority in religion is in that higher life of the reason, the conscience and the heart, through which an ideal of excellence is progressively revealed, it follows that as culture advances, as ideals become higher, and knowledge of the universe increases, the forms of theological conception must gradually expand and undergo such modification as will bring them into accord with the deeper insight of the Spirit and the wider outlook of the Understanding. Hence it is inevitable that progressive Culture and Dogmatic Religion, with its stereotyped forms of dogma and ritual, should violently clash; and it is no less inevitable that in all such conflict it will be by Culture that in the end the victory will be won.

But how about Rational Religion—the religion, that is, which makes its final appeal, not to any external authority (be it the utterance of a religious teacher, a church or a book), but to that inner rational, ethical and spiritual consciousness, through which the Eternal is believed to reveal Himself to the individual soul? The really significant and tragic feature in the present condition of the civilized world is the widespread inability of Culture and Rational Religion to come to a satisfactory understanding with each other; and the momentous question to which I shall have to ask your attention in the following Lectures is whether the present estrangement of a large section of cultured society from theistic belief is removable by earnest thought and by mutual concessions from both the scientific and the theological side, or whether there is an intrinsic incompatibility between high mental development and firm religious conviction.

LECTURE V.
CULTURE AND RELIGIOUS BELIEF.

II. CULTURE AND RATIONAL RELIGION.

The foregoing exposition of the nature of Dogmatic Religion will explain the collisions which take place between it and advancing culture. If I have rightly placed the essence of Religious Belief in some insight into the nature of the Eternal given in the ethical ideal which carries with it a conciousness of relationship to a source of absolute authority, then it is evident that as human ideals rise and their application to all the relations of life are more clearly discerned, so the soul's conception of the character of God will expand; and with the advance of scientific knowledge the mode of conceiving of God's relation to the Cosmos will also advance. The Dogmatic Religion, then, which consecrates and stereotypes a particular phase of ethical insight and of cosmical science, inevitably comes into conflict with physical and moral science so soon as this science has progressed to new and more adequate modes of viewing nature and humanity. In such conflicts between Theological Dogma on the one hand, and Science and Morality on the other, the victory of the latter is only a question of time; and, as a matter of course, these antagonisms become fewer and less virulent as Culture progresses, and the true nature of the *essence* of Religious Belief, as contrasted with its transient *form*, is increasingly perceived. And herein we see the immense value of the Critical Understanding, which is always at war with superstitious survivals, and by its fresher and clearer insight into the facts of nature and of mind, is always dissolving old and outworn forms of doctrinal conception, and enabling the vital essence of religion to embody itself in higher and more adequate modes of thought and expression.

Now if the Understanding, with its healthy appeal to physical and mental facts, did no more than break up outgrown forms of conceiving the character and activity of the Eternal Being, there could be no real collision between the scientist and the theologian; for the scientist, with his newer and clearer insight into the phenomenal manifestations of God in the spheres of matter and mind, would simply be doing the theologian a high service in thus helping him to truer and more adequate conceptions of the mode of action of the Supreme Being in nature and humanity. The fact is, however, that a great awakenment of the scientific spirit, the special organs of which are the Senses and the Understanding, is not frequently found in conjunction with a high degree of that ideal faculty, or faculty of Spiritual Insight, by the exercise of which the essence of religious truth is discerned. These two aspects of man's higher life are not generally represented in any rich degree in the same individual. On the one hand, we have the men of *Ideals*, the Carlyles and the Emersons, the Robertsons and Martineaus; on the other hand, the men of *Facts*, such as Mr. Darwin, Prof. Huxley, Mr. Herbert Spencer, &c. And further, it is to be observed, that whenever new scientific conceptions of a comprehensive character are attained, it is always at first very difficult, even for the most earnest and impartial minds, to reconcile religious belief with the new modes of scientific conception. Religion has become so apparently identified with its old-fashioned dogmatic form that the attempt to strip off that form invariably appears to many minds as involving the destruction of the vital essence itself. Nor is it at all surprising that in times when there is a great revolt from the sacerdotal pretensions or ungrounded and immoral dogmas of the established religion, that the victorious vindications of the rights of the Understanding should, as the Germans say, *das Kind mit dem Bade ausschütten*, and lead many men to think for a time that all religious beliefs which cannot be reached by the application of the understanding to the particular facts of physical and mental science are mere unsubstantial chimeras of the imagination. Accordingly, in seasons of a great intellectual clearing-up (*Aufklärung*), such as took place at the close of the last century, Criticism, exulting in its liberation from dogmatic control, not only breaks up the outgrown forms of the old religious belief, but declines to admit the reality of any insight save that which the Senses and the Understanding can afford; and proclaims, if not a thorough-going Atheism or Agnosticism, at the most a cold mechanical Deism. And, as we have before seen, this exaggerated and exclusive attention to only such facts as the scientific faculty can discern, is speedily proved to be incomplete and one-sided by the circumstance that it is followed historically by a period of Romanticism in which the ideal side of man's self-consciousness receives an equally one-sided and unbalanced expression.

We, however, are not living in a time when the scientific spirit, or the spirit of culture, is mainly engaged in anti-theological negations as a reaction from a previous stage of theological dogmatism. The contest between Culture and Dogmatic Religion is among us gradually losing all interest, and indeed, in the more educated religious classes, has already been decided in favour of the former. Even in books which, like the recent collection of essays termed *Lux Mundi*, represent the views of what is called the "orthodox" party, the claims of science to give the final decision upon scientific matters are freely recognized, the only exception being in the case of the personality of the founder of Christianity. In respect to him, as we have before seen, neo-orthodoxy still maintains a peculiar position, and insists on regarding him as a being distinct in kind from the rest of humanity; for, while mankind in general are the "created" sons of God, Jesus, we are told by Dr. Fairbairn in his recent work on "Christ in Modern Theology," is "the uncreated or eternal Son." It is clear, however, that when this view of the special incarnation of God in Jesus of Nazareth begins to express itself by describing Jesus as "the greatest religious genius of the world," as is the case in

V. CULTURE AND RELIGIOUS BELIEF. 151

the recent writings of the "new school"[1] of orthodox theology, the conflict between Culture and Dogmatic Religion is virtually over; and it cannot be doubted that this is the position towards which the leading theologians of Christianity in all denominations are consciously or unconsciously moving.

Hence it is that the question of chief interest and permanent importance in the present day is not the relation of Culture to Dogmatic Religion, but to what Kant calls Rational Religion (*Vernunft-glaube*). Even the dogmatic or orthodox theologians are well aware of this, as is evident from the high and increasing appreciation which they give to such books as Dr. Martineau's "Study of Religion," which on philosophical grounds defend the main principles of Theism from the sceptical objections urged by recent scientists and philosophers. I will, accordingly, invite your attention in this Lecture to a brief consideration of the more formidable difficulties which recent scientific knowledge and speculation appear to place in the way of the acceptance of that idea of God which, as I have tried to show in a preceding Lecture, has its main basis in man's immediate ethical and spiritual consciousness. If, as the Theist must believe, the Eternal Being who is the source of man's progressive ethical ideals is also the cause and ground of the physical cosmos, there must be a real unity and harmony between the truth which science seeks to discover, and the real nature and character of that self-existent Being with whom the religious mind believes

[1] See Dr. Lynam Abbott's *Evolution of Christianity*, and Dr. J. M. Whiton's *Gloria Patri*.

itself to hold personal relations. The most profound scientific insight into the constitution of the cosmos can evidently not reach a full solution of the many enigmas which the study of the universe presents to the inquiring mind. It is to be expected that even if there be a fundamental identity of the cause and ground of nature with the object of the soul's religious faith, our limited powers of attaining to a clear understanding of nature's ultimate secrets must always make it difficult, and indeed impossible, for the human mind to see in each physical phenomenon a manifestation of that ethical and spiritual nature which religious insight ascribes to the Absolute and Eternal One. At the most, then, all that can reasonably be hoped for when Science and Religious Faith come to compare their respective results is, first, that the truths which Science believes itself to have firmly established shall not logically contradict the idea of God to which the insight of the moral and spiritual consciousness bears witness; and secondly, that on the whole the general drift and meaning of nature, so far as Science can discern it, shall be confirmatory of the idea which the soul forms of God as the immediate source of its ethical ideals and of the ethical imperative. That there should still remain occasional features in the cosmos which appear to the limited insight of man to be at variance with the character which Rational Religion ascribes to the Absolute Being is not only not surprising, but is precisely the state of the case which our knowledge of the necessarily limited range of the powers of the scientific understanding would lead us to expect. Religious Belief, accordingly, passes into satisfactory and helpful relations with scientific fact and theory as soon as it is seen that the conclusions of Science are on the whole confirmatory of the great outlines of that conception of the Supreme Being which man's ethical aspirations and spiritual sentiments spontaneously form.

But when we ask whether this reasonable amount of agreement and sympathy between theistic faith and scientific views at present exists, we are met at the outset with two loud-voiced assertions—firstly, that the most recent generalization of Science, the Theory of Evolution, has rendered unnecessary the hypothesis of purpose or dominating thought as the unifying principle of past and present cosmical phenomena; and secondly, that the human soul, being simply a further development of lower forms of psychical life, can have no higher ethical and spiritual insight than admits of being explained as a more complex result of those sensational experiences which are present in the earlier stages of biological evolution.

I will devote a future Lecture to the consideration of the force of the cosmological argument, the argument, that is, which rests on an alleged necessity in human thought to postulate the reality of a Ground or Cause of that whole series of co-existent and successive phenomena of which it is the business of science to find as complete a *rationale* as it can. And in the same connection also I will briefly discuss the teleological argument, which rests on the alleged clear presence of marks of intelligent design in the objects of nature and in their processes of development. But in the present Lecture I confine myself to indicating some unverified and unnecessary conceptions which are supposed by many minds to form an essential part of the doctrine of Evolution as established by recent researches.

Recent science sees in the co-existent and successive phenomena of nature infinitely varied expressions of energy capable of passing into different modes, and in many cases assuming more complex and more highly individualized forms as the process of evolution proceeds. Superficial students of the theory of evolution are apt to think that the successive stages by which the lower forms of existence pass into the higher are so related to each other that a knowledge of the lower carries with it implicitly the knowledge of the higher also. But this is wholly a mistake. The passage from the lower to the higher planes of being proceeds after a uniform plan, but no study of the one is adequate to account for the other. The biologist may assume that there already exists in the inorganic atoms that subjective side which, when an organism is formed, gives rise to low forms of sentiency, but he is utterly powerless to discover or to prove the existence of these elements of feeling. No study of the physical stage of evolution would suggest that the phenomena of consciousness were destined to supervene. The principle which manifests these phenomena may have been implicitly or potentially present in the inorganic world; and, possibly, even the physical atoms or monads into which science analyzes the cosmos may contain within them the germinal principle which under certain conditions manifests itself in feeling and consciousness. But even if these grand possibilities are already latent in the physical atom, this circumstance would in no way enable the savant to explain the succeeding psychical phenomena by means of the physical phenomena which preceded, but would simply reveal to him that a material atom was an infinitely more wonderful existence than he had imagined it to be, and that in order to fully understand it it would be necessary to study the highest forms of self-conscious life. Nor is it true, as some evolutionists appear to assume it is, that all the changes which take place in the process of evolution are so gradual as to be imperceptible. The maxim, *natura non facit saltum*, is often quoted by evolutionists as if it universally held good, and yet many of the transitions in the course of evolution are of quite startling suddenness. If, for instance, we suppose, as it appears we must do, all the chemical elements of our solar system pre-existing in their elementary condition in the fiery cosmic mist, there must have been a time when quite suddenly the attractions between these elements overcame the degree of caloric force which held them apart, and the rush of elements into chemical union must have been an entire change consummated with inconceivable rapidity. As Dr. Martineau graphically says:

"It is but a single degree of temperature that, handing a body over from solid to liquid, from liquid to gaseous, enables it to leap from science to science, and seek the new protectorate of hydrostatics and of pneumatics. The same small change it is which in an instant brings into play chemical affinities inoperative before, and with a flash and a clap turns the passive volumes of hydrogen and oxygen into water-drops. In like manner the law of gravitation, after holding good through spaces indefinitely vast, turns into sudden repulsion at inappreciable distances, which again gives way to the close attraction of cohesion on still nearer approach. And the rates of ethereal vibration which give luminosity are strictly limited, and from the extremities of the spectrum we instantly step into the dark."[1]

It is by no means, then, the case that the facts revealed in the lower stages of the evolutionary process furnish an explanation of the higher phases which succeed them. On the contrary, the truth appears to be that we never fully understand the significance of the lower phenomena till we have studied and mastered the higher phenomena which emerge out of them. It may be true, as Dr. Tyndall observes, that matter "contains the promise and potency of all terrestrial life;" but if so, this is so far from signifying that if we would know the higher forms of spiritual life we must study matter, that it leads, on the contrary, to the conclusion that if we would know the deeper mysteries involved in the nature of matter, we must study the highest phases of psychical evolution to which the race has attained. It is the essential features of all the higher modes of being which manifest themselves as the process of evolution goes on that not one of these higher modes is explicable by the lower modes which precede it, but that each higher mode in turn throws a clearer light on the earlier processes out of which it has emerged.

This principle is well applied to the evolution of man by Prof. Josiah le Conte of California, in his able book on "Evolution in its Relation to Religious Thought."

"There was," he says, "a time in the history of the earth when only physical forces existed, chemical affinity being held in abeyance by the intensity of the heat. By gradual cooling,

---

[1] *A Study of Religion*, Vol. II. p. 183.

chemical affinity at a certain stage came into existence, *was born* —a new form of force, with quite new and peculiar phenomena, though doubtless derived from the preceding. Ages upon ages passed away until the time was ripe and the conditions were favourable and *life* appeared—a new and higher form of force producing a still more peculiar group of phenomena, but still, I believe, derived from the preceding. Ages upon ages passed away, during which this life-force took higher and higher forms—in the higher foreshadowing and simulating reason itself—until finally, when the time was ripe and conditions were exceptionally favourable, *spirit*, self-conscious, self-determining, rational and moral, appeared—a new and higher form of force, but still, I am persuaded, derived from the preceding. With every new form of Force, with every new birth of Energy into a higher plane, there appear new and unexpected, and, previous to experience, wholly unimaginable properties and powers. This last is no exception. At the moment of the origin of man there may have been no great change in the grade of *physical structure*, but yet a complete change in the *plane of psychical life*—a change absolutely necessary for further advance. There is the appearance of a new creature with entirely different capacities; a passing out of an old world, a waking up in a new and higher one. In this new one man alone is a child of God capable of separate spirit-life. It is this which constitutes self-consciousness, free-will, moral responsibility; and out of these again grow the recognition of relations to other minds and to God, and therefore ethics and religion. This means voluntary progress; it means also spiritual viability or immortality."

This passage is of interest as showing how possible it is for an enthusiastic believer in Evolution and an able Professor of Natural History to find in his special studies a strong confirmation of his firm faith in an immediate and felt relationship between the individual soul and the Universal Soul. Prof. Henry Drummond, in his recent lectures on "The Evolution of Man" at the Lowell

Institute in Boston, endorses Prof. Le Conte's views, and maintains that the mind as well as the body of man has been developed from a lower order of creation. His words, as reported in the *Boston Herald*, are:

"As there is but one tenable theory of origin—creation, so there is but one tenable theory of progress—evolution. Those who reserve here and there a point in their acceptance of the doctrine of evolution for special divine interposition, logically must exclude the Creator from the series. If He appeared occasionally, He must have been occasionally absent. The question is of an all-God or of an occasional God. The continuation of nature needs a living Will as much as does man's creation."

This view of the evolution of the human soul expounded by Prof. Le Conte and Dr. H. Drummond seems at first sight to differ fundamentally from the doctrine on this subject taught by such eminent thinkers as Hermann Lotze and Dr. Martineau, and it appears to me that there is a certain amount of real difference between the doctrines in question, but at the same time it is a difference which, when clearly understood, does not touch the essential foundation of a theistic philosophy. In Dr. Martineau's "Types of Ethical Theory"[1] there is a very striking section, entitled, "Hitches in the Evolutionary Deduction." The more important of these "hitches" are, in Dr. Martineau's view, two: the first, the emergence in the process of cosmic evolution of Feeling or Consciousness; the second, the emergence in the course of biological evolution of man's Freedom of Will. By singling out these two conspicuous instances of the appearance of entire novelties in the course of Evolution,

[1] Vol. II. p. 393.

Dr. Martineau by no means wishes himself to be understood as meaning that the intervening stages in the evolutionary process are devoid of this incoming of fresh evidences of creative activity.

"My argument," he says, "affirms the general proposition that evolution consists in the perpetual emergence of *something new which is an increment of being* upon its prior term, and therefore more than its equivalent, and entitled to equal confidence and higher rank. This, however, though holding good throughout, has an exceptional forcible validity at certain stages of the evolution, on which it is desirable to pause. Though all the differences involved are something new, and may fall upon an observer's mere perception as equally new, yet, when scrutinized by reason, some may retain their character of absolute surprise, for which there was and could be nothing to prepare us, while others may prove to be, like an unsuspected property of a geometrical figure, only a new grouping of data and relations already in hand. In this sense there may be a more new and a less new; and it is the former that brings the force of the foregoing argument to its maximum."[1]

While Dr. Martineau thus selects the emergence of Feeling and of Free-will as stages in the process of evolution which in no way admit of being connected by any process of scientific deduction with the preceding conditions out of which they unexpectedly arise, a celebrated biological authority, Prof. Du Bois-Reymond of Berlin, in his Essay on *Die sieben Welträthsel*, declares there are at least seven stages in the onward progress of the cosmos where the scientist finds himself not only unable at present to construct any bridge of causal connection between the antecedent conditions and the new

[1] P. 393.

and surprising phenomena, but is even compelled to conclude that these higher phases of existence are intrinsically incapable of receiving an adequate explanation from the scientific study of lower stages of evolution. On this question, then, as to the successive emergence in the world-process of higher modes of existence which no observation of lower modes has sufficed or can suffice to explain, Prof. Le Conte, Dr. Martineau and Prof. Du Bois-Reymond, are evidently in fundamental agreement.

It appears to me, however, that in Prof. Le Conte's mode of describing the appearance at certain points of the world-process of higher and unexpected forms of existence there lies a danger of serious misunderstanding. In common with Dr. Martineau, he holds that the advent of Free-will in the course of evolution cannot be explained as merely a further development of those psychical capacities and powers which manifest themselves in the lower animals; and in like manner he maintains that the advent of Feeling or Consciousness is the appearance of a new and higher form of force; but in both these cases he declares his belief that the new forms of force "are derived from the preceding forms" of organic or inorganic force. And thus he would seem to be only endorsing the well-known statement by Prof. Tyndall, to which I have before referred, that "matter contains the promise and the potency of all terrestrial life." Now I venture to think that this mode of stating the problem is a very misleading one. It assumes that there is something, called "Matter" by Prof. Tyndall and "Force" by Prof. Le Conte, which has an existence wholly independent of, and isolated from, God, or the Eternal Ground and

Cause of all finite existence. But, as I have endeavoured to show in a previous Lecture, such a mode of conceiving of the relation of the finite or created being to the Absolute Being is quite opposed to the ultimate deliverance of our own consciousness. Every man is conscious that he is not a self-existent being, that in all probability there was a time when his individual being was not, and that even now the existence of his individuality is continually dependent upon some deeper Ground of Absolute Being. And not only so, but he is aware also that his rational and moral nature depends for its insight on the immanence in his consciousness of an eternal principle which is the property of no finite individual, but manifests itself in all alike, and thus unifies the various forms of finite existence, and by its common relation to all renders them capable of entering into dynamical, rational and spiritual relations with each other. Accordingly, all the modes of finite being, and all the successive phases under which they present themselves in the course of the evolutionary process, are in one aspect of their reality indissolubly united with that Eternal and Absolute Being of which they are each and all differentiations—differentiations varying, indeed, almost infinitely in the degree of independent selfhood which is delegated to them, but none of them wholly severed from that Absolute Reality out of whose self-determination their existence arises, and by whose perpetual energizing that existence is every moment sustained.

In what scientific thought terms the ultimate atoms or monads of the physical universe, we have the simplest modes of dynamical expression by which the Eternal

One manifests himself in the phenomenal world. If the question be asked whether these elementary dynamic centres of the self-manifestation of the Absolute have any degree of real existence or selfhood of their own, or are, as Dr. Martineau teaches, simply forms of God's own immediate energizing, there are, I think, no means of reaching a decisive answer. Certainly the selfhood of the ultimate elements of matter, or even of the lower forms of organism, as seen in vegetable life, is, if it exists at all (and analogy seems to favour the doctrine that it does exist), so inconceivably faint that it is separated *toto cœlo* from feeling and consciousness as it exists in us. With reference to a possible subjectivity or selfhood in even the lowest cosmical manifestations of the Eternal, the following passage from Lotze's "Microcosmos"[1] fairly describes, I believe, the state of mind into which reflection on the universe in the light of recent science will bring the majority of thoughtful minds:

"If we continue to use the phraseology in accordance with which we designated Reality as the general affirmation which belongs to action as well as existence, then Realness is the special kind of reality which we attribute to or seek for things, as the points from which action sets out and in which it is consummated. This Realness has appeared to us as dependent upon the nature of that to which it is to belong; it is the being of that which exists *for self*. But we want the name *self-existence* in order to characterize in a more general way the nature of mentality, which only reaches its highest stage in the self-consciousness of the being that knows itself as an Ego (*Ich*), and is not, because of this being its highest stage, absent in the being which, though far removed from the clearness of such self-consciousness, yet in

[1] English Translation, Vol. II. p. 646.

some duller form of feeling exists for itself and enjoys its existence. Hence to Realness in this sense we can attribute various degrees of intensity; we cannot say of everything that it is either altogether Real, or altogether not-Real; but beings, detaching themselves from the Infinite with varying wealth and unequal complexity of self-existence, are Real in different degrees, while all continue to be immanent in the Infinite. Hence the distinction between Idealism and the standpoint which we have just taken up consists in this: that the idealistic view, convinced of the selflessness of things, on this account will not allow that they are more than states of the Infinite; while we, agreeing herewith in principle, leave undecided, as something which we cannot know, the question whether this assumption of selflessness is appropriate; holding, however, that it is far more likely to be *in*appropriate, and that all things really possess, in different degrees of perfection, that selfhood by which an immanent product of the Infinite becomes what we call Real."

In this passage Lotze is more particularly distinguishing between his view of the reality of the cosmos, and that Hegelian or idealist view which regards all the objects and events of the physical world as being real only in the sense that they are the objects of thought, human or Divine. He contends, accordingly, that the most probable conclusion is, that while all nature is grounded in, and indissolubly dependent on, the thought and will of the Eternal, each atom and each organism has a certain element of feeling which, although of the most attenuated character, is nevertheless a sufficient basis for ascribing to the objects of nature a minimum of selfhood or independent reality. Had Lotze been occupied in comparing his own view of the cosmos with Dr. Martineau's view, viz. that Space is an objective reality, and that what we call matter consists of the direct energizing of the will of God at different points of space, he would, no doubt, have maintained that, supposing Dr. Martineau's view to be the correct one, the atoms or centres of force are probably, in one aspect, something more than simple modes of God's activity, and carry with them, as the guarantee of their partially independent reality, the most elementary germs of that subjectivity which reaches its full intensity in animals and men.

But whether we accept Lotze's probability, that the objects of even the inorganic world possess the earliest dawnings of the element of feeling, or prefer the more commonly-received doctrine that feeling begins quite *de novo* in the animal kingdom, it remains equally true that no investigation into the properties of matter or the laws of dynamics will avail in the slightest degree to explain the origin of this sentiency; nor, further, will any study of animal feeling or of animal activity at all account for the advent of that rational insight whereby a man is able to rise above his finite self, and of that consciousness of moral freedom and of an absolute ethical imperative which present themselves as biological evolution culminates in man.

So far as Evolution has a bearing on the basis of religious belief, the eminent men whose views I have cited are in substantial agreement. They all maintain that as cosmical development proceeds, new and unexpected, and previous to their actual appearance quite unimaginable, modes of Energy successively emerge; that these new modes present features of a higher character than are seen in the earlier stages, and therefore cannot be

V. CULTURE AND RELIGIOUS BELIEF. 165

regarded as so causally connected with the earlier phenomena that the study of these earlier phenomena will explain, or account for, the dawn and development of the higher phenomena which supervene. If the scientist thinks proper to assert that every feature manifested in physical and mental phenomena must have been implicitly or potentially present all through the process (and this is what Prof. Tyndall's above-quoted statement appears to mean), the answer is, that no intelligible sense can be attached to the word "potentiality" if that which is said to be potentially present in no way manifests itself in either the feeling or the action of the creature in which it is said to exist. In what sense, for instance, can moral freedom be said to be implicitly present in physical molecules, which move only as they are moved, or in the physical life of the lower animals, where action appears to invariably follow the strongest impulse?

Hence, though I am inclined to think that Prof. Le Conte's view of Evolution is substantially the same as my own, I somewhat demur to his form of statement. He says that the later and higher forms or modes of force, such as the spirit of man, though revealing properties and faculties not at all exhibited in the lower modes, are nevertheless "derived from" these lower modes. The more accurate manner of expressing the fact is, I think, to say that neither the lower nor the higher forms of force are in any true sense self-existent, but are both alike constantly dependent for their being on the self-differentiating energy or will of the Absolute and Uncreated God. When, then, we say that the higher form of energy is *derived from the lower*, we can only mean that in the order of God's self-manifestation in cosmical phenomena the lower form of existence is the antecedent of, and preparation for, the higher manifestation which follows; and accordingly the assertion that matter contains potentially all the higher forms of life is merely, I believe, an improper and inadequate way of stating the fact that God's energizing in the forms of force or matter is the basis and logical preliminary of His further energizing in the form of sentient animal life, and of free, self-determining man. When Prof. Tyndall and other savants speak of Matter and Force, they appear to regard them and to reason about them as if they were things which possessed the property of self-existence; and yet one would think that they need only to reflect for a moment on that particular form of Force which we know as our individual selves, to immediately and intuitively discern that such existences as these do not carry the ground and cause of their being in themselves, but are by the very necessity of thought only conceivable as dependent manifestations of an Absolute and Eternal Being. And that this necessary attribution of a dependent existence to all forms of force and finite consciousness is no fiction of the metaphysicians, but rests on the indefeasible deliverance of consciousness, is evident from the fact that such a thinker as Mr. Herbert Spencer, in whose mind the purely scientific impulse and interest is the dominant one, proclaims the certainty of this dependence as the fundamental principle of his cosmical philosophy.

It should be added, however, that there is evidently a real, though from our present point of view unimportant, difference of opinion between thinkers such as

Lotze, who regard the spirit of man as a quite new and direct creation or efflux of the Universal Spirit, which takes place on the occasion of the coming into existence of a suitable physical organism, and thinkers like Prof. Le Conte, who regard the spirit of man as derived from the animal soul. I regard this difference as unimportant, because it appears to come to no more than this: that those who hold the distinct creation of the human soul, do so because it seems to them that the manifestation of Divine Energy under the form of a rational and self-determining spirit cannot be conceived as simply a later and higher phase of that logically connected series of Divine energizings which has passed upward from the physical atom to the animal soul, but must be regarded as belonging to a quite distinct plane of God's self-manifestation. For myself, I do not feel sure that there is any mental necessity for regarding the human spirit as a creation by God in any other sense than that in which every animal soul is a creation by God. In the animal there must be a permanent self to be the seat of feeling, and the basis of connection between past and present feelings; and therefore the upward step to the self-determining spirit of man, with all the grand issues which that power of self-determination involves, may very well be regarded as the supreme and culminating act of God's self-differentiation to which the earlier stages of biological development form the appropriate antecedents and preparatory condition.

But whether the view of Lotze as to the mode of origin of the human spirit, or that of Prof. Le Conte and Prof. H. Drummond be the more correct, these thinkers are quite at one in regarding the whole course of cosmical evolution, of which the rational and moral faculties of man form the climax, as a progressive manifestation of Divine Energy or Creative Will. They all agree that it is futile to seek a *rationale* of the Cosmos and its history in any deductive process based upon the lowest and simplest modes of phenomenal existence; they all assert that it is only in the light of the higher modes of divine manifestation that the lower modes become fully intelligible, and that therefore the surest clue to the interpretation of the cause and purpose of the whole is to be sought in those highest ideals and aspirations of human nature in which the unifying principle which has dominated the whole course of the world's historical development reaches its highest and least inadequate expression.

I conclude, then, that the theory of Evolution, so far from being hostile to a Theistic conception of the universe as the self-manifestation or uttered Word of the Eternal One, presents, on the contrary, precisely those features which render God's expression of Himself in the cosmos at once capable of being progressively understood by the human intellect, and of subserving most effectually the growth and enrichment of man's rational, moral and spiritual character. The lowest modes of Divine creation or self-differentiation, constituting those elementary principles which science describes as Matter and Force, form, through their mechanical and invariable operation, the very foundation which is necessary as a theatre for the exercise and development of those higher modes of sensation and consciousness which reach their acme in the rational and self-determining man. There is good reason for thinking that in all cosmical life the Eternal Being surrenders somewhat of His own essence and direct causality that He may call into existence, contemplate and commune with those dependent images of Himself which form the objects of His thought and love. In the case of the human soul, this delegation of real selfhood to the creature, this partial self-sacrifice of the Absolute and Universal Soul in order that the dependent soul may live and become participant of Truth, Righteousness and Love, reaches to such a high degree that man, while still indissolubly linked with the Eternal Ground of all existence and the Source of all high ideals and aspirations, is nevertheless gifted with such real freedom and independence of thought and will that, if the insight of man's moral consciousness is not delusive, the purpose which Eternal Love is engaged in realizing may be temporarily impeded and retarded by the mistaken or sinful self-determinations of those free and rational souls which this same Love has called into existence. And for the development of moral and spiritual life in those highest and freest products of the creative will of God, it appears to be indispensable that they should emerge out of and live amid the conditions of that lower life of animal passions and of mechanical necessity which in the process of evolution naturally precedes them and forms the needful basis for their advent and development. If the chief purpose which dominates and unifies the whole course of evolution is the appearance at the fitting season of creatures so individualized and free that they may be capable of entering into real moral and spiritual relations with the Supreme Being to whom they owe the origin and the maintenance of their life, it is, I believe, impossible to conceive a method of self-differentiation or creation by the Absolute Thought and Will which should be as competent to secure the growth of human characters worthy of the sympathy and love of the Eternal as is that actual process of cosmical and social development out of which we human beings arise, and which, by reason of our essential community of essence with its Ground and Cause, we are enabled in progressive measure to understand and to interpret.

So much, then, for the general theory of Evolution in its bearing on the essential basis of theistic belief. I now pass to a different but kindred subject. Closely connected with current views of evolution is another speculation which of late years has become fashionable in scientific circles, and which, if I am not mistaken, must, in all logical minds that accept it, prove a very serious obstacle to the reconciliation of science with a satisfying form of religious belief. I refer to the so-called "Identity" theory of Mind and Body, the theory, that is, which represents Mind and Body, not as two substances which are capable of acting on each other, but as two aspects or faces of one substance. This view is sometimes called the "new Spinozism," because it is the recent scientific form of Spinoza's doctrine that extension and thought are two attributes of the one self-existent Substance, God. Many recent scientific and philosophical books of note more or less explicitly accept this hypothesis. Mr. Spencer's doctrine of the "Composition of Mind"[1] appears to rest on the sup-

[1] *Principles of Psychology*, Vol. I. p. 163.

position that the ultimate elements of the brain, and the ultimate elements, or "psychical shocks," of sensation, are but two modes of manifestation of the same basal reality. The theory is graphically expounded and its chief implications unfolded in two interesting essays by Prof. Romanes in the *Contemporary Review* for July, 1885, and July, 1886. It is also accepted by some recent Hegelian writers, and the discussion of it forms a fascinating chapter in the treatise on the "Spirit of Modern Philosophy" by Prof. Royce of Harvard; while in one of the ablest of our present hand-books on the human mind, Prof. H. Höffding's "Outlines of Psychology," it is declared to be the only basis on which a satisfactory structure of mental science can be erected. Prof. Höffding argues that both the *parallelism* and the *proportionality* between the activity of consciousness and cerebral activity point to an *identity* at bottom.

"We have no right," he says, "to take mind and body for two beings or substances in reciprocal interaction. We are, on the contrary, impelled to conceive *the material interaction* between the elements composing the brain and nervous system, *as an outer form of the inner ideal unity of consciousness*. What we in our inner experience become conscious of as thought, feeling and resolution, is thus represented in the material world by certain material processes of the brain, which as such are subject to the law of the conservation of energy, although the law cannot be applied to the relation between cerebral and conscious processes."[1]

In order to understand the historical relations of this theory, it is necessary to go back to the great founder of

[1] English Translation, p. 64.

modern philosophy, Des Cartes. In his view, God, or the Absolute Being, creates two substances, Matter and Mind; but as matter is essentially extension, and mind is essentially thought, and thought and extension have nothing in common, matter and mind cannot be conceived as acting upon one another. Des Cartes himself is not very explicit and consistent in his account of how it comes about that the affections of the body and those of the mind so wonderfully correspond with each other. But his disciple Geuliux, whose works have been recently reprinted, explains the apparent interaction of the two by the "theory of Occasionalism," meaning thereby that on occasion, for instance, of the human body being affected by the low temperature of the air, God immediately causes the mind to feel the sensation of cold; and that, on the other hand, whenever the human mind wills a particular bodily movement, it is the causal action of God which intervenes and produces the necessary muscular contraction. Another attempt to explain this seeming interaction of matter and mind is furnished in Leibnitz's well-known theory of "Pre-established Harmony." According to this doctrine, which involves the complete rejection of the freedom of the human will in the libertarian sense, God has so arranged the succession of physical phenomena on the one hand, and of psychical phenomena on the other, that the two lines of evolution, though never causally affecting each other, yet preserve an invariable parallelism. Like the movements of the hands of two perfectly accurate chronometers which are in no way connected, the physical changes and the mental changes invariably correspond; but the only cause of that correspondence is the eternal pre-arrangement by the Supreme Will.

Both these modes of accounting for the apparent interaction of body and mind labour under the defect that the two substances seem to have no natural relationship, but to be forced into an accidental connection and accord by the will of God. Accordingly, to Spinoza, with his intense philosophical passion for the unification of knowledge, this merely arbitrary correspondence between mental and physical phenomena was in no way satisfying. To escape from it he rejected the Cartesian doctrine of two God-created substances, and maintained that there is but one fundamental substance, namely, God himself. This absolute substance may have countless attributes, but only two—extension and thought—are manifested in human experience. But while in this way Spinoza finds in the *essence* and not in the *will* of God a bond of union between body and mind, his theory fails to explain why the human consciousness, which is by its very nature only a mode of God's thinking, should come to know of that other attribute of God, viz. extension, for this latter cannot possibly be accessible to the human mind if it is anything more than a mode of thinking. But if the only extension of which man can know anything is simply the *thought* of extension, one of Spinoza's two Divine attributes falls away, and we are left with the single attribute, *Thought*. Hence there is no difficulty in understanding how it comes about that Spinoza and Hegel are now so often named together as teaching substantially the same doctrine. Spinoza no doubt considered himself a Realist, and continually speaks as if matter or extension, as distinct from thought, were directly cognizible by the human mind; still, if his theory be correct, that the two attributes of God are always parallel to each other, *but never causally interact,* it is inconceivable how man, whose consciousness consists entirely of modes of the attribute, Thought, should come to know of the objective existence of the attribute, Extension; and this inconsistency besets, I believe, all advocates of the "double-aspect" theory who, like Mr. Spencer, aim to combine with that theory a realistic conception of the cosmos.

When we turn from these speculations of the seventeenth century to nineteenth century theorizing on the relation between Body and Mind, we at once notice a curious difference. The writers of the earlier period all philosophize more or less in the interest of rational theology, but in the theories of our own day the theological reference is wanting, and instead of Spinoza's God with His two attributes, we have an Unknowable with two faces or aspects. This difference is partly due to the fact that the "identity" theory, as now held, has had its origin not so much among philosophers as among scientists. It is true that one of the earliest statements of this doctrine occurs in Dr. Shadworth H. Hodgson's thoughtful treatise on "Time and Space," but it was the exposition of it in popular periodicals and lectures by such scientific thinkers as Mr. Spalding, Prof. Huxley and Prof. W. K. Clifford, which gave to the doctrine its present extensive currency. It was only by degrees that the doctrine assumed its present form. When it was first introduced, Prof. Huxley only accepted it so far as the denial of the action of mind on matter is concerned; he still allowed that matter could act on mind, and, accordingly, that the action on our minds of an outer world is the cause of the sensations of colour, sound, taste, &c., which we experience. "The brain," he says, "is the organ of sensation, thought and emotion; that is to say, some change in the condition of the matter of this organ is the invariable antecedent of the state of consciousness to which each of these terms is applied." What, then, is "consciousness" in this theory? It is simply an attendant on certain molecular motions in the brain, but a quite superfluous attendant, which has no causal influence whatever on the bodily movement. In Prof. Huxley's view, the purpose or idea in my mind to write and deliver this Lecture had not the slightest influence in determining the action of my hand on the pen, nor does my aim to be now heard by you count for anything in determining the present action of my vocal organ. As Mr. Spalding puts it, "consciousness is like the steam and smoke which are at times given off by a locomotive, but which have no influence whatever in determining the movement of the engine."

The chief argument employed to establish a doctrine so diametrically opposed to the spontaneous judgment of all mankind, is the doctrine of the Conservation of Energy. If the mind or will acted on the material molecules of brain, it must (we are told) originate some small degree of energy in so acting, and scientific authorities have agreed that the sum-total of energy in the cosmos remains unchanged. But if mind exercises no causal action on body, there appears no reason to suppose that body influences mind, and, accordingly, Prof. W. K. Clifford went further than Prof. Huxley, and maintained that neither side of this seeming duality of matter and mind had any power to affect the other. There is a *parallelism* between brain-states and mind-states, but no *interaction;* the only causal antecedents of molecular brain-charges are preceding molecular movements, and the only causal antecedents of states of consciousness are antecedent states of consciousness. This theory, which Prof. Höffding of Copenhagen declares to be the only one that accords with the facts, leads to the following curious results, which are thus graphically depicted by Prof. James of Harvard, in his important work on Psychology:

"If we knew thoroughly the nervous system of Shakespeare, and as thoroughly all his environing conditions, we should be able to show why at a certain period of his life his hand came to trace on certain sheets of paper those crabbed little black marks which we for shortness' sake call the manuscript of Hamlet. We should understand the *rationale* of every erasure and alteration therein, and all this without needing to acknowledge in the slightest degree the existence of the thoughts in Shakespeare's mind. The words and sentences would be taken not as signs of anything beyond themselves, but as little outward facts pure and simple. In like manner we might exhaustively write the biography of those two hundred pounds, more or less, of warmish albuminoid matter called Martin Luther without ever implying that it felt. And of course, on the other hand, we could give an equally complete account of either Luther's or Shakespeare's spiritual history."

The bearing of this "identity" theory of matter and mind on Theistic belief is very differently represented by different scientists. The late Prof. W. K. Clifford, to whose genius the origination and popularizing of this philosophy of the cosmos is mainly due, is of opinion that the doctrine is decidedly unfavourable to belief in a self-conscious God. The universe, in his view, is composed of "bits of mind-stuff," and this mind-stuff is the reality which we perceive as matter.

"That element," he says, "of which, as we have seen, even the simplest feeling is a complex, I shall call *Mind-stuff*. A moving molecule of inorganic matter does not possess mind or consciousness, but it possesses a small piece of mind-stuff. When molecules are so combined together as to form the film on the under side of a jelly-fish, the elements of mind-stuff which go along with them are so combined as to form the faint beginnings of Sentience. When the molecules are so combined as to form the brain and nervous system of a vertebrate, the corresponding elements of mind-stuff are so combined as to form some kind of consciousness; that is to say, changes in the complex which take place at the same time get so linked together that the repetition of one implies the repetition of the other. When matter takes the complex form of a living human brain, the corresponding mind-stuff takes the form of a human consciousness, having intelligence and volition."[1]

The question, then, which this theory suggests to the theistic philosopher is this: Are we, then, justified in ascribing to the cosmos as a whole a subjective side, or divine consciousness, which is distinct from, and more than the sum-total of, the various subjective states of its constituent parts? Clifford frankly admits that, so far as he can see, the cosmos presents no indications of having any such unitary consciousness. He points out that when we find a highly elaborate brain, as in man, we

[1] *Lectures and Essays*, Vol. II. p. 85.

find a high form of consciousness. As we descend the scale of life, the nervous systems and the brains become simpler in form, and consciousness sinks to a lower level; and when we reach the inorganic world, there is good reason to believe that the subjective side, which pertains to the elementary pieces of mind-stuff, is of an inconceivably faint character. He accordingly argues that, in the absence of any signs of the existence in space of what we may call a cosmical brain, there is no scientific ground for the belief that there exists any other psychical reality in the inorganic portions of the cosmos than the collection of those dim and infinitely multiple bits of subjectivity which are supposed to be present in the ultimate constituents of the material world.

Prof. G. J. Romanes,[1] on the other hand, though he enthusiastically adopts the "mind-stuff" theory of the cosmos, yet at the same time vigorously protests against Clifford's anti-theistic conclusions, contending that the theory in question, so far from militating against the hypothesis of a World-soul or universal consciousness, is rather favourable than otherwise to the Theistic position. He thinks it was very unreasonable in Clifford to assume that a structure like the human brain is the only possible physical concomitant to that high state of subjectivity which is ascribed to the consciousness or supra-consciousness of God. His view is, that the physical cosmos as a whole may very well be regarded as the physical aspect of God's subjective life, and that while the "identity" theory is quite compatible with the existence of such a

[1] *Contemporary Review*, July, 1886, "The World as an Eject."

supreme consciousness, the evident organic unity of the cosmos, the marks of purpose which abundantly present themselves in nature, and the high improbability that the consciousness of a creature such as man should be the highest form of subjectivity in the universe, all concur in rendering probable the existence of a transcendent consciousness which may be related to the finite forms of human consciousness as this latter is related to the faint elements of subjectivity which are on this theory supposed to belong to the ultimate constituents of the physical world. Following Mr. H. Spencer, Prof. Romanes argues, that this hypothetical cosmical mind must be regarded as "impersonal," since personality in his view implies limitation, and that therefore the mind of God can only be "symbolically" conceived by the mind of man.

Now while fully admitting the force of Prof. Romanes' reasoning in favour of the being of a World-soul or Universal Mind, I cannot but think that the belief in such a Being, so far from being strengthened, is very much weakened, if we accept this "mind-stuff" theory, and regard the cosmos, with its uniform laws, not as constantly originated and maintained by God's self-determination or will, but simply as the eternal or uncreated counterpart of the consciousness of God. Prof. Romanes asserts that the "double-aspect" theory "leaves us free to regard all natural causation as a direct exhibition of psychism," and that the invariability of the sequences of physical causation "becomes but the expression of intentional order; and the iron rigidity of natural law becomes but the sensuous manifestation of an unalterable consistency as belonging to the Supreme Volition." But what possible meaning can be attached to this expression, "Supreme Volition," if every movement in the universe has for its only intelligible cause the previous movements, while the so-called "Supreme Volition" is only its parallel concomitant? Surely Prof. Romanes must have forgotten the very essence of the theory he is expounding and defending, for on that theory no causal interaction between the subjective and the objective side of God's being is conceivable, and the "intentional order" of physical nature which his language seems to assign to the activity of a conscious or super-conscious God, is on his own theory to be ascribed to the previous series of physical movements which form its causal antecedents. The believer in the "identity" doctrine, even if he should think himself justified in maintaining that there is a Universal Mind which thinks and puts forth volitions, must at the same time hold that these volitions, so far from determining the order of natural phenomena, are simply the uniform parallel accompaniments of that order; and the term Will or Volition, whether applied to man or to God, becomes utterly meaningless if every subjective state, human or divine, is simply the invariable concomitant of a series of physical events, the necessary laws of which are eternally inherent in the ultimate constitution of the cosmos. It is only, I believe, by treating "concomitance" as if it were the same thing as "cause," that Prof. Romanes succeeds in giving a Theistic appearance to this "double-aspect" philosophy of the universe.

But not only does this doctrine utterly preclude the

possibility of ascribing to the Eternal Spirit any causal or volitional control over the physical order of the cosmos, but it also inevitably tends to fix the attention on the *material* aspects of the world as furnishing the only intelligible *rationale* of the sequence of phenomena. As Mr. Shadworth H. Hodgson, who was one of the earliest advocates of the doctrine, himself admits, it is only the items of the nervous or physical changes which are in *causal continuity*, and the successive mental states are simply *juxta-posed*. As the material series of changes is the only one of which we can give any scientific account, and in which any intelligible causality can be discovered, this conscious-automaton theory virtually turns consciousness out of doors as a superfluity so far as causality and scientific explanation are concerned. As Prof. James humorously remarks, "One may bow consciousness out or allow her to remain as a concomitant, but one insists that matter shall hold all the power." And I may add, that if God's being is thus linked indivisibly and eternally, as Prof. Romanes' theory supposes, to an infinite material mechanism or organism, there can be little doubt that it would be only the material aspects of such a deity that human reflection could take a real interest in, or could study with any hope of increased insight.

And if this "double-aspect" theory of the cosmos is an obstacle rather than a help to theistic belief, it is certainly anything but satisfactory as a *rationale* of man's ethical experience. Prof. Romanes truly says, that if this view be accepted, it settles for good and all the Free-will controversy. Undoubtedly it does this most effectually. But the strange feature in his exposition is the assertion that it settles the dispute by "doing justice to both sides in this time-honoured controversy." The ground on which Prof. Romanes asserts that this view reconciles the conflicting claims of Freewill and Determinism, is that it represents mental states as caused only by previous mental states, and bodily states as caused only by previous bodily states, or rather declares that there is one causality in the case with two aspects. How he has succeeded in coming to the conclusion that mental volitions which are thus tied down to uniform agreement with their invariable physical concomitants can be in any sense morally free, is a psychological enigma which I feel myself wholly unable to solve. And, indeed, I believe that he is the only public advocate of this form of cosmological doctrine who maintains that it is at all compatible with the existence of genuine moral freedom and responsibility in man. The only other writer of note who has discussed this "identity" theory in its relations to moral freedom is the Hegelian Prof. Royce, of Harvard University, in his attractive treatise on the "Spirit of Modern Philosophy;" and the idealist device to which he is driven in order to harmonize the theory with man's feeling of moral accountability is, I think, a clear confession of the impossibility of reaching any satisfactory reconciliation. After describing the theory and endorsing it, Prof. Royce continues :

"But how, one may ask, can I be in any sense thus free? After all, is not my consciousness viewed as a fact in time tied hopelessly to this describable nervous mechanism of mine? The

V. CULTURE AND RELIGIOUS BELIEF. 183

world involves a physical order that necessarily contains just this organism. What the organism itself will do in given circumstances, is therefore physiologically determined by the whole order of nature and by the whole of past time. And my will moves no atom of this mechanism aside from its predestined course. And yet I, whose will is just so much of the world of appreciation [which in Prof. Royce's theory means the self-conscious side of the cosmos] as constitutes the inner aspect of this describable mechanism,—I shall be in some sense free? How explain such a paradox?"[1]

Prof. Royce's mode of escape from this paradox can only be fully appreciated by minds that are already familiar with the Neo-Hegelian philosophy of religion of which I shall attempt some estimate in a future Lecture. As persons existing in time we are, as Prof. Royce says, "tied hopelessly to this nervous mechanism of ours," but in the view of the absolute idealist our real existence is not in time. We are, in Prof. Royce's words, "conscious bits of the Eternal Self." And in his view this Eternal Self, of which we are pieces, by a timeless act freely chooses the whole condition of things, including time and space and this "double-aspect" nature of reality. The whole system of the universe being thus the free choice of the Eternal Self, we, as bits of that Self, are involved as partners in that timeless act; and thus sharing responsibility for the whole, we are to be regarded as responsible also for that minute fragment of the whole which constitutes our temporal life and individual character. Now I think you will agree with me, that if participation in this timeless act of free-choice by which the universe is constituted—an act of which no

[1] P. 430.

human mind has the least consciousness, and which, perhaps, may have no reality save in the speculative imagination of philosophers—if this is all that can save us from the depressing consciousness of being tied down hopelessly to this nervous mechanism of ours, the chances of our shaking off the incubus of fatalism while holding this "double-aspect" view of the cosmos, are of quite infinitesimal minuteness.

I hold, then, that this theory, at present so fashionable in the scientific world, and to some extent in the philosophical world likewise—for there exists in America a widely-circulated quarterly journal, named the *Monist*, the chief business of which is to expound and propagate it—is not only opposed to the immediate deliverance of every one's consciousness, but is also subversive of all such religious belief as the mind and heart of man desiderate, and of all rational basis for man's moral freedom and responsibility. What, then, are the grounds on which this theory, so momentous in its ethical and religious implications, is professedly founded? The advocates of the doctrine allege two reasons for its acceptance, firstly, that Matter and Mind are so wholly unlike that the one cannot be supposed to act upon the other; and secondly, that such interaction would interfere with the now generally accepted doctrine that the sum-total of energy in the universe remains constant.

The first of these alleged difficulties in the way of supposing that the will of man influences his cerebral states and determines his voluntary muscular movements, is the difficulty which, as I before noticed, Des Cartes started, and which Geuliux and Leibnitz sought in different ways to overcome by the alleged action of God, either at the beginning of the history of the cosmos, or at each particular point in human and animal experience where body and consciousness appear to act on each other. But while these attempts still leave mind and matter as merely arbitrarily juxta-posed, and not as intelligibly related, so the old Spinozism and the new Spinozism, or "identity" theory, also utterly fail to furnish any explanation why reality should have these two utterly unlike and unrelated aspects; for no real affinity or connection between the two is established by asserting that they are the two faces of one unknowable substance. My own view is, that the whole difficulty started by Des Cartes is based upon a false conception of the nature of what is called Matter, and that in reality there exist neither two kinds of substance, matter and mind, nor one Unknowable Substance, with matter and mind as its respective aspects, but rather one in part Knowable Substance, namely, Spirit, and that what we call dead or brute Matter is only Spirit in its lowest form of self-manifestation. In other words, the universe of finite things and finite souls arises out of the self-differentiations of the Eternal Spirit, and these finite creations only differ from each other in the degree in which the determining activity of the Absolute and Eternal Mind imparts to them a lesser or greater degree of independent selfhood or individuality. Schelling was not, I believe, far from the truth when he declared, "the feeling of life wakes in man, dreams in animals, slumbers in plants, and sleeps in stones;" for all forms of finite existence are of the same nature as that Eternal Life in which they originate. The Absolute Spirit partially withdraws His determining causality in increasing measure from portions of His own being and energy, that the cosmos may have a real existence, and that spirits akin in nature with Himself may, at the fitting stage of evolution, arise, and in virtue of their moral freedom enter into real rational and spiritual converse with that Eternal Source of Truth, Righteousness and Love, who ever remains immanent and active in the reason, the conscience and the heart.

No one whose reflections have penetrated deeper than the superficial appearances of things will be inclined to dogmatically maintain that there exists an essential difference between matter and spirit, body and mind. Kant's attitude on this question is lucidly expounded by Ueberweg in his "History of Philosophy."[1] In his "Critique of the Pure Reason," Kant says that the difficulty of understanding the interaction between soul and body is increased by the assumption that the two interacting substances are heterogeneous; and he proceeds to argue that this assumption is wholly unwarranted, resting as it does on the false supposition that the external appearance of matter, which is all that our senses can discern, constitute the entire reality. Could we penetrate to that inner nature of matter which underlies the visible phenomena, we should find, he concludes, that this inner reality is perhaps *not so unlike the soul itself.* And the result of Lotze's profound study of the nature of matter is strongly confirmative of Kant's opinion.

[1] 2nd ed. p. 427, Eng. trans.

V. CULTURE AND RELIGIOUS BELIEF. 187

"Those," he says, "who were staggered by the idea of a possible action and reaction between the soul and the differently constituted content of matter, may now have their scruples removed by the perception that in fact two different beings do not here face each other, but that the soul as an indivisible being, and the body as a combined plurality, form kindred and homogeneous terms of this relation. The soul acts not on the body so far as matter, but on the supersensible beings which only afford us the phenomenal appearance of extended matter by a definite form of combination; not as material, and not with material instruments, does the body exert its influence on the mind; but all attraction and repulsion, all pressure and impact, are, even on that nature which to us seems utterly devoid of animation, even where they act from matter to matter, only *the manifestation of a spiritual action and reaction which alone contains life and energy.*"[1]

Lotze's view may on the surface appear to resemble that very "identity" theory of body and mind which I am endeavouring to refute, for Lotze thinks that in all probability every elementary particle of man's bodily frame, as well as every ultimate atom or monad of nature, has an interior life which may involve the faintest dawning of sentiency. It might, therefore, seem that his theory of the cosmos and the "mind-stuff" theory are, if not identical, at least closely akin. But the fact is quite otherwise, for on the mind-stuff theory the consciousness of man and animals is the result of a *collection* or *combination* of the subjective elements which belong to each bit of mind-stuff which contributes to form the nervous system or the brain; but in Lotze's view this doctrine of a complex consciousness, made up of separate pieces of consciousness, is inconceivable and absurd. He, rightly I think,

[1] *Mikrokosmus*, Book III. chap. iv., Eng. trans. Vol. I. p. 364.

regards all consciousness or sentiency, as in its essential nature simple and indivisible, and maintains that, just as physical science shows that the ultimate elements of matter ever preserve their impenetrable individuality through all the changes of composition in which they take part, so the inner life, whether of an atom of the bodily frame or that of a highly evolved soul, is strictly its own, and is intrinsically incapable of resigning its own separate individuality in order to become merged in some more complex mental life. There is, indeed, I apprehend, no more conclusive refutation of this "double-aspect" theory of the cosmos than the fact that it involves the impossible conception that separate bits of subjectivity somehow manage to lose their individuality and to combine to form a higher unitary consciousness. Hence, while in Lotze's view there is probably a certain dim and dawning sentiency in every ultimate particle of the human body and brain, yet the subjective states of these elements of the organism never pass beyond the atoms or monads which possess them, and therefore no more contribute to the consciousness of the soul to which the body is organic than your consciousness enters directly into my consciousness or my consciousness into yours.[1] Lotze's view is indeed diametrically opposed to the theory of "identity" as represented by Prof. Höffding and Prof. Royce. And I need hardly remind you that the two theories stand in quite opposite relations to the belief in the Immortality of the Soul. If the soul is no more than a compound of the separate bits of subjectivity

[1] Compare some admirable remarks on this point in Prof. Seth's *Hegelianism and Personality*, p. 216, et seqq.

belonging to the particles of mind-stuff which constitute the brain, there is every reason to expect that when the brain at death is resolved into its chemical elements, the consciousness, which is nothing more than the psychical aspect of the brain, will in like manner break up again, and the bits of mind will only continue to exist as the subjective sides of the physical molecules, which in process of time may again become the constituents of animal brains, and so help to form other modes of consciousness. Such is the only immortality which the "double-aspect" theory of the cosmos is able to provide. The theory, on the other hand, which regards every psychical monad as well as every human soul as having its own individual and inalienable sentiency or consciousness, is not only quite compatible with a doctrine of personal immortality, but even points to such a doctrine as the most natural and probable sequel to the infinite capacities and affections which manifest their presence in the higher forms of individual consciousness.

The important bearing, then, of this prevalent "identity" theory, not only on ethics and religion, but also on the hope of immortality, is my excuse for dwelling so long upon a doctrine which I believe the future historian of philosophical thought will not regard as of primary importance. I have endeavoured to show that no such theory is needed in order to furnish a *rationale* of the correspondence and apparent interaction of body and soul. And now, finally, I will ask your attention to the other argument which its advocates adduce, namely, that the common view of body and mind as acting upon each other must be discarded, because it is a virtual denial of the perfect accuracy of the scientific doctrine that the energy of the cosmos is a constant quantity. On this I would remark, in the first place, that it is yet very far from having been proved that the sum-total of "force" manifested in the universe undergoes no change; and scientific men, in view of the fact of the so-called "dissipation of energy," are very much exercised in mind by the difficulty of accounting for the fact that in past time, which we cannot help conceiving as of infinite duration, the energy of the universe, if it be an unchangeable quantity, has not reached that condition of equilibrium or uniformity of temperature which means the entire cessation of all possibility of life and work. But apart from this fundamental difficulty, there is still a difference of opinion among competent inquirers as to whether self-conscious beings do not give forth in their activity and volition more force than they actually receive in the form of food. Only a few months ago, there appeared in the oldest of the German philosophical journals, *Fichte's Zeitschrift für Philosophie und philosophische Kritik*,[1] two elaborate articles—"Ueber die Einseitigkeit der herrschenden Kraft-theorie"—in which the author, Dr. Nicolaus Van Seeland, adduces what appear to be solid reasons, based on careful observations made in hospitals and elsewhere, for the opinion that not only in the movement of the limbs, but also in many other instances, such as in the effort called forth in the recovering from illness, in the building up of character, in literary and artistic creations, the human Self actually gives forth more energy than it receives, and thus in a slight degree adds to the

[1] The volume for 1893.

sum-total of cosmical force. As to whether Dr. Van Scoland's arguments are perfectly conclusive, I do not feel competent to say; but they are certainly worthy of consideration, for there appears to be no antecedent impossibility or improbability in the manifestation of some measure of fresh force by an active Self. The celebrated mathematician and physicist, Euler, remarks, in one of his "Letters to a German Princess:" "Although impenetrability creates force, yet one cannot ascribe to it a certain definite force, but it is rather capable of putting forth all degrees of force, great or little, according as circumstances demand; and it is an inexhaustible source of the same." If, then, a material atom can exert an indefinite amount of energy according to the degree of external pressure which it resists, there is no absurdity in supposing that the psychical monad or soul under certain circumstances may in its volitional activity manifest a portion of that inexhaustible energy which it appears to possess. But be this as it may, even if we accept the current doctrine of the conservation of force, Sir John Herschel has clearly shown that any creation of force needed for the action of mind on body is so small that in the aggregate it might entirely elude scientific observation. In a paper on "The Origin of Force," he writes:

"The actual force necessary to be *originated* to give rise to the utmost imaginable exertion of animal power, may be no greater than is required to remove a single material molecule from its place through a space inconceivably minute—no more in comparison with the dynamical force *disengaged* directly or indirectly by the act, than the pull of a hair-trigger in comparison with the force of the mine which it explodes. But without the power to make *some* material disposition, to originate some movement, or to change, at least temporarily, the amount of dynamical force appropriate to some one or more material molecules, the mechanical results of human or animal volition are inconceivable. It matters not that we are ignorant of the mode in which this is performed. It suffices to bring the origination of dynamical power, to however small an extent, within the domain of acknowledged personality."[1]

This being the state of the case, it is, I think, evident that Science has shown no sufficient ground for rejecting the unanimous and irrepressible testimony of the human consciousness, that our brain changes and our muscular movements are not merely the parallel concomitants of our volitions, but are really the effects of which our personal self-determinations are in some way the efficient causes. And if there are good reasons for considering our bodily activities as the results rather than as another aspect of our mental activities, so, in like manner, the countless phenomena of the cosmos are not to be regarded as necessary and eternal physical sequences, to which God is "tied down" by the inherent necessity of his nature, but are rather to be contemplated as the dependent products of His self-determining will and purpose,— products which owe their origination and their continuance in existence to that Eternal Spirit, of whose essential thought and energy they are the finite and visible expressions.

Though, then, recent Science, in its doctrine of Evolution and its speculative view of the relation between Matter and Mind, appears on the surface to be incompatible with the reality of man's moral freedom and

[1] *Familiar Lectures on Scientific Subjects*, p. 468.

with the Theistic conception of the soul's personal relationship to God, I trust that the foregoing considerations will help to show that there is no irreconcilable antagonism here, but merely a temporary misunderstanding which further insight into nature on the one hand, and into the facts of man's ethical and spiritual insight on the other, will, as in similar cases in the previous history of scientific and theological thought, gradually clear up and remove.

But for the establishment of wholly satisfactory relations between Science and Rational Religion it is not enough that there should be no basal contradiction between religious belief and influential scientific ideas; there is the further need that the impression which the cosmos as a whole makes upon the mind should be suggestive and confirmative of the religious conception of God as the ultimate Ground and Cause of all finite existence. In the next Lecture, accordingly, I will discuss the force of the cosmological and teleological arguments through which most theologians believe the reason of man possesses a legitimate passage from "Nature up to Nature's God."

Lecture VI.
GOD AS GROUND AND CAUSE.

The influences which awaken and sustain religious belief are manifold. These influences affect different minds with different degrees of cogency, and it is to be noted that they rarely operate singly, but generally conspire together in producing a conviction of the being and character of the Absolute and Eternal One. Hence it often happens that stimulants to faith which, if isolated from each other, would fail to give rise to complete satisfaction, may, when they blend together, prove quite adequate to overcome all negative considerations.

You will have gathered from the preceding Lectures that I regard the moral consciousness, with its progressive ethical ideal and its unconditional imperative, as the main source of that form of Theism which vital religion always tends to assume as men become civilized and distinctly recognize the paramount authority of the Conscience and the transcendent worth of moral character. But though the moral faculty of man is the deepest, and ultimately the most influential, element in human nature, it does not manifest its presence clearly in the earlier periods of the life either of individuals or of society. The faculty which in the lower stages of mental development pre-eminently asserts itself is the perceptive faculty, and therefore the form which religion first assumes is that which is shaped by the impression which the external world makes upon the human consciousness. I have already pointed out in the second Lecture that one of the modes of religious awakenment to which the visible cosmos gives occasion is that tranquillizing and consoling sense of personal relationship and communion with an Infinite Presence of which all men are in some degree susceptible. But although in poets, such as Wordsworth and Coleridge, this feeling of immediate companionship with the Spirit of Nature reaches an intensity which converts it into a form of religious sentiment and belief, in the majority of mankind and in the lower phases of mental evolution it does not become a prominent element in religious experience.

The earliest and most conspicuous form in which the visible aspect of the cosmos calls forth Theistic ideas is through suggesting to the human mind the question, What *causes* these changes which go on before our eyes, and in some cases affect ourselves either injuriously or beneficially? Now this demand for an adequate *Cause* of phenomena is, no doubt, one of the chief sources of the earliest theistic ideas. And when human thought has reached maturity, this same consciousness that the collective phenomena of the cosmos must have a Cause, remains as one of the grounds on which theistic belief is founded, and under the name of the Cosmological Argument has played a great part in the countless treatises in which thinkers have sought to explain and justify the belief in a Self-conscious Power as the adequate Cause of all the changes in the universe. I hope to be able to make clear to you in the course of this Lecture that the question of Causation which the human mind cannot avoid asking may receive two answers which differ in kind from one another; the one of these is superficial and provisional, the other is fundamental and final; and it is, I believe, to the confounding together of these quite different answers that the Cosmological Argument, as commonly formulated, has in the present day lost, and rightly lost, the confidence of a large proportion of thoughtful minds.

The superficial or provisional answer to the mind's question, why certain movements or changes take place in the universe, is the answer given by the untutored savage; but, as we shall afterwards see, it is not given by him alone, but is virtually repeated over and over again by highly-tutored theological and philosophical writers all through the history of thought; and very few of these writers betray any suspicion of its inadequate character. The uncivilized man sees certain movements on the earth or in the heavens, and is impelled by the constitution of his mind to ask himself how they come about; and the answer which first suggests itself is, they must be produced by a being with a will like mine, only more powerful than mine. I am conscious, he says, that I move my limbs, and I see that my limbs move surrounding objects; it is a will, then, like mine that gives the first start to these changes in nature. If the savage is in the very lowest stage of reflection, he will not have learned to think of his mind or self apart from his bodily frame, and in that case he will suppose that the spirit, whose activity he imagines in order to account for the movements of the clouds, the winds, the waves, &c., is indivisibly united with the natural objects in which it appears to energize. But if his reflection has advanced so far that either through the experiences of dreams and the consequent belief in "doubles" and "ghosts," on which Mr. Spencer lays so much stress in his account of the Evolution of Religion, or in some other way, he reaches the conception of the soul or self as separable from the body, he will then distinctly conceive of the changes in nature as the work of spiritual beings capable of moving from place to place and causing like phenomena in different localities. The religious impression which the external world thus makes on man in the lowest stages of culture is thus graphically described by Dr. Martineau:[1]

"In the apprehension, then, of the human observer, using his most human faculty, this visible world is folded round and steeped in a sea of life, whence enters all that rises and whither return the generations that pass away. This is religion in its native simplicity, so far as it flows in from the aspect of the physical scene around, and ere it has quitted its indeterminate condition of poetic feeling, to set into any of the definite forms of thought which philosophers have named. Doubtless it is an ascription to Nature on the part of the observer of a life like his own; in the boundless mirror of the earth and sky, he sees, as the figures of events flit by, the reflected image of himself. But for his living spirit, he could not move, and but for a living spirit, they could not move. Just as when standing face to face with his fellows, he reads the glance of the eye, the sudden start, or the wringing of the hands, and refers them home to their source within the viewless soul of another; so with dimmer and more

[1] *Seat of Authority in Religion*, p. 2.

wondering suspicion, does he discern, behind the looks and movements of nature, a Mind that is the seat of power and the spring of every change. You may laugh at so simple a philosophy; but how else would you have him proceed? Does he not, for this explanation, go straight to the only Cause which he knows? He is familiar with *power* in himself alone; and in himself it is *Will*, and he has no other element than Will to be changed with the power of the world. Is it said to be childish thus to see his own life repeated in the sphere that lies around him, and to conceive of a God in the image of humanity? to project, as it were, his own image upon the space without, and then render to it the homage of his faith?"

The conclusion which Dr. Martineau reaches in this eloquent passage is, I believe, substantially the same as that which I hope to reach presently; but the mental road to Divine Causation by which I feel myself compelled to travel does not appear to me to be entirely identical with that by which I arrive at a belief in the existence and activity of my fellow-men. I cannot but think that there are clear marks of immaturity of thought in the view of the uncultured worshipper that the changes in nature are the immediate volitional manifestations of such a Mind as man knows himself to be. The difficulty is, that every human mind, I believe, feels itself to be, not a self-subsistent, but a *dependent* existence; and therefore, if we refer the phenomena of nature to the will of a Being "in the image of humanity," we have not yet reached a final response to our rational demand for an adequate and ultimate Cause; seeing that a mind in the image of humanity is a dependent mind, and therefore the Theist who formulates the Cosmological Argument in this way appears to me, as I said in a pre-

VI. GOD AS GROUND AND CAUSE.

vious Lecture, to lay himself open to the question which we are told precocious children sometimes ask, "Who made or caused God?"

But do I here really differ from Dr. Martineau? If my reflections have led me altogether astray from that intellectual route from nature to God which a thinker, for whom I feel profound admiration and reverence, has, after so careful and lengthened a survey of the subject, finally laid down, I should be distrustful of the correctness of my own procedure.

I venture to think, however, that when the above passage is read in the light of other portions of Dr. Martineau's writings, it becomes evident that in his view the nature of the "Cause of causes" wholly transcends that of the finite causes or souls whom He calls into existence. Dr. Martineau would assuredly admit that the individual human mind is a dependent existence, and would maintain that God, to whose self-differentiation he refers the existence of human souls, is self-subsistent and eternal. If I understand him aright, then, he believes that the centres of force in nature, which constitute what we call "matter," and also all finite minds, derive their existence from that voluntary act of self-sundering, as it were, by which the Eternal and Absolute One makes over or "plants out," to use Dr. Martineau's expression, certain portions of His own energy and causality, and thus eternally calls into existence, out of the substance of His own being, physical worlds and finite minds, that He may ever possess objects of His thought and love. If this be a correct account of Dr. Martineau's opinion on this ultimate matter, the difference between his judgment and that to which I am led is, after all, little more than a verbal one, and turns upon the question whether it is appropriate to term the Cause and Ground of all nature and of all dependent minds a "Mind" in the same sense in which we apply that word to ourselves. As I remarked in the last Lecture, the truth appears to me to be that man's finite and dependent self-consciousness affords in its positive aspects a valid clue to the essential nature of that Infinite Self-consciousness, or Perfect Personality, who is the Eternal Ground and Cause of nature and humanity. But while we may fairly say that in what is *universal* in our consciousness—in our laws of thought, our ethical ideals, our spiritual affections—we participate in the very essence of God, and so know or feel Him directly, we are not able to penetrate into that inner subjective life of the Eternal out of which all the elements of our own higher life proceed, and in which they find their centre and their unity.[1]

To turn now to the question of the Causation of the Cosmos: it is clear that if we look upon the universe as

---

[1] Compare Prof. Otto Pfleiderer's view of the necessary limitation to man's insight into the inmost nature of God, in his article on "The Philosophy of Religion," in the *Philosophical Review* for January, 1893: "No subject is entirely exhausted by its external effects; it has also an inner side, a being for itself which reflects and unites its manifold effects into a persistent unity. The laws of logic demand that the same thought be applied to God. Here, indeed, we have reached the limits of what is Knowable. We comprehend only that side of God which is turned towards us, His essence in so far as it manifests itself as the active principle of the universe. The inner nature of God, His being-for-himself, the inner reflection of his causality, we can as little know as we can perceive the side of the moon turned away from us."

a boundless concatenation of centres of force or energy, each one of which is acted upon by others, and so, by their reciprocal effects, produce all the changes of natural phenomena, two quite different modes of Causation may be suggested to the mind by this idea of the world. We may think of one stage of the series of successive phenomena, and inquire how it was caused by the preceding stage, and in this view of "cause" one portion of the visible universe becomes the cause of the changes in other portions. And this is the only kind of Causation with which Science has to do. But instead of thinking about the way in which changes in one portion of cosmical phenomena are brought about or caused by previously existing modes of energy, we may think about the Ultimate and Self-existent Cause which brings into existence, and sustains in existence, the entire infinite series of finite causes, originates all the centres of force or atoms, and confers on them their particular properties, and so co-ordinates them that in the aggregate they form an evolving cosmos. Now it is this latter kind of Causation with which philosophy and theology have to do. With regard to the former kind of Causation, which concerns Science, the modes in which bodies act, or appear to act, upon each other, is simply a matter of observation or experience. We do not certainly know whether there is really any direct action of body on body or of atom on atom. We gather from our own consciousness that we act efficiently, directly on our brain and indirectly on our limbs, but there is no necessity of thought which compels us to think, when we see a body in motion, that it must have been put in motion by another body. We see that it appears to be so in all the cases which we have observed, and so we come to believe that it is universally so; and science seeks to discover laws, or uniform modes of reciprocal action, by which it can unify the changes in the universe.

By the constitution of our thinking faculty, we are constrained to refer all phenomenal change to the action of some *power* which, like the human self or will, is not itself merely phenomenal;[1] and physical Science attains its goal in proportion as it is able to explain the series of natural phenomena by the interaction of these atoms or centres of energy of which the human will is the highest form with which we are acquainted. But while the claims of Scientific Causation are satisfied in the degree in which scientists discover for phenomenal changes adequate sources of energy, there still remains a *deeper* question of Causation—the question, namely, What is the Cause of each and all of these countless centres of activity, which by their concurrent action give rise to cosmical phenomena? Judging from the only one of these centres of energy whose inner nature we know, viz. our own spirit or will, we cannot but conclude that these myriad atoms or centres of force depend for their existence and for their essential properties on a deeper Ultimate Cause. Each individual mind is compelled, by its very nature, to believe that it is neither self-existent nor self-originated, and therefore it must depend upon some principle or being whose nature it is to be self-subsistent or eternal.

[1] *Vide* Dr. Martineau's masterly paper on "Is there any Axiom of Causality?" in his *Essays, Reviews and Addresses*, Vol. III.

Now, if we carefully distinguish between these two meanings of the word "Cause," we shall, I think, come to see how it is that the Cosmological Argument has of late lost much of its cogency as one of the proofs of the reality of God. As I shall afterwards point out, the argument is still valid if it rests on the second, or philosophical, meaning of the word Cause; but in the way in which the argument is generally presented it confuses the two uses of this word. This confusion of thought I will now endeavour to illustrate.

It is reported of the great physicist Faraday that he kept his rather peculiar religious tenets and his great scientific knowledge quite apart, as if the two sets of ideas were localized in different compartments of his mind or brain. If this be the inevitable dilemma into which every man who is at once scientific and religious must find himself at length driven, it must be admitted that such a relation between science and religion is not only a very uncomfortable one, but it is also a condition of unstable equilibrium which must, in the long run, determine itself in favour of the constantly accumulating and mutually corroborating facts of science. Let us, accordingly, inquire whether it is not quite possible to look at the cosmos, both scientifically and religiously, without feeling this painful jar of incongruity. In other words, can we or can we not regard the ultimate Ground and Cause of the universe as that very Being with whom the religious mind seems, at all events, to experience a real union and relationship?

The problem before us will become clearer if we attend carefully to the word "Cause," and ask ourselves whether it is always used in the self-same sense. Take, for instance, the exclamation of the Hebrew prophet: "Lift up your eyes on high, and see who hath created these things that bringeth out their host by number." This is precisely the question in regard to the universe which the religious mind puts to itself, and the answer which it gives to itself is: "It is Yahve, or God, the Eternal One whom my soul adores, and to whom I feel my inner consciousness most intimately related." God, then, from the religious point of view, is the *cause* of these celestial galaxies. But now suppose that La Place and Kant (when the latter happened to be in a scientific rather than a religious mood) looked up at the spectacle of the star-lit heavens; they would probably also ask themselves a question, which verbally would seem to come to the same thing as the utterance of the prophet; they would say to themselves, What is the *cause* of these countless orbs in the sky? But now, instead of the mind of the physicist or the philosopher thinking of Yahve as the Cause, their scientific imagination runs back to an immense cosmic mist; they seem to see the contraction of this vast nebula, outer rings gradually detaching themselves from the rest of the mass, then breaking up and forming planets; satellites arising on the same principle, and the glowing sun remaining at the centre.

Now the question before us is, Do the religious answer and the scientific answer to this inquiry about causation really clash? The theologians who first formulated the Cosmological Argument for the being of God would probably have replied, "No! these answers do not necessarily clash," for Kant and La Place want a *Cause* for this cloud of diffused matter out of which the planets and the sun were gradually formed; and however far they go back in their physical explanations, they will require a Cause for that condition of things which their scientific imagination postulates as the earlier state of the universe out of which the present state has by slow stages been evolved. Sooner or later they must, it is alleged, come to a *First Cause*, and that Cause will be identical with the Yahve in whom the Hebrew prophet found an immediate and satisfactory answer to his soul's demand for Causation. Very few competent thinkers in the present day would accept this as a genuine reconciliation of the scientific and the theological accounts of the causation of natural phenomena. The La Place or Kant of to-day, having reached his cosmic mist, does not feel that he is thereby a step nearer to that primeval epoch when Yahve uttered His creative word, and the primitive cosmos, from which all scientific explanations are bound to take their start, suddenly came into existence. If the theologian's only chance of finding Yahve's causation is at an assumed *beginning* of cosmical phenomena, almost all competent scientists would now, I believe, agree in assuring us that such a search after the God whom Theism desiderates is indeed a forlorn hope.

It is a noteworthy fact, however, that some theologians of eminence even in the present day continue, apparently through the force of habit, to set forth the Cosmological Argument in this utterly inconclusive form. Prof. Flint, for instance, in his valuable treatise on "Theism," says:

"We may believe either in a self-existent God or in a self-existent world, and must believe in one or the other; we cannot believe in an infinite regress of causes. The alternatives of a self-existent cause and an infinite regress of causes are not, as some would represent, equally credible alternatives. The one is an indubitable truth, the other is a manifest absurdity. The one all men believe, the other no man believes."[1]

For want of clearly seeing that the word "Cause" has two quite distinct meanings—a scientific meaning, and a philosophical or theological one—Prof. Flint has, in this passage, expressed his argument so confusedly that, instead of being a conclusive answer to the non-theistic scientist, it is really, if taken literally, a positive confirmation of the sceptic's position. For the "infinite regress of causes," which the scientist in question regards as the fact which renders the hypothesis of a God unnecessary, refers, of course, to scientific causes; that is to say, to the modes of force which succeed one another in the universe, and which, from the scientific point of view, are said to *cause* one another. The shrinking nebula, for instance, causes the intense heat of the central mass; the heat of the sun causes the evaporation of the ocean; evaporation causes the formation of rain-drops; rain-drops cause the invigoration and growth of vegetation, &c. &c. Now the scientist whom Prof. Flint is aiming to refute, maintains that this regress of causes is an infinite regress, and that therefore the assumption of God as a Cause is quite uncalled for, seeing that Science can get on as well or better without Him. As I understand the matter, the proper answer to such a

[1] P. 120.

scientist would be: I quite admit the probable truth of what you say about this infinite regress of causes, as you term them, but what I maintain is, that the existence of this infinite regress of causes, in your scientific sense, is precisely the fact which demands for its adequate explanation the belief in God as the ultimate Ground or Cause, in the philosophical or theological sense. Prof. Flint declares that what the scientist means by an infinite regress of causes is a "manifest absurdity;" to my mind it appears to be not only no absurdity, but to be in all probability the actual state of the case. I find nothing inconceivable or improbable in such an infinite regress; indeed, the difficulty with me would be to conceive of a regress of scientific causes which is not infinite.

I contend, accordingly, that the theistic Cosmologists who argue in favour of the reality and causality of God after this fashion have got entirely upon a wrong track; they have been seeking for God in a direction where the religious mind never expects effectually to find Him. The Cause which the man who is in a religious mood is thinking about, and yearning to be in perfect sympathy with, is a *present Cause;* and unless the Cause in nature is the same present Cause as the Cause who is now manifesting Himself in the soul's ideals, and who is felt in the very heart of hearts, Science and Religion are not harmonized, and man *quâ* religious and *quâ* scientific is still divided against himself.

While, then, Prof. Flint speaks of the belief in a self-existent Cause on the one hand, and in an infinite regress of scientific causes on the other hand, as *alternative* beliefs which cannot be simultaneously held, and one of which is an absurdity, I maintain, on the contrary, that there is no alternative in the case, that both beliefs are rational, and, so far from being incompatible with each other, are so related that in an intelligible universe each implies and logically necessitates the validity of the other. If there is an Eternal Being whose essence includes those universal principles of reason, righteousness and love, which disclose themselves in the higher forms of our own self-consciousness, then it is no more than reasonable to expect that this Absolute Being should *eternally* manifest His inner nature in an infinite cosmos of inter-related physical and psychical agencies, all of which continually depend for their existence and their intelligible unity on that self-determining Causality, whereby He in part differentiates His own substance into a world of dependent things and finite souls.

The Cause, then, with whom religious sentiment and theological thought concern themselves, is by no means one of, or in a line with, that series of causes in which the scientific mind is especially interested. The Theist's God is the Cause of all causes, the Soul of all souls. He is literally what the words of the poet declare Him to be, the

"Centre and Soul of every sphere,
Yet to each loving heart how near!"

Yes; of every atom, of every animal soul, of every human spirit, He is the central principle; He is the perpetual Ground and Cause of their being, and apart from Him they could not for a moment exist. The final explanation of their existence and of their mutual relations is in that ever-present Eternal Life out of which their finite and dependent life emerges, and by vital connection with which alone it continues to be.

There is only one possible way, then, by which a final reconciliation between scientific and religious thought can come about, and that way is by looking for the Cause and Ground of the cosmos, not at some supposed beginning of things (for there is no reason to think that there ever was any such beginning, or that the Eternal was ever without his self-manifestation in nature and in rational finite spirits), but by looking for Him in the deepest core of the present cosmical reality. Here and now, if anywhere and any when, we shall effectually find Him of whom we are in search. He is at the deepest heart of the self-conscious spirit, He is the living soul of every particle of matter, and by reason of His immanent presence it is that the material world contains "the promise and the potency" of all the higher forms of life. But some of my hearers may be inclined to ask me: How, then, about what we call Scientific Causation? Are not La Place and Kant, Darwin and Spencer, quite justified in tracing the process of Evolution backwards as far as science and the scientific imagination is able to travel? Undoubtedly they are. Nay more: it follows, from the view I have above stated of the *eternal* relation of God to the universe, that the scientists are justified in assuming that, if they possessed unlimited insight into the relations of phenomena, they would see that this backward journey is an endless one, and that the imagination, when it reaches the extreme confines of our present physical knowledge, is just as far off as ever from the point where scientific explanations become intrinsically impossible and theological explanations have to be called in to take their place. Theistic explanation and causation, and Scientific explanation and causation, belong to different planes of thought; there is no time-relation between them, and if the immediate Causality of God is not necessary to account for the simplest present fact of physics or psychology, it may equally be displeased with an explanation of the natural phenomena which occurred in those inconceivably distant epochs into which our present geological and astronomical insight enables us to peer.

Two separate questions, then, must be answered before we are in a position to fairly estimate the theistic value of this Cosmological Argument—of the assertion, that is, which the Theist makes, that cosmical facts and events require, as the only possible rational explanation of their existence, the Causality of an Eternal and Absolute Being with whom the human spirit may feel a personal relationship. One of these questions is: What is the nature of those *causes* the infinite series of which is supposed by non-theistic scientists to supersede the necessity of believing in the reality of any other Cause? and the other question is: What is the relation, if any, of these scientific causes to that Ultimate Cause, or God, on whom theistic belief reposes? I believe the answers to these two questions will make it clear that when scientists and theologians speak of Causation they are thinking of two opposite sides of cosmical reality, and that so far is the Scientific idea of causation from clashing with or from superseding the Theistic idea of causation that this latter

VI. GOD AS GROUND AND CAUSE.

is simply the other aspect of the scientific idea, and must be thought along with it in any final rational explanation or conception of the cosmos as a whole.

Let me now, accordingly, invite your patient attention while I attempt to answer the first of the above questions, that is, to analyze what is meant by Scientific Causation. I will not in the present Lecture criticize that view of Scientific Causation which is put forth by those who advocate Absolute Idealism, or Hegelianism, and maintain that all that we commonly call real things and forces in nature are but modes of thinking in the human or Divine self-consciousness; that stones and trees, for instance, and even animals, in so far as they have merely feeling and not thought, have no other reality than that which is conferred on them by their being groups of thought-relations in some self-consciousness. In this view the only beings that have any reality for themselves are those rational self-conscious minds in the case of whom the Eternal Self-Consciousness reproduces itself under certain organic conditions. Now, for my own part, I cannot doubt that the feeling of the lower animals is quite real for the animals themselves, and not merely for God or man who thinks it; and by analogy I am led to believe that the physical objects or forces which environ and limit my activity have also a certain degree of reality independent of the fact that they are objects of God's thought. I cannot but conclude that what we call force or energy in nature is *something more* than a form of God's *thinking;* it has a certain reality conferred upon it by what we can only conceive of as God's *willing*. In other words, I believe that dynamic energy cannot

P 2

be resolved into simply a mode of thinking. But this Absolute Idealism has attracted of late so much attention in academic circles, partly through the genius of the late T. H. Green, and partly by three or four series of Gifford Lectures which have been delivered by members of the same school, that I have thought it better to devote a future Lecture to discussing the worth of Hegelianism as a philosophy of religion.

Our first question, then, is, What do scientific men mean when they speak of Cause? As a logical consequence of Locke's view that Sensation is the chief source of Knowledge, Hume maintained, and the two Mills and Prof. Bain endorsed the opinion, that Cause means only uniformity of relation among phenomena. When, for instance, I say that the shriek of the steam-engine frightened the horse, and that the horse took to flight and knocked a man down, I, on this theory, only mean that the sensations and ideas representing the noise of the engine is, under given circumstances, uniformly followed by the sensations and ideas representing the running horse, and these sensations in their turn by the mental image of the falling man. Now Kant accepted from Hume this notion of Causation as merely a relation between presentations in our minds, only he maintained that the order in which these presentations succeed each other is a *necessary*, and not merely an *empirical* order, that the human mind by its very constitution must apply to its sensations this category of Causation. But while, in the more original portions of his great Critique, he speaks of Causation as merely a way of conceiving the order of sensations to which the human mind is tied down by its own nature, in other passages he uses the term "Causation" in a quite different and more usual signification; for, when charged with teaching an idealism resembling Berkeley's, he maintained that the sensations which form the matter of thought, not being originated by the thinking mind itself, must be *caused* by something other than the thinking mind, and that this "something other" must be the things-in-themselves which have a reality independent of the thinking mind. Out of Kant's first account of Causation has sprung all the future systems of German Idealism; out of his second account of Causation has sprung the realism of Herbart, and that ideal-realism of Hermann Lotze, which is now so influential in Germany, and bids fair to be the dominant philosophy in this country and America in the course of a decade or two.

To the sensationalist's notion that Causation only means a uniform time-relation among phenomena, and does not imply the action of any efficient force in things, I believe Dr. Martineau's admirable account of the idea of Cause in his "Study of Religion," and his profound paper, read before the late Metaphysical Society, on the question, "Is there any Axiom of Causality?"[1] has given the *coup-de-grace*. Dr. Martineau virtually adopts Kant's second view of Causation, and conclusively shows that by the word "cause" we always understand something more than a relation among phenomena, or the impressions of our senses, and imply that the changes in nature are caused by some really efficient power or force which our outward senses cannot discern, but which

[1] See note on p. 202, *supra*.

we always mentally supply after the analogy of our own consciousness of efficient volitional Causation. To use my previous illustration, when we say that the horse knocked down the man, we mean that there was a certain power or force in the horse invisible to the observer's senses, but none the less real, which had its seat in the horse, and which, acting upon the body of the man, caused it to fall. And in like manner, the mind cannot help thinking that when bodies collide there is an active energy operating there which is none the less real because it is not a visible phenomenon, but is conceived by the human mind after the analogy of its own effort in producing muscular movement. Not only does the human mind instinctively import this idea of efficient power into the object which it calls the Cause, but science cannot even give an intelligible account of the changes in the universe without using such words as Force, Energy, Tendency, Pressure, &c., all which words answer to no sensuous experience, and can only be conceived after the model of the mind's own causal activity. All the force, then, which Science takes cognizance of in nature is implicitly assumed to be of the nature of Will-force.

This, indeed, is admitted by Mr. Herbert Spencer, for he says that when we seek to analyze our conception of the Power of which nature is the expression, we find that we necessarily conceive the Power to which we ascribe changes of form and movement after the fashion of our own mental activity. Force, he says, by which we ourselves produce changes, and which serves to symbolize the causes of movement in general, is the final disclosure of analysis. He declines, however, to allow that the force which we encounter when we strive against physical obstacles can be precisely the same in kind as the energy we ourselves exert in willing. "If I lift a chair," he says, "the force which I am obliged to postulate in the chair cannot be of the same kind as the force which I exert, because, if so, the chair would have to possess nerves and muscles such as the human being possesses." This difficulty of his vanishes, I think, if we consider that all that our mind appears to do in such volition is to produce a change of position in some group of molecules of the brain; and the feeling which we have of graduated effort when we are striving to overcome resistance (and which is entirely distinct from the later feeling which accompanies the muscular contraction), is presumptive evidence that the psychical monad or self, which is the seat of our individuality, acts upon the monads of the brain, and graduates its effort in proportion to the resistance to be overcome.

As all Force, then, is presumably of the same nature as Will-force, it appears to be by far the most probable theory that not only are the souls of animals of the same kind as our own, but that all the elements of the organic, and even of the inorganic, world are essentially of the same nature. And further, recent science affords good reason for believing that it is by the action of these elementary atoms, monads, or centres of force (whether they be called physical or psychical), that all the changes in the cosmos are produced. Even the force of attraction called Gravitation is probably no exception to this principle. On the surface it looks as if in the case of this mode of force the rule which elsewhere obtains in nature, viz. that the change of position in an atom or monad is caused by a previous change in some contiguous monad, is broken, and instead of it we seem to have a purely exceptional action from a distance without the operation of intermediate agencies, a mode of action which cannot possibly have a purely scientific explanation. But certainly this was not the view of Sir Isaac Newton himself, for in writing to Dr. Bentley, in reply to the charge that the theory of gravitation implies that a thing can act where it is not, he says:

"That one body should act on another at a distance through a vacuum without the mediation of anything else by and through which their action and force may be conveyed from one to another, is to me so great an absurdity that I believe that no man who in philosophical matters has a competent faculty of thinking can fall into it. Gravity must be caused by an agent acting constantly according to certain laws."

Our only experience of personal causation is in the action of the psychical monad, the soul, on its physical organism through the mediation of the brain, and on its own ideas through the same medium; and in like manner, if we move other bodies, it is only by contiguity that the motion is effected. Hence all changes that we know of appear to be caused by a certain pushing or propelling; and recent Science quite bears out Newton's view that neither molecular nor molar matter is capable of exercising efficient causation at a distance. Though Newton had discovered a most important descriptive law, he was well aware that he had not yet reached the real dynamical law; and I need hardly remind you that it has from Newton's time up to the present been one of the chief matters of interest to the scientific mind to discover what are the intermediate agents the action of which suffices to give a dynamical *rationale* to this grand phenomenal law. In all probability, then, the changes in the cosmos are all brought about, not by what we may call the direct agency of the Supreme Being, but by the interaction of those elementary monads (physical and psychical) whose modes of energy it is the business of the scientist to investigate.

At a superficial view, then, it certainly does seem as if Science were more and more enabling the human mind to dispense with the necessity of God's causal action in nature, and were proving itself competent to find the causes of all events in existing modes of force. Neither science, nor indeed ordinary common-sense, looks immediately to God's action for the scientific explanation of any natural event. All it asks for is the action of adequate force, adequality directed to effect the phenomenon. It is in the supposed reciprocal causality of molecular forces, or molar groups of force, that science and common-sense seek the explanation of physical facts. If we see a flying kite in the air, we think of the force of the wind, of the attraction of gravitation, of the cohesion in the string, of the muscular contraction in the hand or arm of the boy who is holding it, and also of the action of the mind or will of the boy on his muscles; and if we wish to account further for the action of any one of these agents, we do not call in a *deus ex machinâ*, a sudden supernatural intervention, to explain it, but simply search more carefully into the action of the molecular forces which have concurred in effecting the change in question. Hence, the tendency of modern science is to regard the cosmos as the manifested effects of the constant activity of innumerable dynamic agencies which reciprocally affect each other's movements, and thus change the visible forms of bodies.

And if it is asked what appears to be the inner nature of these centres of force, or physical and psychical atoms or monads, we have seen, that so far as we can penetrate by analogy into their inner condition, the probability increases, that they are, as Leibnitz and Kant and, more recently, Lotze have said, perhaps, after all, not very unlike our own spiritual nature; that is, it seems likely that each one of the ultimate energies of nature is a psychical principle, essentially of the same kind as the human self or will, though, in the lower kingdoms of nature, these monads act only blindly and automatically, each in accordance with its special dynamic character, when stimulated to action by neighbouring monads.

As I argued in the last Lecture, I see no reason for accepting, but very cogent reasons for rejecting, the doctrine of the identity of body and mind as being only two parallel aspects of a primitive and otherwise unknowable reality; but I believe there are excellent scientific and philosophical grounds for holding that the constituents of the cosmos, from the ultimate element of the ether-vortex up to the flower in the meadow, the bird floating in the air, and man building churches and worshipping the Supreme, are one and all differentiations of that eternal substance, God, in whom every particle of the whole has its ground, and from whom it derives its special character. Every atom of nature is instinct with energy and life; it is, as it were, a portion and visible manifestation of the Eternal Life. In the inorganic world the Self-existent Ground of all reality imparts to the monads only the capacity for physical force, the lowest aspect of His own essence; in the organic world sentiency is by degrees manifested, but still the atom or the organism can, upon stimulation, act only in one definite way; but in the inner life of man a far higher phase of the nature of the Eternal is imparted, and we reach a being who, by virtue of the conscious immanence within him of eternal reason, can rise above his own individuality and finitude, and in his moral and spiritual experience consciously participate in some essential features of the eternal life of the Absolute Being. In man, too, Moral Freedom emerges; and Dr. Martineau has thus truly expressed the essential distinction between man and the lower products of God's causality: "Man is included in what God has caused, though excluded from what He *is causing;* so that, while author of all our possibilities, He is not responsible for our actualities." I do not understand that Dr. Martineau's meaning is that God "plants out" human spirits, and then leaves them to exist simply of themselves. At every moment of their lives and of their ethical decisions, God is the immediate Cause and Ground of their being, and were He to cease to energize they would cease to exist; still, His creative causation is clearly distinguishable from that free moral self-determinations, in virtue of which a man becomes, in a true sense, responsible for the formation of his character.

We are now, I hope, in a position to give an intelligible answer to the first question, viz. What is meant by

VI. GOD AS GROUND AND CAUSE.

Scientific Causation? From the point of view of Science the universe presents itself as an infinite series of changes of form and movement, preserving such an amount of uniformity in their modes of succeeding each other that the human mind is able to classify them, and, from the present condition of the cosmos, to infer, with ever-increasing clearness, the earlier conditions, and to foresee, in some measure, the conditions which will be realized in the time to come. Now when we look at this infinite series of changes in the light of our knowledge of ourselves as the seat of volitional energy, the most probable *rationale* of the origin of cosmical phenomena is that they proceed from the activity of innumerable centres of energizing, which science terms atoms, and philosophy terms physical and psychical monads. The human will is the highest that we know of among these finite sources of energy, and from our own self-consciousness we have some clue as to the inner or subjective side of these monads into which the Infinite and Eternal Substance is differentiated. As the putting forth of energy in our case is accompanied by a high degree of self-consciousness, analogy makes it likely that all the centres of energy in the universe have some measure of subjectivity. In the case of the inorganic world this subjectivity must, if it exists, be inconceivably faint; but as vegetable and animal organisms arise, the subjective states of their dominant monads become more and more vivid. Whether animal and human souls are, in the order of the creative activity of the Eternal, simply continuations and further developments of the inner or subjective sides of the material monads, as some high authorities, such as the late Prof.

VI. GOD AS GROUND AND CAUSE. 221

Teichmüller,[1] maintain, or whether, on the other hand, they are, as such profound philosophers as Hermann Lotze and Dr. Martineau think, differentiations *de novo* of the Eternal Substance, is a question to which I do not feel able at present to give a decisive answer. But in either case these souls are, like all the energies of nature, essentially of one kind; all monads alike, being products of the self-differentiating causality of God, are modes of God's Eternal Substance and Eternal Life, to which He imparts a certain degree of delegated individuality; and, as is the case with all monads, the activity of souls is accompanied or followed by changes in the relations of the other monads with which they are immediately associated.

This differentiation of His Eternal Substance by which God calls into existence a physical and psychical cosmos, is, as we have seen, in all probability a process of Divine Causality co-eternal with the Absolute Himself. Hence we and all things in existence have a two-fold relation; the one mode of relation we may call scientific, the other religious or theological. In the former respect we are related to our past, to the evolutionary process through which we have become what we are; in the latter respect we are immediately dependent every moment of our being on the causality or will of the Eternal. As Lotze most truly says:

"We see good reason for the assumption that in the Divine activity there is unity and coherence; and for this reason the creative act of the next instant is a consequence of the creative

[1] *Vide* Gustav Teichmüller's treatise, *Ueber die Unsterblichkeit der Seele*, 2nd ed. p. 147.

act of the preceding instant; and we see good reason for denying that the world of one instant *perpetuates itself by its own agency and by its general laws into the next instant.*"

This view of Lotze's is only the philosophical form of the same thought and sentiment which prompts the poet to say that the world—

> "An every fresh and new creation,
> A divine improvisation,
> From the heart of God proceeds."

You will observe, then, that Scientific Causation and Philosophical or Theological Causation, though indivisibly connected, are two quite different aspects of reality; and the error in the ordinary presentation of the Cosmological Argument (which has made that argument in recent years far more a source of scepticism than of religious belief) arises from confounding together these two distinct modes in which God's activity is related to the world. The grand function of Science is to unravel, if possible, the principles or uniform modes of procedure which obtain in these successive transformations of form and inner subjectivity which the universe presents, and as far as may be to intelligibly connect the facts at one stage of evolution with the facts at an earlier or later stage. In this process of exposition it is seen that the dynamic condition at any one instant is intimately and rationally connected with the dynamic condition of the preceding instant, and this in turn with a still earlier state of things; so that the scientist cannot help coming along his line of thought to precisely the same conclusion that the theologian reaches by another route—to the conclusion, namely, that there is no beginning to this series of modes of physical and psychical life which constitutes the universe; or, theologically expressed, that this Cosmos, with its wealth of loveliness and of physical and psychical life, is the eternally-begotten Word and Son of God, through whom we may well suppose the thought and love of the Eternal find at once expression and satisfaction. When, then, the Cosmological Argument takes the form of asserting that the universe, with all its powers and properties, must at some remote point of past time been called into existence by what is called a *First Cause*, it naturally fails to carry conviction to any scientist of the present day. Nay, it not only does not convince him, but it is apt to produce in his mind a distrust of theology and all its pretensions; for he feels that it is an impertinence to arbitrarily stop short his scientific researches with a dogmatic "thus far shalt thou go and no farther," and he is sure that if the life of Theism is at all essentially connected with the discovery of this beginning of cosmical phenomena, then Theism may be regarded as virtually defunct.

But when we turn from the scientific to the theological or Divine aspect of the world, the case is wholly altered, and the Cosmological Argument, when it takes the shape of asserting that a unitary Ground and Cause is needed to account for and render intelligible this entire infinite series of dynamic activities and phenomenal changes which constitute the universe, rests still, I believe, upon a solid foundation of logical necessity. For, in the first place, I will appeal to each man's consciousness whether he does not feel, as Mr. Herbert Spencer admits he does, that his individuality is in no way self-existent, and that he is compelled by the necessity of thought to think of himself as dependent on that which is absolutely real. And while our own self-consciousness reveals to us that we carry in our own finite nature no adequate cause of our personal existence, so it is also in regard to every one of those centres of energy which Science regards as the causes of phenomena. Not one of these causal agencies with which Science deals bears the slightest mark of self-subsistence; all demand as the explanation of their existence that they should arise out of a deeper causality, out of that Absolute who carries within Himself the ground and reason of His own eternal reality.

And while our self-consciousness thus immediately testifies to the dependent nature of ourselves and of all the series of dynamic causes whose modes of action Science investigates, this necessary reference of all finite things and finite minds to their source in the unifying Absolute is corroborated by the circumstance that all these multiform causes or modes of energy conspire, without any consciousness or purpose of their own, in producing and evolving an intelligible universe. The very possibility of Science depends upon and testifies to the logical coherence and consistency which links into a rational unity the infinite multiplicity and variety of cosmical phenomena. And not only so, but as I pointed out in a previous Lecture, Hermann Lotze has, I believe, conclusively shown that no action of body on body, of monad on monad, is unintelligible unless we assume some deeper unity to which all the monads, or centres of energy (be they physical or psychical), are all in common related, and through the intermediation of

VI. GOD AS GROUND AND CAUSE. 225

which a change in the inner state of one monad produces a change in the internal activity of contiguous monads. Were it not for the fact that each atom and each human mind are on one side of their being in immediate and vital connection with that Absolute and Eternal One to whose beneficent self-differentiation they owe their existence, no action between one body and another, or between the soul and nature, can be made in the slightest degree conceivable. If we say one thing or atom acts on another by projecting from itself some influence which passes over to and affects the other, we are employing words to which no clear signification can be attached. "Can the quality of one body detach itself from this body, become the quality of no body, then transfer itself from this nothing, and become the quality of the second body?" It becomes evident, then, argues Lotze, that there can be no complete independence in the case of the plurality of things in the world; but all elements between which a mutual relation of cause and effect can appear, must be to a certain extent parts of one only true and absolute Being.

And while the ordinary phenomena of cause and effect in the physical world thus show that the causes of which science treats are not the ultimate reality, and that, in order that they may interact, all monads and minds must have their common ground and cause in God or the Absolute, this conclusion is confirmed when we think of the interchange of ideas between mind and mind. This interchange only becomes possible through the fact that the universal laws of thought which belong to the essence of God are immanent in all human souls.

Q

And in the case of our own self-consciousness, it is just because we are not merely individual minds, but are through the immanent Divine reason indivisibly united with the eternal life of God, that we are able to pass from the merely personal to the universal point of view, to impartially compare ourselves with others and pass judgment upon our own worth. And in like manner, were it not for the immanence of the Infinite Love in our spirits, the higher forms of human affection, with their marvellous power of annihilating all self-seeking, would be unknown. All these considerations powerfully endorse the intuitive judgment which we cannot help forming, that our finite life and the life of all finite energies and finite minds is immediately dependent on, and indivisibly connected with, that Universal Self-existent Life which in the case of self-conscious man reveals itself in the ideals of truth, beauty and goodness which immediately assert in the soul their universal character and their absolute worth. Through this immediate connection between our individual souls and the Eternal Life of the Universe which is immanent in our self-consciousness, it comes about that all influences which appeal to that side of our nature where our finite being blends with the Universal Being, awaken in us religious sentiments and religious belief. As I remarked in the previous Lecture, God, to be thoroughly believed in, must be *felt;* and hence it is that the most vivid realization and proof of God's being and character is not derived immediately from arguments about God, but rather from contact with some noble nature which kindles the latent divinity in ourselves, from the biography of some pure and heroic soul, from some grand poem or work of art, from the soul-stirring strains of divine music, or from the beautiful and sublime aspects of nature. All these high influences carry us out of the narrow and vulgar region of our own individual self, with its petty aims and petty passions and ambitions, and admit us in some measure into that life of the Absolute, that Eternal Life in which alone the human spirit finds unalloyed joy and satisfaction.

I am here, however, anticipating the subject of the next Lecture, in which I shall consider the Absolute, not as the Cause and Ground of all cosmical existence, but as the Source of our Ideals. It is not possible, however, to wholly dissociate these two modes of insight into the relation which man's individual life bears to the Absolute Ground of all existences. Were we conscious of no pressure of the Ideal in our inner life, we might, it is true, through our immediate feeling of dependence on a deeper reality, and the rational consideration that we and all other finite beings could not exist and be interrelated to each other without the causality and intermediation of the Absolute, reach by logical necessity a belief in a self-existent unifying ground and cause of the world. As a matter of fact, however, we not only feel our dependence for existence on an Absolute Reality, but we are also aware in our self-consciousness of the presence and unconditional authority of rational, ethical and æsthetic ideals which we cannot but associate with the essential character of that Absolute Being out of whose substance and causality our existence arises. In the present Lecture, however, I wish to exclusively emphasize the necessity of thought which constrains us to refer all the scientific causes or dynamic agencies which constitute the universe to the Absolute Causality of the Eternal. We have seen that all these causal agents in the cosmos with which science has to deal appear to be of one Substance, and of that Substance we have experience in our own inner life. These differentiations of the Absolute Spirit exist in all degrees of selfhood and partial independence, from the condition of blind inorganic centres of forces, which may or may not possess a dawning subjectivity, up to the human self-consciousness to whom the Eternal so richly imparts His own essential and universal nature that the soul can rise above itself, and to some extent see the world of men and things, not merely from an individual, but from a universal point of view. The question, then, will arise, Is this Absolute Being, of whose substance our personal wills and all the centres of energy in nature are originally portions, to be Himself regarded as a Will and Personality? I have already touched on this important matter, and will recur to it in the final Lecture. But in relation to our present subject, I may note that we are surely justified in concluding that the Eternal self-differentiating Causality of the Absolute, to which finite wills and all things owe their existence, is essentially of the same nature as our own volitional self-determinations, although from the finite and dependent nature of our personality we cannot form an exhaustive conception of the transcendent causality of God. That, however, we are approximating to complete insight when we think of the Absolute Being after the fashion of our own self-consciousness and will, is confirmed by the reflection that the relation of His Eternal Unity to the infinite variety and endless succession of the dependent existences and causes which make up the universe appears to be closely analogous to the relation which our personal self-identity and unity bears to the indefinite plurality of our present and past states of consciousness. Accordingly, this idea of God as the necessary abiding Cause and Ground of the endless evolution of cosmical changes, anticipates and renders intelligible that sense of personal relationship between the finite spirit and the Eternal Spirit which constitutes the essence of vital religion.

If, then, the infinitely varied phenomena of the Cosmos all have their ground and unifying principle in that Absolute Being, of whom we are immediately conscious as the underlying reality and cause of our own existence, we should expect that He who is the source of our intelligence and of our ideals should afford evidence of His rationality and of His realization of rational ends in the present features and in the historical evolution of the universe. That nature exhibits clear evidence of such rational purpose in its Ultimate Cause is the contention well-known under the name of the Teleological Argument, which has been thus regarded as confirmatory of the Cosmological Argument, the value of which we have just been discussing. Upon the publication of Mr. Darwin's theory of Natural Selection, it was popularly supposed that his discoveries and speculations with regard to the gradual passage of one species of animal out of another, and of the acquisition by each species of the forms and attributes most appropriate to its surroundings, had for ever invalidated the argument from Design, and rendered quite needless all appeals to constructive reason for the explanation of biological evolution. Accordingly, a sort of panic arose among the theologians; and the thinkers who favoured a non-theistic view of the inner nature of the cosmos were jubilant. In a short time, however, it became abundantly evident that the flutter had been in the main occasioned by a false alarm. Some of the leading scientific teachers of the day, among whom Prof. Huxley was prominent, clearly saw and pointed out that whatever havoc the theory of the Survival of the Fittest might make among the special instances of contrivance adduced by Paley and the Bridgwater Treatises, it still remains true that, if account is taken of the universe as a whole, and the question is asked whether the whole process of biological development, including the fortunate tendency in the offspring to variation, is intelligible apart from the assumption of a rational principle at the heart of the process, the position of the Teleologist remains substantially unaffected by all that Darwin and the Darwinians have established.

The limits of this course of Lectures do not admit of my entering in detail into this controversy; and indeed this is the less necessary for two reasons,—firstly, because Dr. Martineau has, in "A Study of Religion,"[1] defended at great length the validity of the Design Argument, and has brought to the subject such logical clearness of statement, and such a wealth of admirably selected illustrations, that anything I could say would be very far inferior both in form and in conclusiveness; and secondly, because the perfect consistency of a teleological view of the universe with all that Darwin and his followers have

[1] Vol. I.

discovered is freely admitted by some of the ablest and warmest sympathizers with the theory of Organic Evolution. Prof. Romanes, for instance, writes:

"I need scarcely wait to show why it appears to me that the world-object furnishes overwhelming proof of psychism; for this truth has been ably presented by many other writers. There is first the antecedent improbability that the human mind should be the highest manifestation of subjectivity in this universe of infinite objectivity. There is next the fact that throughout this universe of infinite objectivity—so far at least as human observation can extend—there is unquestionable evidence of some one integrating principle, whereby all its many complex parts are correlated with one another in such wise that the result is universal order. And if we take any part of the whole system—such as that of organic nature on this planet—to examine in more detail, we find that it appears instinct with contrivance. So to speak, wherever we tap organic nature, it seems to flow with purpose.... Assuredly no human mind could either have devised or maintained the working of even a fragment of Nature; and therefore it seems but reasonable to conclude that the integrating principle of the whole—the Spirit, as it were, of the Universe—must be something which, while, as I have said, holding nearest kinship with our highest conception of disposing power, must yet be immeasurably superior to the psychism of man."[1]

In like manner Prof. Huxley declares that the evolution of the cosmos, so far as science has investigated it, appears to be best described as "a materialized logical process." The following passage, taken from an admirable chapter of Prof. Schurman's Winkley Lectures on "Belief in God," justly calls attention to Mr. Darwin's own inability to account for common facts of organic

---

[1] *Contemporary Review*, July, 1886, p. 54.

change on the assumption of blind or undesigned variation:

"Must we not," asks Dr. Schurman, "think of the primitive germs of life as endowed with a constitution capable of variation only along certain pre-ordained lines of development? Such, at any rate, is the view of Professor Huxley. And from Darwin's own standpoint it seems to me that the conception of design in the organic world should not have been thrown over until he had found an answer to that conundrum which, on Nov. 25th, 1859, he somewhat profanely propounded to Mr. Huxley. 'You have,' he says, 'most cleverly hit on one point which has greatly troubled me; if, as I must think, external conditions produce little *direct* effect, what the devil determines each particular variation? What makes a tuft of feathers come on a cock's head, or moss on a moss-rose?' Until that query is answered, the proof that the eye has 'come' by way of natural selection instead of having been 'specially made' is no proof that its coming was unintentional. And when the query is answered, it will be seen that though we have in the eye a result which is brought about only in accordance with the inexorable laws of causation, it is a result that cannot be exhaustively explained on a merely mechanical or blind necessitarian theory of the universe."[1]

The degree of conviction which the Design Argument brings to any particular thinker will be largely influenced by the general philosophy of the universe which that thinker accepts. If on other grounds, such as those which I have endeavoured to set forth in the former part of this Lecture, the belief that both matter and mind are finite modes of an absolute spiritual life, is already attained, the thinker will find the presence of Design in nature so much in accordance with what his theory leads him to expect, that the Teleological Argument will not only be itself received as valid, but will

[1] P. 204.

VI. GOD AS GROUND AND CAUSE. 233

come as a confirmation to the previous belief. But when the elements of matter are looked upon, as they seem to have been by Darwin, as something essentially unlike to spirit, the difficulty of conceiving of purpose as immanent in the physical cosmos is immensely increased. Thus Darwin, in answer to Prof. Asa Gray, who had asked him what would convince him of design, replied: "If I could be convinced thoroughly that life and mind was in an unknown way a function of other imponderable force, I should be convinced."[1] Accordingly, it appears probable that, if Darwin had heard of and accepted the view taken in this Lecture, that all existences, both physical and psychical, are finite modes or differentiations of the one eternal spiritual Substance or Life, a serious obstacle to his recognition of design in nature would have been removed.

I conclude, then, that the force of the Design Argument is in no way destroyed by recent scientific discoveries; and that in so far as the principle of variation and natural selection operates in biological evolution, it is to be regarded as itself one of the features of that rational process by which life on this planet has moved upward to its present level.[2] But while some eminent

---

[1] See Prof. Schurman's *Belief in God*, p. 209.

[2] In connection with this subject, I would invite attention to a treatise now in the press, entitled, *Nature* versus *Natural Selection: an Essay on Organic Evolution*, by Rev. C. C. Coe, F.R.G.S. In this able work, the part which "the struggle for existence" really plays in biological development is very carefully estimated; and by a cogent line of argument, based on facts admitted by eminent naturalists, the conclusion is reached that Natural Selection cannot be the chief agent in determining the process of Organic Evolution.

scientists, such as Prof. Huxley, are not disposed to deny that there are reasons for thinking that an absolute intelligence must be immanent in the original molecular constitution of a world which by inherent necessity has evolved all the ascending series of animal life, they still reject the Theistic interpretation of the universe, on the ground that the process of animal evolution is characterized by principles the very reverse of those moral principles which are now recognized as right in all civilized societies. Prof. Huxley has forcibly expressed this view in the Romanes Lectures which he recently delivered at Oxford. The consideration of this objection to religious belief belongs to my next Lecture, in which I shall endeavour to set forth the evidence for Theism furnished by man's Moral Consciousness, that is, by the presence and development in our nature of authoritative Ideals.

Lecture VII.
GOD AS THE SOURCE OF IDEALS.

I ENDEAVOURED to show in the last Lecture that Science and Religion, in their demand for an adequate Cause for cosmical phenomena, look at the objects and events in nature from an entirely different point of view—Science seeking to investigate and make intelligible the dynamical elements and dynamical relations which give rise to the successive phases in the evolution of the world, but always dealing with modes of energy, which are not self-subsistent, while Religion looks to that Absolute and Supreme Causality in which each and all of the physical and psychical centres of energy in the universe have their common ground and their unifying principle. We saw that if this view be correct the Eternal is not to be regarded simply as a *First Cause* acting creatively at some remote period in the past, but rather as the present and eternal Cause in whom all the forces which science investigates have their source and maintenance. The feeling of the constant dependence of all finite existences on this self-existent or Absolute Being, and of the soul's personal relationship to Him, gives the religious answer to the human mind's quest for ultimate Causation. As, then, Religion and Science are severally concerned with quite different aspects of the causal problem, they need not, if each confines itself to its own sphere, come into collision; each gives the complementary insight which the other requires—the former thinking of God as the inner cause and ground of every centre of energy, and of the cosmos as a whole, the latter seeking for the rational principles which shall give unity and intelligibility to the infinite series of dynamic activities in which the Eternal Will successively expresses itself.

In the earlier, or perceptive, stage of religious belief, the God or Gods are closely associated with particular dynamic phenomena, external to the soul; and in the heavenly bodies, the might of winds and ocean, or in the succession of the seasons, the religious mind recognizes the causal energy of the Eternal. But later on, when reflection sets in, all forms of dynamic energy are seen to be but varied manifestations of one central reality, and therefore the truest and deepest insight into the being and character of that Eternal Reality is looked for in the inmost consciousness of the individual soul. In thus seeking for God at the very centre of their own being, different thinkers and different nations have been variously affected by what they saw therein. One class of thinkers have been most struck by the discovery in their inner life of a fundamental thinking faculty, or Reason, which, though immanent in the individual, is felt to be universal and self-existent, and to manifest its presence in all finite souls alike. Another type of mental structure has fastened upon the Moral Consciousness, with its unconditional imperative, as the fundamental revelation of the being and character of the

Ultimate Reality. Hence different peoples have apprehended with clearness two distinct aspects of the Eternal. The Hindoos and Greeks, for instance, saw His outer manifestation in the sum-total of objective phenomena, and His inner unity in that universal Reason which is consciously felt at the centre of every rational soul; while the Semitic races, on the other hand, and especially the Hebrews, chiefly recognized the Eternal in the subjective consciousness of His personal relationship to their own inner life, and discerned His universality and self-existence, not so much in the Reason, as in that inner voice of Duty which is uttered in the individual soul, but which is felt to wholly transcend the finite and the particular, and to carry with it a quite infinite and absolute authority.

In the history of religious thought we clearly see the operation and development of both these modes of apprehending the essential nature of God; the former mode leading to Pantheism and to the undervaluing of the importance and worth of the individual soul, the latter mode leading to the comparative neglect of the objective cosmos, and consequently of science and philosophy, and to the concentration of all warm interest on the moral and spiritual relation of each particular soul to the Divine source of the ethical imperative within. These two typical modes of regarding the relation of the human soul to God and to the universe, which we may broadly characterize as the Greek and the Hebrew, have each their influential representatives in the present day; and I hope to be able to show, in what remains of these Lectures, that it is in the synthesis of these two aspects of the Eternal that a vital and progressive Theism consists. I may add, that it is just because in the case of Jesus of Nazareth what was deepest and best in both the Hebrew and Greek thought of God found combined expression, that his character and teachings have been so influential in the past, and bid fair to be still more inspiring in the future; for it is evident that only now, in the nineteenth century after his birth, are the grand features of his personality and his thought being effectually liberated by reverent criticism from the disfiguring disguises in which superstition and ecclesiastical dogmatism have so long enwrapped them, and set free to captivate by their intrinsic majesty and beauty the inmost heart of the highest culture of our time.

But to return to my main subject. It will help us to understand the real relation of Hindoo and Greek thought about God to the Hebrew thought, if we first inquire into the mental conditions out of which the former arose. The great fact in man's inner life which impressed the reflective Hindoo mind was the presence of a universal principle of Reason in the individual's consciousness, whereby man is able to transcend his own finitude, and to impartially view and estimate himself as one among the innumerable finite things and souls of which the cosmos consists. The old English poet, Samuel Daniel, was impressed with this same sense of the greatness of man as being a partaker in the universal Reason when he exclaimed:

"Unless above himself he can
Erect himself, how poor a thing is man!"

It is simply in virtue of the felt immanence in our finite

VII. GOD AS THE SOURCE OF IDEALS.   239

nature of the Infinite and Eternal Ground of all existences that man is able to rise above himself; to see his own individuality, as well as all other finite existences, in some measure from God's point of view; to have glimpses of the Ideal—that is, of the truly Real—as seen from the standpoint of the Eternal. The reflective Hindoo, accordingly, looking into his own inner life, finds at the core of his own secondary and dependent existence a deeper and Eternal Self, the uncreated Cause of all created causes, the Soul of all souls. It is of this central unity and ground of all existences which the mind discerns within its own personality that the profound Hindoo thinkers, who composed the Upanishads, speak so often.

"The key-note of the old Upanishads," says Prof. Max Müller in his Hibbert Lectures,[1] "is 'Know thy Self,' but with a much deeper meaning than that of the Γνῶθι σεαυτόν of the Delphic oracle. The 'Know thy Self' of the Upanishads means, Know thy true Self, that which underlies thine Ego, and find it and know it in the highest, the eternal Self, the One without a Second, which underlies the whole world. This was the final solution of the search after the Infinite, the Invisible, the Unknown, the Divine, a search begun in the simplest hymns of the Veda, and ended in the Upanishads, or, as they were afterwards called, the Vedânta, the end or the highest object of the Veda."

And the essential supremacy of this inner unity, this Eternal Self (which is but the Hindoo way of abstractly expressing the same immanent Reality, which Jesus describes in all its concrete fulness by the words, "the Father within me"), is thus vividly set forth in the

[1] P. 317.

following quotation given by Prof. Max Müller from one of the Upanishads:

> "Verily, the worlds are not dear, that you may love the world; but that you may love the Self, therefore the worlds are dear.
> Verily, the Devas are not dear, that you may love the Devas; but that you may love the Self, therefore the Devas are dear.
> Verily, creatures are not dear, that you may love the creatures; but that you may love the Self, therefore the creatures are dear.
> Verily, everything is not dear, that you may love everything; but that you may love the Self, therefore everything is dear."[1]

Evidently the author of this passage is inspired by a perception of precisely the same deep truth which Richard Lovelace, the cavalier poet, expresses in the words:

> "I could not love thee, dear, so much,
> Loved I not honour more;"

for "honour" is just one of the aspects under which that Eternal Self reveals His presence in the inmost heart of every rational being.

This Supreme Unity, this Eternal indwelling Self, which the mind discerns by reflection, gradually took the place, in the more thoughtful and speculative minds among the orientals, of the many Deities who in the popular religion were supposed to manifest their presence and activity through the various phenomena of nature. And hence all philosophy and religion, in the view of cultured Hindooism, tended to pass into contemplation of this abstract Unity. In meditation on this Eternal Self, and mystic union with the same, the only road to salvation was supposed to lie.

Now Buddhism was virtually a grand ethical protest

[1] P. 329.

against this merely contemplative and mystical method of seeking salvation, and against the superstitions which always attend this passive mysticism. It is only by the fashioning of moral character, teaches Gautama the Buddha, that you can escape from the illusions of existence; and therefore all speculations about the Gods, and indeed all questions concerning their reality, are practically worthless and unedifying. Hence Buddhism presents a tolerably exact parallel to the present reaction in many minds against all metaphysical theology, and to the consequent endeavour to confine religious interests to the purely ethical realm.

There is, however, this important difference between the Buddhistic and the modern ethical revolt against the current theology. The Ethics of Buddha rests upon the Brahmanic notion of the illusory and worthless character of individuality, so that practically the Buddhist, like the Brahman, seeks to escape from this undesirable condition of individual life; but, unlike the Brahman, he thinks, as do Von Hartmann and other modern pessimists, that moral discipline and culture, and not mere philosophic meditation, is the most effectual way of losing that irrational longing which ties the soul to this unsatisfactory finite existence. Accordingly, both in Brahmanism and Buddhism man's ethical ideal is not regarded as a real revelation of the essence and character of the Eternal Self; for in their view the end of Ethics is not to realize in increasing fulness a sense of personal relationship to the Divine Self, or the Father within us, but either to so fuse the human self with the Eternal Brahma as to virtually destroy all distinct sense of individual personality; or else, as in the case of Buddhism, to achieve that total extinguishing of the desire to live which appears to be equivalent to personal annihilation. The tendency of both these systems of Hindoo thought is to weaken and efface all personal passions and affections, and so to destroy that distinct consciousness of individuality which, in their view, was not a privilege, but rather an undesirable condition from which they sought redemption.

One of the chief features in human nature, which gives an absolute value to individuality or separate personality, is the capacity of the soul to feel a quite infinite affection for other souls, and a quite infinite aspiration to realize an ideal. It is a noteworthy fact that Gautama, notwithstanding his practice and inculcation of the highest benevolence both to mankind and to animals, never clearly recognized that the *spiritual* affections and passions whereby man is related to the Infinite and the Eternal are totally different in kind from the *animal* and *selfish* desires from whose tyranny he sought to rescue the soul. He apparently never clearly saw, as Jesus saw, that Spiritual Love, so far from being a passion which conflicts with the Reason and fetters the soul to what is finite and disappointing, is really like the Reason itself (of which, in truth, it is only another aspect), the self-manifestation in man of Him who is Universal and Eternal, and that, consequently, the true freedom, the blessedness and the insight of the finite soul, are only realized by progressive self-surrender to this immanent and self-revealing Deity. Hence Prof. Kuenen, in his admirable Hibbert Lectures on "National Religions and Universal Religions," truly says of Buddhism:

"It seeks not to convert, but to rescue—to rescue from delusion and desire. The moral life is not its *end*, but its *means*. The reality was (happily!) too strong for it, and compelled it to recognize as an independent magnitude that to which it could on principle assign no such lofty place. But its want of a positive ideal avenges itself. It cannot have a future unless it has and gives a prospect in the future. It is not the present inactivity of Buddhism, but its devoted zeal in earlier times, that astonishes us. We gratefully observe that at first compassion overbore quietism. But that quietism, in its turn, has at last maimed compassion, who shall wonder?"[1]

Now there can be no question, I believe, that for the entirely different estimate now generally formed of the value of individuality the modern world is chiefly indebted to the influence of Hebrew and Christian thought. It is because the Hebrew genius (in the utterances of its great prophets) attached supreme and independent importance to the Conscience, as the real centre of individual character, where man and the Eternal enter into the closest personal relations, that the Hebrew and the Christian never dream of seeking the true end, or ideal, of human life in the loss of individuality. As seen from the point of view of the moral consciousness, man can never be regarded as simply a transient mode of the existence of the Eternal Self. It is because the Conscience makes known the possibility in man of *resisting* the injunctions of the moral imperative, that it reveals a clear distinction between the Will or Personality of

[1] P. 285.

God and the will or personality of man, and thus confers upon the latter an independent value and importance which it always tends to lose when the relation between man and God is viewed solely from the standpoint of the pure reason or intellect. Just as the feeling of *resistance* renders most men quite unable to doubt the reality of an external world, so does the consciousness of spiritual resistance, as presented in the discord felt at times between the human will and the invitations and injunctions of the Ideal, i.e. of the indwelling God, make it impossible for any one in whom ethical experience is vivid to remain satisfied with any theory which treats the human spirit as merely a transient mode of the Universal Spirit. Wherever the Conscience is regarded as revealing a supreme authority, there complete Pantheism becomes impossible, and individual spirits become of quite infinite significance and worth.

Systems of philosophical and theological thought, such as the chief Hindoo systems, some Greek and German systems, and the system of Spinoza, which contemplate man's relation to God and nature mainly from the intellectual point of view, recognize no possibility of any real or ontological antagonism between the will of God and the will of man. Vice and Virtue tend to be regarded as merely necessary phases in the development of the life of the individual; and as man in this view has no real power of origination, he practically becomes of value simply as playing a brief part, and subserving a temporary purpose, in the necessary evolution of eternal fate or eternal thought. The noblest Pantheistic religions, such as Stoicism in Greece and Rome, which regard self-consciousness and reason as the very substance of all reality, emphasize a most important truth, the immanence of God in all souls and in every object of nature; and undoubtedly they succeeded for a long time in inspiring and sustaining a high ethical ideal and warm ethical enthusiasm. Still, in the long run, such systems inevitably work out for themselves the logical consequences which are implicit in their essential nature; for if each individual and his character is no more than a phase of the self-manifestation of the Universal Spirit, all individuals will be regarded at length as of quite secondary value, and interest in the moral progress of society will resign its place to mere speculative interest in that Eternal Being who is the only permanent reality.

It is to the Hebrew race, then, I apprehend, that the world owes a great debt of gratitude for saving modern culture from the two extremes which so often meet, of Pantheism and Materialism. Looking for the relation between man and God at the very point where the two most certainly meet, viz. in the sense of Duty, the Hebrew saw in wilful wrong-doing something far deeper than vice; he saw *sin* there, and sin meant to him a real estrangement and opposition for the time between God and the individual soul.[1] Hence Pantheism was for him

---

[1] "Without ever formulating a theory, the teachers of post-exilic Judaism were inclined to lay the greatest stress upon man's unfettered choice between good and evil, upon his unrestricted capacity to obey the law and to transgress it. Man's will was free."—Mr. C. G. Montefiore's *Hibbert Lectures* on "The Origin and Growth of Religion as illustrated by the Religion of the Ancient Hebrews," p. 518. For the antithesis of this view, see Mr. F. H. Bradley's recent work on *Appearance and Reality*, passim.

impossible. He could not view his own moral being as simply an emanation or inevitable development from self-existent thought. He was conscious that he was able in moments of temptation to obey or resist the Divine Voice; hence he and his character had an independent or absolute interest and value in the view of the Eternal. The Hebrew conception, however, of the action of God on the individual spirit, was seriously defective in this, that the Ideal, in the earlier stages of Jewish thought, was conceived as reaching the individual soul in the form of an external commandment, rather than as inherent in the very constitution of the soul, in virtue of the soul being of the same substance as God. It was not till late in their history that the Hebrew seers saw what the Pantheistic thinkers of India and Greece had long seen, that the human spirit is a reproduction or differentiation of the Absolute Being, and that therefore in the awakening of the conscience we have not to do with an external commandment, but with the conscious realization of the authority of that Divinity who is already implicitly present in the very nature and essence of the soul.

The human mind, accordingly, reaches, I think, most nearly to a correct apprehension of the true relation of the soul to God, when it combines what is best and most vital in the Hebrew ethics and religion on the one hand, and in Greek and oriental religious thought on the other; that is, while preserving with the Hebrew the sense of the freedom and absolute worth of the individual soul, and of the fundamental character of sin and holiness, yet realizing, with the Pantheist, the essential divinity of human nature, the immanence of the

VII. GOD AS THE SOURCE OF IDEALS.

Universal and the Eternal in the depths of each man's personal life.

In the last Lecture I considered how far the external world is capable of awakening in man the belief in an Eternal Cause and Ground, but, as I then said, religion never adequately realizes itself in the human consciousness till we recognize in our inner life the presence of Ideals which appeal to us with the authority, not of any individual mind, nor of any social combination of individual minds, but with a quite absolute imperative. As it is characteristic of man as a rational being that he can rise above his finite individuality, so in the moral life of man Ethics proper shows itself in the form of an Ideal of conduct which, although it emerges out of our own individual consciousness, has yet a quite universal significance. This felt invitation and injunction to higher levels of thought and action has clear characters which indicate that it does not originate in that finite and particular nature which we share with the animal, but has its source in that universal and rational nature which belong to us as consciously participating in that Eternal Life, of which our souls are a reproduction. All our personal experiences which are occasioned by the finite impressions made upon us by the external world are capable of eliciting in us ideas which are more than finite, and which could not be produced by any addition or accumulation, either in our own case or through heredity, of merely finite sensations. The experiences of finite extension gradually elicit, but do not constitute, the idea of Infinity; nor does the accummulation in imagination of finite durations constitute the idea of Eternity.

In like manner, in the case of our æsthetic and ethical sentiments and judgments, the particular experiences of life awaken by degrees Ideals of the True, the Beautiful and the Good, which are distinctly recognized as not belonging in a special sense to each one of us individually, but to be the emergence in our consciousness of the perception, more or less vivid and adequate, of a universal or absolute beauty, of a universal or absolute good. This higher, or, as I may call it, Divine element in our consciousness, is both in its origin, and indeed all through its history, associated, and in a measure limited and dimmed, by narrow views, passions and considerations of expediency which appertain to us as individual finite beings seeking our immediate or remote personal pleasures and satisfactions; but I maintain that so soon as the animal passes into the properly human stage of existence, this ideal insight into a good, which is not merely mine or yours, but which is absolutely worthful, begins in some elementary form to manifest itself as a real factor in man's consciousness. The savage whose sympathies or hereditary tendencies have led him to identify in some degree his own personal self with the tribal unity, not only feels, when his own individual desires and the interests of the tribe happen to clash, that there is some amount of pain (as the Darwinians would say) resulting from allowing the occasional personal appetites to override the more permanent social affections, but he also feels the incipient presence of something more than this; he feels that he is bound by some authority, which is quite distinct from either his natural appetites or his natural sympathies, to hold in check his own cravings when the well-being of his tribe demands it.[1] In like manner, in regard to valiant behaviour in war and fortitude in bearing pain, the more conspicuous elements in these virtues are no doubt explicable as the outcome of animal passions: but there is more than this; the yielding to fear or to bodily torture is not only repressed by the savage's thought of the consequences to his reputation, but he also feels bound to repress it by that element of self-respect or honour in his consciousness which authoritatively asserts itself.[2] So in more advanced stages of civilization, when self-indulgence is seen by any one to be undermining and paralyzing his higher faculties, there are no doubt strong prudential and social considerations which influence him to put a curb on his lower appetites: but these are not all; for if these were all, the profligate, on observing the wreck of his better nature, would only charge himself with imprudence arising from short-sightedness; there is also the consciousness that he has violated a law of his nature which is unconditionally binding upon him. It is true that the actions which a man performs at the bidding of this universal or absolute imperative are in most cases in accordance with the moral code of the persons among whom he lives, and they are also actions which on the whole are found to be conducive to the general welfare of society; but for all that, in so far as they are

---

[1] See the admirable chapter on the "Nature of Moral Authority," in Dr. Martineau's *Types of Ethical Theory*, Vol. II.

[2] In relation to this subject, Mr. Huxley's candid admission, in his Romanes Lecture, that there is more in the sentiment of 'ought' than evolutionist theories avail to explain, is most important and significant, as coming from such an unexpected quarter.

truly moral acts of the individual self, they imply the recognition of an absolute obligation; they contain the elements of the sense of duty, and of the attendant reverence for a felt authority, which, though it expresses itself in the individual consciousness, is recognized as having a source which is not individual and particular, but universal and eternal.

The late Prof. Rauwenhoff of Holland, in his recent original, and in many respects very valuable, treatise on the "Philosophy of Religion," aptly expresses the idea, which I am seeking to convey, in the following words:

"The consciousness of Duty is something entirely unique in us. Far from always agreeing with inclination, it is for the most part opposed to it; and not only to the inclinations which at the very beginning of man's moral life are recognized as perverse, but also to those inclinations from which life is wont to derive its most beautiful blossoms and fruits. It forbids the great social and religious reformer at times even to seek a place where he can lay his head; it obliges him prematurely to sacrifice to the hostility of his opponents his own life, which if he could have preserved it might have been of inestimable value to his fellow-men. It asks nothing about the calculations of utility and expediency. Inexorably and pitilessly it pursues us with 'Thou must!' (*Du musst*), and if we give no heed to it there comes into the 'Thou must!' a more emphatic tone, and it passes over into an imperative 'Thou shalt!' (*Du sollst*). Through the whole of our life (if our higher nature be not stupefied and deadened by absorption in pleasure or in some ruling passion) this 'Thou must!' accompanies us, and as we reach any stage of ethical development we still feel the pressure of the Ideal summoning us to a still higher point of moral perfection."[1]

---

[1] Dr. Hanne's German translation of Rauwenhoff's *Wijsbegeerte van den Godsdienst*, p. 233.

VII. GOD AS THE SOURCE OF IDEALS. 251

Rauwenhoff adds: "Not all men feel this. It happens even in the case of intense mental work that the object of study may so completely pre-occupy a man that he has heart for nothing else than for his literature, his art, his music, his natural science, or whatever else it may be." But estimable, he says, as from one point of view such all-engrossing devotion to one aim may sometimes be, man, nevertheless, becomes in this way little more than an instrument; and as concerns the other sides of his soul's life, he is practically as insensible as a sleep-walker is, except to the one idea on the realization of which his mind is concentrated. "But whenever a man wakes up from this one-sided absorption, he begins to pass this absolute judgment on himself, and the Ideal of a more perfect life appeals to him in tones which he cannot choose but hear."

The Ideal which is here spoken of by Rauwenhoff is not something which arises independently of experience; it is only an occasion of experience that it presents itself; and the fuller and richer the experience, the more pure and elevated the ideal is likely to become. But what is here contended for is, that experience and reflection do not *make*, but *awaken* or *elicit* the Ideal; the actual, the individual, calls forth something higher than itself; and the very ideal which social intercourse serves to bring into clear consciousness may even turn out to be an ideal which morally constrains a man to take a course which involves the breaking of the closest and most precious social ties.

What relation, then, do these ideals of truth, of beauty, of goodness, of infinite love, which speak to us in tones of absolute authority in which nothing finite, nothing merely individual, mingles—what relation, I ask, do they bear to that Supreme Ground and Cause which is discerned at the central core of each man's consciousness? Surely they must be regarded as an expression of the inmost essence of human nature, and therefore as a revelation of the true character of that Eternal One out of whose substance the spirit of man is formed. It may be objected that these ideals are very different at different stages of mental and moral development. No doubt they are, for the elevation of the ideal is in necessary relation to the state of culture amid which it arises; still all the evidence goes to prove that as human nature, under the influences of civilization, evolves its higher faculties and aspirations, the ethical ideal, as it unfolds and purifies itself from lower admixtures, becomes more and more identical in all the higher forms of humanity, thus showing that it is not the result of individual or local accident, but is the making explicit that which is already implicit in the original constitution of man.

Rauwenhoff regards the reverence we feel for the moral ideal as the very essence of religion, and he would deny the name "Religion" to any cultus in which this was not a chief feature. Religious faith means, in his view, the faith we have in the moral order of the universe; the conviction that somehow (though the "how" may be beyond our comprehension) the man who follows the leading of the moral ideal will find that he and the purpose of the universe are at one; and he maintains that, though we cannot pretend to determine the ends

VII. GOD AS THE SOURCE OF IDEALS. 253

towards which nature is working, there is clearest evidence that the cosmos is an organism, that the forces in the universe have a definite direction imposed on them, and that Darwinism has proved nothing that weakens or refutes the Aristotelian doctrine that an idea to be realized dominates the whole course of evolution, and that this idea is essentially the idea of moral perfection.

But though Rauwenhoff has such faith in the moral order of nature, he will not allow that we are justified in assuming that an Eternal Self-consciousness is the ground of this moral order. It is admissible, he holds, and indeed not only admissible, but very desirable, that we should think the Cause and Ground of all things under a personal form; but we must always remember, he says, that all such theological conceptions are but poetic symbols of a reality which transcends the range of human thought. But as Prof. Pfleiderer[1] points out, Rauwenhoff himself admits that we cannot conceive of this moral order except as the expression of a highest Will, and also adds that we must cherish and put our trust in the truth of this, though "not as a logical conception, but as poetry." If Rauwenhoff only means that the attempt to conceive of the Ground of the Universe as an Eternal Self-consciousness and Will gives us no exhaustive conception of the reality, he is doubtless right. All that is maintained is, that this mode of conception is not simply the only possible one, if we

---

[1] See an excellent article by Dr. Otto Pfleiderer on "Die religionsphilosophischen Werke von Rauwenhoff und Martineau," in the *Jahrbücher für protestantische Theologie* for 1889.

are to have any conception at all, but that there are good reasons in the constitution of our own minds, in the existence within us of authoritative ideals, and in the feeling of personal relationship between the human spirit and the Eternal, for holding that in conceiving of God after the type of our personal consciousness we are gaining a true, though only partial, insight into the infinite reality. Rauwenhoff thus agrees with Kant in recognizing our moral consciousness as the real basis of man's belief in God; but whereas Kant is obliged by the principles of his philosophy to reach the belief in God by roundabout inferences from the reality of moral obligation to an Immortality which shall allow of unending approach to perfection, and to a Supreme Being who shall secure moral retribution, Rauwenhoff and Dr. Martineau most justly, I believe, find in the moral consciousness itself immediate and firm ground for theistic belief.   Even Prof. H. Sedgwick (though he is in close sympathy with the empirical school of philosophical thought) not only admits that the feeling of "ought" is unique, that is, is irresolvable into feelings of pleasure, pain or sympathy, but he also agrees thus far with Dr. Martineau, that no empirical explanation can be given for the recognized moral principle that we are bound to sacrifice our selfish interests when the welfare of our fellow-men demands it. Social influences alone cannot have generated that ideal of conduct which, as we have seen, at times imposes on a man the obligation to incur social obloquy, and even to sacrifice his life without the slightest calculation as to whether society will or will not be the gainer by his death.

VII. GOD AS THE SOURCE OF IDEALS.

If, then, religious belief has its chief source in man's conviction of the divine authority of his moral ideals, how comes it about that established theology has been so often the bitter foe of the most truly conscientious men? I have already given an answer to this question in the previous Lecture on "Culture and Dogmatic Religion." This terrible mischief has arisen from the fact that established churches are ever tempted to forget that the only legitimate foundation of their existence and of their authority is in the moral consciousness of mankind, and hence they generally attach a factitious authority to mere forms of doctrinal opinion, to particular books and persons. When we consider the unwarranted pretensions of nearly all existing established religions, we see the justification of Schiller's well-known distich:

"Welche Religion ich bekenne ? Keine von allen
Die du mir nennst !—Und warum Keine ? Aus Religion."

It is through locating ultimate authority, not on its legitimate throne in the highest ethical and spiritual insight of mankind, but in some supposed exceptional revelation, that established churches have so often succeeded in blunting and perverting the natural conscience of their adherents, and have substituted in its place an unnatural ecclesiastical conscience. As Dr. Martineau eloquently says, in his "Seat of Authority in Religion:"[1]

"It is in vain to tell me how conscientious the ecclesiastical persecutors were. There lies the very charge I make against the Church—that it has put into the conscience what has no business to be there; has treated error of thought as if it were

[1] P. 157.

unfaithfulness of will; and misguided the affections of men by rendering it possible for them to hate what is most lovable, and honour, if not love, what is most hateful. The whole conception of an "orthodoxy" indispensable to the security of men's divine relations is an ethical monstrosity in the presence of which no philosophy of duty is possible and every moral ideal must be dwarfed or deformed."

There is, happily, good reason for hoping and expecting that these attempts to override and supersede the natural ethical judgment by the pretence of a superior ecclesiastical authority will not long continue to deform the civilization of our time. Every fresh generation sees with greater clearness that whatever else true religion may involve, it certainly involves the recognition of the highest ethical ideal as man's only reliable insight into the nature and will of God. That every year will bring educated persons nearer to this identifying of Religion with what is highest in Ethics can hardly be questioned; the only doubt which the present condition of culture suggests is whether in the future Ethical Ideals will take the place of theology, and reverence for these ideals replace the faith in that God, in whose essential nature Theism believes that these ideals are eternal realities. This important practical question calls, accordingly, for serious consideration.

The, in many respects, admirable founder of Positivism maintains that it is impossible for the human mind to make a real synthesis of humanity and nature; that is, to discover any one principle or being out of which both arise; for nature, he holds, in itself has no features which are in harmony with human ideals. But still Comte

VII. GOD AS THE SOURCE OF IDEALS. 257

maintains that religious thought must somehow manage to harmonize and unify the inward and the outward aspects of human life so as to conceive of a Unity the thought of which shall serve to kindle inspiration and enthusiasm. As he maintains that the human mind cannot reach this unity (as Theism professes to do) by a real or *objective* synthesis, it must take the next best course, viz. unify the two by the play of poetic imagination, or, as Comte expresses it, by a *subjective* synthesis.

"The logic of religion," he says, "when freed from scientific empiricism, will not confine itself any longer to the domain of hypotheses which are capable of verification. It must in the end find its completion in the domain much wider and not less legitimate, which, without offending the reason, is peculiarly suited to develop the feelings. The utterances of true poetry are better adapted to our moral wants, and are as harmonious as those of sound philosophy with the intellectual conditions of this relative synthesis. They ought, therefore, to obtain a great extension and influence in our efforts to systematize our thoughts; and Positivism permits of their doing so without any danger of confusion between the two distinct methods of thinking which openly consecrates the one to Reality, the other to Ideality."[1]

In precisely the same spirit Frederick Lange, the author of the valuable "History of Materialism," endeavours to show that it has not been *truth*, but *illusions*, which have kindled spiritual enthusiasm and founded the great religions of the world. He is, no doubt, quite justified in contending as he does that in the beliefs that have swayed so many souls at the birth-period of a new and influential religion, many of the ideas which

[1] Prof. E. Caird's *Social Philosophy and Religion of Comte*.

have most strongly acted on the emotions and the will have not been ideas which the science of that age, or indeed of any age, could verify. But when Lange proceeds to argue that, therefore, mere Ideals, which are not supposed to correspond to any reality, will suffice to kindle and sustain religious fervour and ethical zeal, he overlooks the essential point, viz. that whether these beliefs were or were not consistent with the highest culture of the age that held them, they were, at all events, *beliefs which were regarded by the believers in them as in true accord with the deepest reality;* and had these believers come to see that their beliefs had no other foundation than in the poetic imagination of the prophets who uttered them, the religious movement to which they gave rise would assuredly have forthwith collapsed. As Heinrich Lang of Zürich pertinently remarked in reply to Lange, Religions have ever fallen when people no longer believed in them; that is to say, when people have come to see that their doctrines are only poems and not truth.

"That is not the fate of poems which profess to deal with creations of the imagination. Has Homer's *Iliad* become discredited since the Gods and heroes have no longer been believed in? Has Goethe's *Iphigeneia* passed into oblivion because nobody thinks the story on which it is founded a fact? Poems hold their own if they æsthetically satisfy, religions fall when they are no longer believed in.'[1]

It is quite futile, then, for Positivists to suppose that a merely subjective or imaginative synthesis of the ground of nature with human ideals will avail to create

[1] *Versuch einer Christlichen Dogmatik.*

and sustain a real and effective religious faith. And if we carefully consider that Worship of Humanity with which Comte and his disciples have sought to replace Theism, we cannot, I think, avoid the conclusion that it lacks the essentials of a satisfying and effective religion. As I indicated in a former Lecture, it is only by personifying or hypostatizing the abstract idea of Humanity (after the fashion of a Platonic Realist), and hence introducing as all-important one of those very metaphysical conceptions which, according to Comte's fundamental law, cultivated society is supposed to have done with for ever, that the *Grand-être* can at all perform the function of an object of worship. And when we leave this metaphysical fiction and contemplate the fact, we find that the aggregate of individual human beings is about the least inspiring object of reverence that man's speculative imagination ever devised. It is not in the contemplation of human beings in the mass that any religious sentiment or faith takes its rise.

Such faith is kindled (as Comte himself was very well aware when he drew up his interesting Calendar of the Saints of Positivism) by contemplating the lives and characters of those among mankind who have been the purest and noblest representatives in their respective spheres of that Divine Ideal which is implicit in the depths of every human soul. Such men are, no doubt, the real redeemers of humanity. But why are these select spirits of such surpassing interest, of such infinite worth? Why is the contemplation of their lives and their thoughts such a perennial source of inspiration, such an efficient means of awakening religious faith and ethical enthusiasm? Surely it is because in them that Ideal which is dimly present and operative in every human mind incarnates itself in a living concrete character; and the divinity thus realized in a grand personality fertilizes and fructifies those germs of divinity which are inherent in every soul, because every rational soul is the offspring or reproduction of Him in whom all true ideals have at once their source and their realization. Did we suppose that the ideas of the thinker or poet, the creative genius of the artist, the divine love of the saviours of the world, were but splendid developments of the merely individual and accidental resources of their particular minds, we should indeed wonder at and admire them for their exceptional splendour; we should note how grandly they overtop the average level of their fellow-mortals; but in such a case they would be quite ineffective to awaken in us religion. What kindles faith and enthusiasm as we come into personal contact, either through the living voice or through literature, with these divinest of our brethren, is the inspiring consciousness that in them that divine ideal, which in us is but a vision and an aspiration, has become a concrete possession of mankind, and under this influence the ideals of truth, beauty and love (those features of the authoritative Universal in our souls) become invested with quite new life and interest, and for a season at least we feel assured that the Ideal is after all the most truly Real. As this Divine side of our nature is thus called forth into clear and intense self-consciousness, the finite Self spontaneously recognizes with joy its deep inner relationship and communion with that Eternal Self who is felt to be revealing Himself and His essential character in that aspiration, hope and faith which the vivid presentment of the Ideal never fails, in some measure, to call forth in the human mind.

Thus the cosmological demand for an adequate Ground and Cause for all finite existences, of which I spoke in the last Lecture, blends with the ethical and spiritual insight of our highest moods, and in their union they generate in all rational souls some degree of that strengthening religious belief which enabled the world's representative Theist to say, "I am not alone, for the Father is with me."

Because the spirit of man, in those elements of our self-consciousness which reveal the Universal and the Ideal, is of the same substance with the Eternal and Absolute One, the inmost life of man and the life of God so indivisibly blend that it may almost be said, in a certain sense, that they are identical. If we say with Tennyson, "our wills are ours to make them Thine," we may also say "our Ideals are Thy Reality, and Thou dost reveal them in our inner life that we may, by moral effort and by self-surrendering love, weave them into the very texture of our character, and so make them increasingly Real to us as they are eternally Real to Thee." The law of conduct which the beauty of the Ideal invites, and which the moral imperative enjoins, is, as Kant and T. H. Green truly held, felt to be imposed upon us by ourselves; but it is at the same time felt to be imposed upon us by the Eternal Self or God, who is at once the Ground of all cosmical life and of our individual existences.

And it is, no doubt, because the positive ethical Ideal is the same in all spirits that have reached the same level of mental and moral culture, that nearly all schools of ethical theory, however much they may differ in their way of accounting for the genesis and mode of development of the ethical ideal, agree that the supreme principle in Ethics is the principle of Spiritual Love. Love, in its purest essence, is the emotion which attends the conscious realization of a deep oneness or identity of nature between one finite soul and another, and between the finite Self and the Eternal Self. Every expression and actualization of the Ideal in human life, whether it be in the higher reaches of "divine philosophy," in poetry, in art or music, or, chief of all, in the possession of the soul by spiritual love, all awaken the sense of a deeper unity beneath individual variety and plurality. Ethics is simply the growing insight into, and the effort to actualize in society, that sense of fundamental kinship and identity of substance in all men, while Religion is the emotion and the devotion which attends the realization in our self-consciousness of an inmost spiritual relationship, arising out of that unity of Substance which constitutes man the true son of the Eternal Father.

It is because of this essential identity of substance which relates all finite souls to each other and to God, that I cannot but think that the leaders of the "Ethical Culture" movement, among whom are some of the noblest of men, are unconsciously standing in the way of the realization of the divine end which they have at heart when they attempt to dissociate ethical enthusiasm and effort from that deep sense of metaphysical unity and spiritual relationship with the Absolute Ground of all existence of which our ethical insight and sense of moral obligation is only a partial, though most important phase. Apart from the faith, the hope, and the consciousness of infinite sympathy and support which springs from the religious feeling of immediate personal relationship and communion with the Eternal Ground and animating Spirit of the cosmos, of whose essential nature man's ethical ideals, in so far as they become purified and perfected, are the ever-present expression, the sphere of ethical interest and enthusiasm is unreasonably and unnaturally narrowed, and is divorced from conscious relation to that deeper and central life of the universe in which all that is true in science, beautiful in literature and art, noble and heroic in conduct, ecstatic and uplifting in religious aspiration and devotion, find their common ground, their unification, and their innermost vitality.

Our apprehension of God may be faint or vivid, but it is not to be explained as gained by inference from the action upon us of something external to ourselves. It is the gradual emergence in man's self-consciousness of a clearer vision of that Eternal Self whose essential character becomes clearer as the ideals of the human mind and heart become higher and purer. Two great principles are admitted by nearly all moralists to hold supreme rank in the ethical scale, the principle of Righteousness or Justice, and the principle of Benevolence or Love. By many theologians God's Justice and God's Love have been regarded as antagonistic principles. Jesus, however, clearly saw, and the world's greatest thinkers agree with him, that Justice, or moral retribution, the principle that "as a man sows so shall he reap," so far from admitting of real opposition to the principle of true Benevolence, derives its very being and eternal validity from the fact that Infinite Love is at the helm of the universe. The insight, then, into the Divine Being, which our moral consciousness gives, is that God is at once eternal Justice and eternal Love, and that He is eternal Justice because He is Eternal Love.

But is it so? Does the actual universe as interpreted by science, do the facts of individual life and of human history, accord with and endorse this *à priori* insight of the conscience and the heart, that Love, or the aim to communicate the highest possible good, has been and is the regnant principle in the universe? The answer to this question cannot fail to be influenced to an immense extent by the view which the answerer takes of the validity of that ethical insight which we have been discussing. If the belief that God is Love were reached, as an induction from the study of nature and history, then, of course, to take this belief with us as a clue when we have to deal with the stern reality of Natural and Moral Evil would be mere reasoning in a circle. It appears to me evident that the belief that Love belongs to the essence of God's nature is, in general, based on the principle, which each religious mind verifies for itself, that man most truly realizes his own higher nature when his conduct is at the free disposal of rational self-forgetful love; and the mind spontaneously infers, and feels itself justified in inferring, that the principle which speaks with highest authority in the individual consciousness is also the principle which is dominant in the universe. The human mind is thus generally predisposed, or, if you prefer

VII. GOD AS THE SOURCE OF IDEALS.

to say so, prejudiced, through faith in its own ethical insight, in favour of the conclusion that both nature and humanity have their origin in the causality of a Being whose aim is to confer the highest possible good on the aggregate of sentient and self-conscious beings whom He creates, or, as I have preferred to phrase it in these Lectures, into whom He differentiates, in some measure, His own substance.

The most important recent attempt to prove that the universe, apart from man, is wholly devoid of any ethical character, is the Romanes Lecture on "Evolution and Ethics," recently delivered at Oxford by Prof. Huxley; and in the brief treatment of the problem of Evil which I am able to give here, I will have chiefly in view Prof. Huxley's representations. Now it is to be noted first that Prof. Huxley takes no account whatever of the above ethical prejudgment concerning the character of the Cause of the universe. It appears to him, for instance, a somewhat surprising and regrettable feature in the philosophy of the Stoics, with whom in other respects he finds himself in general sympathy, "that they perfected, if they did not invent, that ingenious and plausible form of pleading, the Theodicy, for the purpose of showing, firstly, that there is no such thing as evil; secondly, that if there is, it is the necessary correlate of good; and moreover, that it is either due to our own fault, or inflicted for our benefit."[1]

I doubt very much if Prof. Huxley, whose evident devotion to truth and to humanity all must admire, is himself altogether free from this tendency to form for

[1] P. 24.

himself a Theodicy. It appears very probable, from the statement made on the last page of his printed Lecture, viz. that "the man who hopes to abate the essential evil in the world must cast aside the notion that the escape from pain is the proper object of life," that our eminent biologist is not wholly without the faith that if the Absolute has not kept pain and sorrow out of the cosmos, it is probably because the existence of pain and sorrow is a necessary condition of the attainment of a higher good.

He tells us that he cannot see why, among "the endless possibilities open to omnipotence," that of "a sinless happy existence"[1] should not have been selected. But why does he not say that he cannot see why, among the possibilities open to the Eternal, that of a perfectly comfortable existence, containing at the same time rich opportunities for the manifestation of self-sacrificing love and moral heroism, should not have been selected? Clearly it is because he cannot but regard this particular combination as *not* being among the possibilities open to what he calls "omnipotence." And I should feel much surprised to learn that Prof. Huxley does not in his inmost heart endorse the satisfaction which the Theist feels in the thought that "among the possibilities open" to Him, the Absolute has chosen that one which allows the rational spirit to approach to, and to experience, that highest blessedness which is cheaply purchased at the cost of long-continued self-sacrifice, pain and sorrow.

When Mr. Spencer looks forward to an ideal condition of things in which there shall be little or no pain, and

[1] P. 25.

little or no opportunity for self-sacrifice, and Spinoza speaks of suffering as "a passage to a lower state of perfection," it may well be questioned whether these great thinkers have at all realized what the universe would lose if its Eternal Ground and Cause had no other and higher aim than the complete avoidance of suffering. As Dr. Momerie justly and eloquently writes:

"I say we may well thank God for the existence of such suffering. 'We will not complain,' says Thomas Carlyle, 'of Dante's miseries: had all gone right with him as he wished it, Florence would have had another prosperous lord mayor, but the world would have lost the Divina Commedia.' Again, we do not know much about Shakespeare's life; but we do know from his sonnets that he had suffered vastly. The most striking instance, however, that I am acquainted with of the way in which poets 'learn in suffering what they teach in song,' is to be found in Tennyson. The only great poem he has written is, 'In Memoriam;' and that, as you know, he wrote soon after the loss of his friend, Arthur Hallam. See now the inspiration he derived from suffering. Why, there are single stanzas in 'In Memoriam' worth ten thousand times as much as all his other poems put together. And it is not only those who will have a niche in the Temple of Fame that are teachers of sorrow's divine lessons. I have known women of whom the world will never hear, whose whole life was one protracted grief—who, by their patience, their faith, their cheerfulness, their unselfishness, have preached to all who came near them sermons more eloquent by far than were ever delivered from any pulpit—sermons in comparison with which the discourses of Chrysostom or Savonarola must have been tame and dull."[1]

As Miss F. P. Cobbe expresses it in her beautiful hymn, "All noblest things are born in agony." Struggle and anguish in some form and measure is the inevitable

[1] *The Origin of Evil, and other Sermons*, p. 21.

lot of those whose devotion to the Ideal is of the right genuine sort; and the idea ever haunts my own mind, though I have no direct proof to offer in its justification, that the suffering of those divinest sons of God who most richly share in His true inward peace and blessedness, has its supreme counterpart in the inmost being of that Eternal Father who may be truly said to be ever sacrificing Himself that Nature and Humanity may live, and of whose infinite sympathy with the joys and woes of His dependent offspring we may believe that our finite experiences can give but a faint inkling.[1]

With regard to the presence of Moral Evil, the usual explanation which spontaneously occurs to most minds appears to me to be an adequate one. Appalling as is the blackness and deformity which Sin introduces into the cosmos, yet the absence of it from the world would surely not exhibit a nett profit to mankind, if with it departed, as must needs depart, all true moral freedom,

---

[1] See on this subject a thoughtful volume of sermons, *Religion in Life*, by Rev. Edwin Smith, M.A., p. 94, and also a tract by the late Rev. T. T. Lynch, entitled, *Amongst Transgressors*. In a striking sermon (which the author conceives to be written from Hegel's point of view), the following remark occurs: "The only true and profitable way of studying God is through ethical principles. Any conceptions of God which impose ethical limitations on Him, or that are ethically valueless for us, are worse than useless, for they are false. The former of these two canons excludes the Unitarian God, for the God of the Unitarians cannot comply with the central and essential ethical principles, viz. the sacrificing of self to find self."—*Liverpool Pulpit*, March, 1893, p. 34. I am quite unable to see why a monopoly of this mode of thinking about God is claimed either for the old-fashioned Trinitarians or for the new-fashioned Hegelian ones. It so happens that I know some Unitarians who not only have this conception of God, but lay great stress upon it.

all genuine responsibility. To ask why wrong-doing is in the world is virtually to ask why Evolution did not stop short at the animal stage and not press upwards into human experience. In Dr. Martineau's words: "To set up an absolute barrier against the admission of wrong, is to arrest the system of things at the mere natural order, and detain life at the stage of a human menagerie, instead of letting it culminate in a moral society."[1]

Who that earnestly reflects would really wish for a world in which all that is truly ethical should be lacking, and where all those sentiments of moral admiration and of moral reprobation and indignation which impart the highest interest and sublimity to the grand drama of each individual life and of the history of mankind, should be transformed into mere æsthetic judgments concerning the inevitable phases of relative beauty and ugliness in the course of cosmical and biological evolution? It must be remembered, too, that if the possibility of Moral Evil were absent, the conscious relation between the human soul and the immanent Father would lose all those essential elements of aspiration and felt personal sympathy for the existence of which a certain dualism of will and personality is an indispensable condition.[2]

[1] *A Study of Religion*, Vol. II. p. 108.

[2] The above inadequate treatment of this great problem of the existence of Moral Evil is intended only as an introduction to the study of the subject. Those interested in it will find the clearest and fullest presentation and discussion of all the phases of the question in Dr. Martineau's great work, *A Study of Religion*, Vol. II. They should also read Dr. Momerie's admirable sermons on the *Origin of Evil*, from which I have quoted above, and also the Rev. George

And now I will turn to what is called Natural or Physical Evil. Does this Evil fatally collide with that character which the intuitions of our ethical consciousness prompt us to ascribe to the Eternal? The main purpose of Prof. Huxley's Romanes Lecture is to prove that the cosmical principle which dominates the process of Evolution up to the point when man appears and begins to feel an elementary moral ideal, is diametrically opposed to that course of action which the moralized man regards as right. "Let us understand," he says, "once for all, that the ethical progress of society depends, not on imitating the cosmic process, still less in running away from it, but in combating it."[1] Now if this is a correct way of expressing the principle of cosmic evolution, we find ourselves confronted with an astounding conception of the universe. Here is a cosmos which

St. Clair's Handbook on *Evil, Physical and Moral*. One of the ablest attempts to solve the problem is the Rev. Charles Voysey's volume of sermons on *The Mystery of Pain, Death and Sin;* and the following passage from a letter written to Mr. Voysey by a deceased brother of his, an Anglican clergyman, happily expresses the main feature of the Theistic solution: "Why was it that evil was permitted to come into the world? .... The explanation lies in half a-dozen words; that the highest manifestation of any nature can only take place, i.e. its highest qualities can only be in exercise and the depth of its resources and the sufficiency of its strength only fully called out, in dealing with what is antagonistic to itself. Any nature less or meaner than Divine would have left evil and antagonism out of his Creation—as a parent would keep it out of his nursery, or a master from his school, and would have revelled in the contemplation of scenes of happiness and order. But the higher nature lets in the evil, the disorder, the trouble, knowing the inexhaustible and matchless force of its resources to deal with it and subdue it."

[1] P. 34.

bears all the marks of being a unitary system: we have learned from Prof. Huxley in one of the articles he has contributed to the *Nineteenth Century*,[1] that there is no better way of describing the course of evolution than as "a materialized logical process;" and in the Lecture before us we are told that, in the view of science, the cosmos "assumes the aspect, not so much of a permanent entity, as of a changeful process, in which nought endures save the flow of energy and *the rational order which pervades it*."[2] But strange to say, this system of rational order, which up to a certain stage exhibits not the slightest traces of a dominant benevolence, or, indeed, of any benevolence at all, all at once begins to evolve a being whose fundamental principles of conduct are in complete antagonism to the whole spirit of the process which has generated him. This cosmic nature, which we are told is "no school of virtue,"[3] manages somehow to present as its culminating product a race of beings who (to use Prof. Huxley's words) "do not doubt that, so far forth as they possess a power of bettering things, it is their paramount duty to use it, and to train all their intellect and energy to the supreme service of their kind."[4]

Surely, then, the evolution of nature as thus presented to the hearers and readers of the Romanes Lecture is hardly a process to be characterized as "rational order." For myself, I cannot but think that the Cosmos is marked by much more unity of purpose and inherent rationality than Prof. Huxley gives it credit for. Is, for instance,

[1] February, 1888, p. 164. [2] P. 4 (the italics are mine).
[3] P. 27. [4] P. 31.

the relation between man's animal appetites and passions, and his gradually developing ethical ideal, of such a nature that it is an accurate and adequate account of the matter to say that "the cosmos works through the lower nature of man, not for righteousness, but against it?"[1] In some respects the lower nature of man, as well as of animals beneath him in the biological scale, appears, as in the parental and social instincts, to be an anticipation of, and preparation for, ethical principles of conduct; and even when passion and greed collide, as in self-conscious man they so often do, with the ethical imperative, this very antagonism, so far from having no ethical significance, is the indispensable condition of that free self-formation of moral character on the part of rational agents which seems to be the final result for which the cosmical process has been all along preparing, and towards which it has through its whole course been tending.

John Stuart Mill, in his Essay on Nature, has depicted the apparently unmoral or malevolent features of the cosmos in the darkest possible tints; yet in his final Essay on Theism he writes:

"Endeavouring to look at the question without partiality or prejudice, and without allowing wishes to have any influence over judgment, it does appear that, granting the existence of design, there is a preponderance of evidence that the Creator desired the pleasure of his creatures. . . . . Even in cases when pain results, like pleasure, from the machinery itself, the appearances do not indicate that contrivance was brought into play purposely to produce pain; what is indicated is rather a clumsiness in the contrivance employed for some other purpose. The author of the machinery is no doubt accountable for having

[1] P. 27.

VII. GOD AS THE SOURCE OF IDEALS.

made it susceptible of pain; but this may have been a necessary condition of its susceptibility to pleasure; a supposition which avails nothing on the theory of an Omnipotent Creator, but is an extremely probable one in the case of a contriver working under the limitation of inexorable laws and indestructible properties of matter. The susceptibility being conceded as a thing which did enter into design, the pain itself usually seems like a thing undesigned; a casual result of the collision of the organism with some outward force to which it was not intended to be exposed, and which, in many cases, provision is even made to hinder it from being exposed to. There is, therefore, much appearance that pleasure is agreeable to the Creator, while there is very little or any appearance that pain is so: and there is a certain amount of justification for inferring, on grounds of Natural Theology alone, that Benevolence is one of the attributes of the Creator."[1]

Hermann Lotze has, I believe, conclusively shown that the mechanical necessity, which everywhere marks the lower planes of cosmical existence, is an indispensable foundation for the advent of an intelligent and morally free being such as man is, for it alone furnishes the needful condition alike for scientific knowledge and for

[1] *Three Essays on Religion*, p. 190. It is to be noted, that even if the development of animal species is mainly conditioned by the "struggle for existence," this struggle by no means involves any great amount of suffering. Mr. Wallace, who ranks with Darwin himself as an authority on this matter, writes: "Now that the war of Nature is better known, it has been dwelt upon by many writers as presenting so vast an amount of cruelty and pain as to be revolting to our instincts of humanity..... Now there is, I think, good reason to believe that all this is greatly exaggerated; that the supposed 'torments' and 'miseries' of animals have little real existence, but are the reflection of the imagined sensations of cultivated men and women in similar circumstances; and that the amount of actual suffering caused by the struggle for existence among animals is altogether insignificant."—*Darwinism*, pp. 36, 37.

the free formation of moral character. The fallacy involved in the popular assumption (in which one is surprised to find such a thinker as Prof. Huxley apparently acquiescing), that God, in manifesting His love in the eternal creation of the cosmos, has wholly unlimited possibilities, is admirably exposed in the following passage from Dr. Martineau's "Study of Religion:"

"Do you ask, What business have 'imperfections' in the work of an infinite Being? Has he not power to bar them out? Yes, I reply, if he lives out of his boundless freedom and, from moment to moment, acts unpledged, conducting all things by the miscellany of incalculable miracles, there is nothing to hinder his Will from entering 'where it listeth,' and all things will be 'possible to him.' But, if once he commits his Will to any determinate method, and for the realization of his ends selects and institutes a scheme of instrumental rules, he thereby shuts the door on a thousand things that might have been before; he has defined his cosmical equation, and only those results can be worked out from it which are compatible with the values of its roots. If the square of the distance gives the ratio of decreasing gravitation, the universe must forego the effects which would arise from the rule of the cube. If, for two transparent media, the index of relative refraction is made constant, the phenomena are excluded which would arise were it variable. Every legislative volition narrows the range of events previously open, and substitutes necessity for contingency; and a group or system of laws, in providing for the occurrence of one set of phenomena, relinquishes the conditions of another. It is vain, therefore, to appeal to the almightiness of God, unless you mean to throw away the relations of any established universe and pass into his unconditioned infinitude; in the cosmos he has abnegated it; and there is a limit for what you may demand from it as within its compass. The limits, it is true, which are assigned to its play are *self-imposed:* but, in order to any determinate action at all, *some* limits had to be assigned:

and unless you can show that to a different scheme better possibilities and a less mixed good would have attached themselves, a tone of complaint which can only be justified by such comparative criticism is out of place."[1]

As to the existence of pain in animals, it is quite conceivable, as J. S. Mill points out, that the liability to it is an indispensible condition of the enjoyment of pleasure. The psychological principle of relativity appears, indeed, to indicate that such a necessary relation between pleasure and pain is not only conceivable, but is the real state of the case; and the beneficent mission of want and suffering in directing the animal's conduct aright, and in preserving it from greater ills, has been a common theme of moralists from ancient times.[2]

---

[1] Vol. II. p. 85, 1st ed.

[2] There is another aspect of nature which has often been noticed by theists as indicating the *ethical* as well as the *logical* unity of the cosmos. It is so admirably expressed in a recent sermon by the Rev. J. Thomas, M.A., and is so strongly confirmative of the conclusion which we have reached by another route, that I feel impelled to append the passage: "Selfishness is self-destructive. This law arises from the fundamental ethical principle that ethical life is the realization of self through what is other than self. Indeed we find this law of inter-dependence everywhere, revealing that *even the physical creation is ethical at heart.* All things thrive in proportion as they relate themselves to the world around them, in proportion as they surrender themselves to their environment. While the branches surrender their independence, and lose themselves in the tree, they grow beautiful with leaf and flower and fruit; but, as soon as they detach themselves from the general life, they begin to wither and rot, and men gather them into bundles, and burn them. While the members surrender their individual life to the one life of the body, the rich blood courses through them and they become strong and vigorous, but a severed member soon becomes a withered, shapeless thing. So the selfish man ethically destroys himself by selfishness. It is as we lovingly

There remains one more aspect of this grand problem of justifying the ways of God in the cosmos to the questioning intellect and the ethical insight of His offspring, man; it is the presence of God in History, and the question whether the facts of History support the theistic position that those forces, or springs of action, in human nature, which the ethical consciousness declares to be intrinsically the higher, do, as human nature and social organisms develop, become more and more the regnant principles which control and subjugate the relatively lower passions and affections of mankind. Along the line of argument which leads to an affirmative answer to this question I cannot in these Lectures travel; but this is no cause for regret, for even should I attempt so to do, you would find me a far less competent and interesting guide than the one that is ready at your hand in Dr. Martineau's powerful chapter on the "Triumphs of Force in History."[1]

I may conclude this outline-sketch of a Theodicy with the repetition of the remark which I made in introducing the subject, viz. that I am not contending that, apart from the insight into the nature of the Eternal which man's ethical and spiritual experience affords, the out-

surrender ourselves to the larger life of the world, realizing that we are but parts of a Divine whole, in and through which we must find our true life, that our thought will expand into a nobler conception of life, our sympathies will be quickened, enlarged, enriched, refined and purified, and our action will become more holy, vigorous, intense and comprehensive. In proportion as we give shall we receive, and the power of perfect sacrifice is also the power of perfect life."—*Liverpool Pulpit*, March, 1893.

[1] *A Study of Religion*, Vol. II. p. 116, 1st ed.

VII. GOD AS THE SOURCE OF IDEALS. 277

ward aspects of the world of nature and of the world of humanity would furnish wholly conclusive evidence that God is Love. What I do contend for is, that the main features of natural and human evolution are confirmative of this Theistic faith, and that there appear to be no established facts, physical or mental, which even to our very limited vision are necessarily incompatible with that belief in God's essential character which the pressure of the Ideal in our own inner life continually inspires and sustains.

Lecture VIII.
ABSOLUTE IDEALISM.

The historian of religious thought in this country will have to chronicle, as a somewhat important feature in the speculations current during the latter half of this century, the appearance in England and Scotland, especially at the great educational centres of Oxford and Glasgow, of an importation of German philosophy, which has taken strong hold of many reflective minds, and during the last ten years especially has given a particular colour to much of our ethical and theological literature on both sides of the Atlantic. I refer to the movement of thought called "Rational" or "Absolute" Idealism; a movement which, it is admitted, has its origin in the writings of Hegel.

At the time when Hegelianism was first introduced into this country, some thirty years ago, it had almost ceased to be taught as a philosophical system in Germany, though no doubt it had left a marked and permanent impression on philosophical speculation. But philosophical thinkers in Germany had become dissatisfied with Hegel's system as a whole, and the prevalent interest had passed over either to such forms of spiritual realism as Hermann Lotze's views presented, or to those psycho-

VIII. ABSOLUTE IDEALISM. 279

physical researches to which Prof. Wundt at Leipsic and his disciples have given such celebrity. In the sphere of religious and theological thought, likewise, the Hegelian philosophy has, in Germany, largely given place to a theological theory in some respects essentially opposed to it, especially on the basal question of the freedom of the will, viz. the system of religious thought put forth in the writings of the late Albrecht Ritschl of Göttingen, and developed by Prof. Hermann and others. It is to this school of theological thought rather than to the Hegelian that the majority of the younger theologians of Germany now look for light and guidance.

There are, I believe, clear indications that Hegelianism as a philosophy of religion is already losing its interest in this country, and in all probability its fate here will only repeat what has happened at an earlier date in its native land. The logical development of its principles, in the writing of Prof. Alexander and of Mr. F. H. Bradley, leads to issues which will hardly satisfy any theistic thinker, and the present determined opposition to it by able men who have been trained in its principles, such as Prof. Andrew Seth, Prof. James Seth, Prof. Schiller and others, are all signs which indicate incipient disintegration. The appointment, however, of several thinkers of this school to the Scottish Gifford Lectureship, will, probably, cause it to remain for some time to come as an influential factor in the speculative religious thought of English-speaking nations.

On the surface it seems somewhat strange that the Hegelian mode of dealing with ultimate problems should have had any special attraction for the Anglo-Saxon mind, for, while British thought delights to keep very close to the facts of sensation, Absolute Idealism appears to soar into quite transcendent regions of speculation. Appearances here, however, are very deceptive. Genuine Hegelianism has very close affinities with the popular view of Evolution, and with prevalent scientific ideas. It is true that it lays down as its fundamental doctrine that all objective phenomena require for their existence a unifying principle of thought, which by thinking them gives them the only reality they possess. But when the scientist or the psychologist has once allowed that all his facts have on one side this philosophical or theological aspect towards the unifying thought, the Hegelian theory will not trouble them with any more call for the recognition of the activity or causality of God. In the Hegelian view the Absolute exhaustively manifests Himself in physical and psychical phenomena, past, present, and to come; and all that can be known of nature and God is to be learned by the progressive study of these phenomena. Direct action of the Universal Spirit on the finite spirit in response to prayer or aspiration, such as most Theists recognize, has no intelligible meaning from the Hegelian point of view. Every experience of the soul's communion with God has its only possible explanation in its inevitable relations to the other psychical facts of a man's inner life, and, therefore, its *rationale* falls wholly within the scope of psychological science. And as Hegelianism also rejects Free-will in the true sense of that term, it makes all nature, physical and psychical alike, a necessary process of evolution with the inevitable sequences of which no causal action, either of God's spirit or of man's spirit, can in the slightest degree interfere.

This will help to explain, I think, the fascination which Hegelianism, like Spinozism, to which it is very closely akin, exercises over the predominantly scientific mind; but it still remains a problem why it should have any great attraction for the theologian and the preacher. The explanation, I believe, is that very few preachers do really embrace the genuine Hegelian doctrine. While they imagine they are preaching Hegelianism, they are frequently much more in sympathy with the different theological position of Schleiermacher. Schleiermacher had such immense influence in Germany, because he was the great modern representative of that most real side of religious experience called the mystical. There are some striking similarities between his system and that of Hegel, but they are more apparent than real. Both of these great thinkers agree in their tendency to disparage what they call the "mere individual"; both insist on the principle that alike in Ethics and Religion "we must die to live," and declare that the essence of religion consists in transcending the ideas and the affections which belong to us as finite individuals, and in surrendering ourselves freely to the spirit of the Whole; both alike accept the fundamental principle of Pantheism, that there can exist no real and fundamental dualism of Will in the relation of man to God. In other respects, however, the followers of Hegel and those of Schleiermacher part company. With the disciples of Schleiermacher religious experience resolves itself finally into Feeling—

feeling of dependence on and communion with the Universal and the Eternal; with the disciples of Hegel the very highest religious experience resolves itself into clear Thought; and whereas the sympathies of the former are predominately with the Mystics, the sympathies of the latter are increasingly in the direction of Positive Science, physical, psychical and sociological; for, as Prof. Seth points out, "there never lived a man more wedded to hard fact than Hegel, and he had an instinctive aversion to seeking the Divine in some ideal beyond the confines of the world that now is."

My own impression is, that ere very long those theologians and preachers of this country who now look upon Hegel as the world's greatest thinker, will follow the example of their German *confrères*, and will recognize the truth that a system of philosophy which allows of no room for the immediate personal action of the Eternal upon the human soul, and which, by admitting no possibility of real antagonism between the will of God and the will of man, makes *sin* no fundamental *reality*, but simply a relative *appearance* (as Mr. F. H. Bradley calls it), is not the philosophy which either accords with, or renders intelligible, the deepest facts of man's ethical and religious experience. What Absolute Idealism really comes to, when its principles are fully understood and its necessary implications unfolded, may be seen in the writings of Prof. S. Alexander, in Mr. F. H. Bradley's "Ethical Studies," and still more clearly in this writer's recent metaphysical treatise on "Appearance and Reality," an important work which, in some of its features, vividly reminds one of Spinoza's writings, though it lacks that mystical doctrine of the *intellectualis amor Dei* which renders the Fifth Part of Spinoza's *Ethica* so fascinating to some religious minds.

In reading Prof. E. Caird's most interesting and instructive Gifford Lectures on the "Evolution of Religion," and his brother's captivating presentation of Hegel's views in his "Introduction to the Philosophy of Religion," I do not know whether I feel more delighted with the many precious and beautifully expressed thoughts which these writings contain, than I feel disappointed at the fact, which appears to me evident, that the truth and importance of much of the doctrine, and the gracefulness of the style, unintentionally serve to hide, rather than to reveal, the real nature and intrinsic character of the philosophy of ethics and religion which underlies these eloquent utterances.

Let me endeavour to explain what I mean. To do so, it is necessary to give in outline the view of God, man and nature to which the line of thought in the previous Lectures has brought me; and, therefore, I must beg you to excuse some repetition of what I have before said. Starting with our own consciousness, we have seen that this finite life of ours is felt to be continually dependent for its existence on an Absolute or Self-existent Being. We have noticed, also, that we are surrounded on all sides by energies which limit and restrict our activity, and we necessarily assume that these centres of force are, like ourselves, dependent sources of activity; we refer them, therefore, to the same Absolute Ground and Cause to which we refer our own existence. The cosmos, then, appears to consist of an infinite aggregate of centres of energy, some of which, under certain conditions, rise to sentiency, and others to clear self-consciousness. These all appear to interact, and by their interaction to produce all the variety of cosmical phenomena. To study what are called the causes of phenomena is the function of Science, and Science is satisfied when it has reached certain finite sources of dynamic energy which are adequate to account for the phenomena it is its business to investigate. We further saw that Science cannot answer the final questionings of the human mind. When Science has reached its finite causes and their laws of operation, it has not touched the ultimate problem. While it has been discovering and enumerating the various causes and laws of phenomena, Religion has been asking what is the fundamental Ground and Cause which is eternally keeping in existence all these infinitely numerous dependent sources of energy, or centres of force. As Lord Gifford truly says: "The human soul is neither self-derived nor self-subsisting. It would vanish if it had not a substance, and its substance is God."[1] As the forces in nature affect our consciousness, and our wills affect them, the natural inference is that they are of a nature like our own soul, and that, in fact, what we call matter is simply spirit in its lowest mode of manifestation. All the varied dynamic energies of nature are, then, of one substance, and that substance is Spirit. When, then, the religious mind looks round and asks for the absolute or independent Cause of all this infinite variety of dependent scientific causes—for the Cause, that is, which so constitutes and unifies them all that they form, not a chaos, but a

[1] Prof. Max Müller's *Anthropological Religion*, p. 392.

rational cosmos—the answer necessarily is, that this Absolute Cause must be that deeper Self which we find at the very heart of our own self-consciousness. If, then, all the dynamic centres or souls in the universe are spiritual in their nature, and the Eternal Self is at the inmost core of every one of them, the only reasonable and satisfactory account of their relation to Him is that the Absolute and Eternal One (who, by reason of His creating our finite minds, must have all the essential elements of self-consciousness in Himself), in virtue of the action of His Will, creates out of His own substance, by an eternal act of self-differentiation, this infinitely varied aggregate of spiritual energies to which our souls belong. But as the Eternal Self is immanent in the self-consciousness of each of us, so He is equally immanent in every other monad, soul or centre of force in the universe. And not only does this follow from the fact that we feel Him within us, and therefore must assume His presence in all other finite natures, but it is likewise powerfully confirmed by the conclusive arguments in which Lotze has shown that the action of monad on monad, of mind on nature, and of nature on mind, only becomes intelligible on the hypothesis that all finite existences, partially individual as they are, are yet on one side of their being in continuous union with that Eternal Ground out of whose self-differentiation they arise. Were not the self-same God identically immanent in every atom and in every soul, not only would not interaction be possible in the physical world, but also in the psychical world all knowledge, all duty, all spiritual love, would be wholly inconceivable and impossible. We saw that the Eternal is not only immanent in our several spirits as the ground of all our mutual influence and intercourse, but also that He reveals Himself in His universal and essential character in our rational, our æsthetic, our ethical, and our religious ideals and emotions.

So far I reached in the last Lecture; and we have now come to the pivot on which the controversy between the Absolute Idealism, which Prof. Edward Caird so admirably represents, and the Ethical Theism which I am endeavouring to expound, really turns. From what I have said, you will perceive that there is in every finite existence a two-fold nature or aspect; there is the *individual* nature which belongs to it as being a separate differentiated portion of the eternal substance, and there is the *universal* nature which belongs to it in virtue of its continuous union with that Eternal Ground whose voluntary self-determination has given it birth. For our present purpose we have only to do with the mode in which this duality of aspect and nature presents itself in our own rational souls. We have seen in previous Lectures that no adequate account of the facts of our self-consciousness can be given which does not allow that with regard to the universal or ideal side of our inner life we in a certain true sense participate in the very essence of God's being. That is to say, that in so far as absolute truth, absolute beauty, absolute goodness, are apprehended in our imperfect and progressive Ideals, we, to that extent, share the essential nature of God; and hence it is that these Ideals ever carry with them a consciousness of their absolute worth and of their intrinsic authority to command our reverence and our allegiance. It is true that though they are in our nature and in God's nature too, they are not in us as they are in Him. In us they are a revelation of the perfection which *ought to be* realized, in Him they are eternally realized in His essential being; and it is only as the ideal becomes, in virtue of self-surrendering devotion and moral effort, actually realized in our characters, that man's Divine Sonship, which is implicit in him in virtue of his being of the same substance with the Father, becomes an explicit reality.

Were it not for this *universal* side of our nature, in which, so to speak, the Eternal Essence of God flows into and at times absorbs our finite consciousness, we could know nothing of absolute truth, of eternal beauty, of the ethical imperative and of spiritual love. And, on the other hand, were it not for the reality of our *individuality* there could be no sin, no moral heroism, no sense of estrangement from God, no joy of reconciliation with Him. It appears quite clear, accordingly, that an adequate philosophy of ethics and religion must recognize, and do justice to, both sides of our nature—the universal side, in which God reveals Himself in our self-consciousness, and the finite or individual side, in which consists that special selfhood of ours, that Will, which is delegated to us by God that we may freely make it His. Now it is recognized alike by the Ethical Theist and by the Absolute Idealist that the characteristic defect of Deism is, that on the *human* side it treats all men as isolated individuals forgetful of the immanent divine nature which inter-relates them and, in a measure, unifies them, and that on the *divine* side it separates man from God, and makes the relation between them a purely external one.

It is admitted also by both parties that the characteristic defect of Pantheism, on the other hand, is, that it does injustice to man's individuality, and by practically identifying man and God effaces all true moral responsibility in man, and all moral distinctions in the nature of God.

The Theist and the Absolute Idealist, then, are quite at one in asserting that both of these two extremes must be avoided, but each of them asserts that his own religious philosophy is the very one and the only one which hits the happy mean, and so escapes alike the lifeless Deism which isolates man and God, and the unmoral Pantheism which identifies them. Our question accordingly is, Which of the two, the Ethical Theist or the Absolute Idealist, is most successful in making good his pretension? Let me now ask you to consider carefully what Prof. E. Caird has to say on this matter. His clearest utterance is, I believe, the following:

"It becomes possible to think of *man* as 'a partaker in the divine nature,' and therefore as a self-conscious and self-determining spirit, without gifting him with an absolute individuality which would cut him off from all union and communion with his fellow-creatures and with God. I do not deny that there are many difficulties in this view, difficulties with which I have not attempted to deal. But it seems to me that this is the only line of thought which makes it possible to escape the opposite absurdities of an *Individualism* which dissolves the unity of the universe into atoms, and an abstract *Monism* which leaves no room for any real individuality either in God or in man; not to speak of the still greater absurdity of holding *both* of these one-sided views at once."[1]

If I had seen no more than this passage, and were not

[1] *The Evolution of Religion*, Vol. II. p. 84.

acquainted with the context and with other writings by Prof. Caird, I should be inclined to say that I heartily agreed with it. All through the long note, of which what I have quoted is the concluding paragraph, there are clear indications of the great influence which Hermann Lotze's writings have had over the author's thought. Evidently Lotze and Prof. Caird are aiming at the same result, namely, to reach a religious philosophy which sacrifices nothing really valuable in man's individuality, and at the same time does full justice to the universal immanence of God in nature and humanity. And if Prof. Caird had devoted a lecture or two to making clear his philosophical position in relation to Lotze or to Dr. Martineau, instead of giving so much space to extreme Deists and extreme Pantheists (specimens of whom are comparatively rare), he might have done a most essential service in extricating many perplexed minds in the present day out of their mental entanglements. For the fact is, that Hermann Lotze, as a careful student of the various forms of German Idealism, went through precisely the phase of philosophical development in which the two eminent brothers Caird now find themselves, but after a careful survey of that speculative region he came to the conclusion that it was not suitable for a permanent mental settlement, and so he journeyed on; and, as I have before said, I cannot help thinking that before very long a large section of the Neo-Hegelian party will, in like manner, strike their tents, and, following the example of Lotze, will seek a *Weltanschauung* in which their moral and religious consciousness will find greater satisfaction.

What, then, caused Lotze to move on? Simply this,

that reflection forced him to the conclusion that the words "sin" and "moral responsibility," without the possibility of real choice, without the presence of any *alternative*, are *voces et præterea nihil*, a delusion and a sham! It was in vain that the siren voice of Idealism whispered in Lotze's ear: "Surely if you make the choice yourself, if you are not determined to choose by some influence external to yourself, if your moral decision is the expression of your character, it is your own choice, and therefore you are properly accountable for it." To this "soft" Determinism, as Prof. William James, of Harvard, aptly calls it, the reply is: "If my conduct follows, as Absolute Idealism says it does, in this inevitable way from my character at the present moment, and my character now is determined with like inevitableness from my character of yesterday, and I have never had the slightest option in regard to the kind of character conferred upon me, then you may call my behaviour at any time *æsthetically* beautiful or ugly if you like, but *morally* good or *morally* bad it cannot be." And when the Idealist replies that "an indeterminate choice" is really quite incomprehensible by the human mind, Lotze answers: "Of course, it is incomprehensible and inexplicable, for if it were comprehensible and explicable by the human intellect, if, that is, it could be seen to follow necessarily from the pre-existing conditions, it, from the very nature of the case, could not be a morally "free" choice at all."[1] But, adds Lotze, this exercise of really

---

[1] "Denn angenommen, die Freiheit sei, so liegt es in ihrem Begriffe selbst, dasz es einen 'begreiflichen' Vorgang ihrer Entscheidung nicht geben kann, weil dies voraussetzen würde, dasz die Entscheidung

free choice is not the only fact the "how" of which is wholly incomprehensible by the human mind. We cannot comprehend how the mind moves the muscles, or how a moving stone can set another stone in motion; and if the Hegelian should reply that bodies have no reality save as groups of thought-relations, there still remains for him the insoluble problem how the Absolute calls into existence those "reproductions" of Himself which form our individual selves. It is, therefore, wholly futile to seek to invalidate man's consciousness of freedom of choice in moments of temptation on the ground of its "inconceivability."

If the final cause or supreme end of the Absolute in calling the cosmos into being was to produce a universe of which Aristotle, or Hegel, or Mr. Spencer, or some other intellectual giant, would be able to give a complete account which should be exhaustively intelligible by man, then, of course, the conferring of the faculty of free moral choice on His "reproductions" would have been eschewed as being quite incompatible with the object aimed at. But if the final cause of the eternal creation of the cosmos is not primarily the present satisfaction of the full demands of man's questioning intellect, but rather the institution

durch eine Reihenfolge einander bedingender Umstände, also nicht 'frei' erfolge."—Lotze's *Grundzüge der Religions-philosophie*, § 61; compare Lotze's *Grundzüge der practischen Philosophie*, § 18, and Lotze's *Mikrokosmos*, Vol. I. p. 288 ff. No student of this subject should miss reading Dr. Martineau's masterly chapter on "Determinism and Free-will," in *A Study of Religion*, Vol. II. Compare with Green's chapter on the "Freedom of the Will," in the *Prolegomena to Ethics*, an acutely reasoned pamphlet on "Freedom as Ethical Postulate," by Prof. James Seth.

of the highest personal relations between the Absolute and His rational offspring, then it is indeed inconceivable how this end could have been gained save by imparting to man a measure of real moral freedom. And if by the conferring of this most precious, but "incomprehensible," gift, scientists and academic philosophers are subjected to a certain amount of dissatisfaction, probably the infinite gain both to God and to humanity may well compensate for an occasional hiatus in those imposing expositions in which some eminent savans and philosophical thinkers seek to give a logically connected account of God and of His modes of manifestation in the universe. It is no doubt perfectly true, as Prof. Caird remarks, that the insistence on the existence of an alternative in any of our moral decisions " offends science by the assertion of a kind of freedom in individuals which seems to be the negation of all laws of causation; and it offends philosophy by the denial that there is any point of view from which the differences of things can be brought back to a rational unity."[1] The expression "rational," however, in this passage may possibly belong to that frequent form of fallacy to which our logical handbooks so properly call attention under the head of "question-begging" epithets. If by "rational unity" Prof. Caird simply means a unity wholly comprehensible by the human intellect, the statement is no doubt unimpeachable; but if this epithet is meant to insinuate that a universe involving the existence of intelligent beings morally free would be, from the Divine point of view, an *irrational universe*, I venture to think that the statement is about

[1] *Evolution of Religion*, Vol. II. p. 24.

as false as false can be; for the conferring on man the faculty of moral freedom is, I apprehend, an indispensable feature in that supremely rational scheme of creation through which the eternal love of God seeks to confer the highest possible blessedness on the creatures who are fashioned out of His own substance and made after His own image.

I am, accordingly, utterly unable to see how Prof. Caird's "Absolute Idealism," which manages to offend neither exclusive scientists nor exclusive intellectualists, can at the same time fulfil the needful function of being a true and satisfactory mean between Deism and Pantheism. So far as I can understand his position, it is simply unmitigated Pantheism, for according to it every moral decision which man comes to, be it called noble or be it called base, is an act for which no human being, but only God, is responsible. For where in Prof. Caird's account of the matter does real human initiation come in? At no single point. The Absolute, manifesting itself through the processes of evolution and heredity, is responsible for every man's special character, and every one's conduct follows inevitably from his character and his environment.[1]

[1] Since the above criticism was written, I have met with the following lucid expression of a similar judgment on the ethical aspect of Absolute Idealism, in a paper entitled, "A Criticism of Current Idealistic Theories," by the Hon. Arthur James Balfour, in a recent number of *Mind* (Oct. 1893): "Now it may seem at first sight plausible to describe that man as free whose behaviour is due to 'himself' alone. But without quarrelling over words, it is, 1 think, plain that whether it be proper to call him free or not, he at least lacks freedom in the sense in which freedom is necessary in order to constitute responsi-

In reading the brilliantly written Gifford Lectures by Prof. Caird, for whose genius and philosophical learning and acumen I have the highest respect, and also the newspaper reports of his eloquent brother's recent Gifford Lectures on "Natural and Revealed Religion," I cannot but feel how much deeper and more ennobling would be the moral and spiritual response which these thoughtful and graceful utterances would evoke in the minds and hearts of their hearers and readers, were it not for this depressing fatalism which pervades them and so seriously weakens their ethical and religious force. In his first Gifford Lecture, Principal John Caird says:

"By its cardinal doctrine of the unity of God and man Christianity dissolved the dualism and bridged the gulf between the finite and infinite which, apart from Christianity, was never spanned, and by its conception of the self-realization of God in

bility. It is impossible to say of him that he "ought," and therefore he "can," for at any given moment of his life his next action is by hypothesis strictly determined. This is also true of every previous moment until we get back to that point in his life's history in which he cannot in any intelligible sense of the term be said to have a character at all. Antecedently to this the causes which have produced him are in no special sense connected with his individuality, but form part of the general complex of phenomena which make up the world. It is evident, therefore, that every act which he performs may be traced to pre-natal, and possibly to purely material antecedents, and that even if it be true that what he does is the outcome of his character, his character itself is the outcome of causes over which he has not, and cannot by any possibility have, the smallest control. Such a theory destroys responsibility, and leaves our actions the inevitable outcome of external conditions not less completely than any doctrine of controlling fate, whether materialistic or theological."

VIII. ABSOLUTE IDEALISM. 295

humanity solved the problem which baffled the greatest minds of ancient times."

There is, undoubtedly, a great and important truth in this statement; but if Principal Caird holds, as it is clear from his later lectures on the "Problem of Evil" he does hold, that moral evil is the product of human volitions, and that these volitions could not possibly or conceivably have been other than they actually were, he empties of all real content his eloquent remarks about "sin," "repentance," "moral responsibility," &c. How he could persuade himself that, with his philosophical theory of human conduct, he could consistently use these words in the sense in which Jesus of Nazareth used them, is a psychological problem which nothing that he says enables us to solve. Christianity, of a truth, does bridge the gulf between God and man, but certainly not by the simple Hegelian expedient of making the will of man only the will of the immanent God under a different name. Jesus surely means by "Sin" something infinitely deeper and more ontological than it is possible for those thinkers to mean who accept the Spinozistic and Hegelian dogma that the real is the rational and the rational the real. I can only suppose that the minds of the lecturer and of his sympathetic hearers were so saturated with the remains of Calvinistic ideas, which for so long a time fettered Scottish theological thought, that the intrinsic incompatibility of this "soft" determinism with Christian ideas of sin and genuine moral accountability quite escaped their notice. Principal Caird can hardly have seen, as I have seen in several cases, how effective this Hegelian Idealism has been in undermining and destroying all real interest in theological thought and in religious devotion. My own experience quite bears out the remarks made not long ago by the veteran German philosopher, Dr. Schaarschmidt—for many years the editor of the philosophical journal, the *Philosophische Monatshefte*—who, in an article, *Zur Widerlegung des Determinismus*, thus gives the result of his life-long study of the various phases of "hard" and "soft" Determinism: "I regard the deterministic view of human nature, be it connected with foreign Positivism and Empiricism, or with native Pessimism and Pantheism, as among the most influential (*folgenschwersten*) errors of the present day;" and the whole drift of his paper is to justify the conviction that "the vitality of Religion, no less than that of Ethics, depends on the recognition of real Freedom of the Will."

I have dwelt at some length on what I conceive to be the fatal defect in this, at first sight, fascinating "idealist" theory of ethics and religion; but I am by no means blind to the great and permanent gains which philosophical thought has derived from the speculative movement which began with Fichte and culminated in Hegel. It cannot be denied that it is impossible to study the Hegelian philosophy, either in Hegel's own works, or in the writings of T. H. Green, the brothers Caird, Mr. D. G. Ritchie, or of the many other able writers of the same school, without feeling that whether we accept its fundamental principles or not, we have derived from the study a most powerful stimulus towards a reconstruction of a large portion of our mental furniture. A careful study of Hegelianism may, and does, I think, suggest the criticism which leads at length to its own rejection as a complete system; but, for all that, it has been a great educational influence, and none who have come under this influence will go out from it with precisely the same philosophical views with which they went in.

Allow me, then, to enumerate one or two of the important gains which present thought appears to owe this Idealism. In the first place, it has helped to lift off from the modern mind that paralyzing notion of the merely relative value of all knowledge which the Kantian philosophy, with all its merits, left pressing like a nightmare upon European thought. As Hegel himself said, Kant tells us what are the ways in which we cannot help thinking, and then adds that for that very reason these ways do not appear to lead to any true insight into the reality. Philosophy, accordingly, owes a debt of gratitude to Hegel for having reinstated thought in its true rights, as being capable of giving man a genuine and progressive insight into the nature of reality. Another direction in which, I believe, Hegelian speculation has effected a permanent gain, is in getting rid of the old notion of Matter as a mysterious substance with properties wholly unlike and incomparable with the properties of Mind. It attempts, indeed, to outflank Materialism by the simple device of allowing the most thoroughgoing materialists to have their full say, and then turning round on them with the remark, But how about your material atoms and brain molecules? they have no real existence save as objects of thought, and therefore the very thought, which you say your atoms produce, turns out to be the essential pre-condition of their own existence. I am inclined to think that this short and easy way of refuting materialism proves, like most very short cuts, to be a misleading road; but, nevertheless, it is largely owing to idealist thinking that the supposed impassable chasm between mind and matter has been bridged over, and the two have been linked together in the different systems of ideal or spiritual realism.

A still greater gain than any I have mentioned to the philosophy of ethics and religion, is the clearer insight which Hegelianism has given into the truth, on which I have insisted so often in these Lectures, that reciprocity of causal action is inconceivable, that the fact of knowledge is inexplicable, and the presence of absolutely worthful ideals in our consciousness wholly unaccountable, unless we believe that beneath the partial dualism which separates mind from mind, and all finite and dependent minds from God, there is a deeper unity of substance which, by its immanent presence in each and all, inter-relates part to part, and vitally connects every part with the unitary life of the Whole. In the earlier portion of this Lecture I have said that, in my view, Hegelians have carried this most true and important idea of the essential unity of God and man beyond its legitimate limits, and by denying that God has given to the Will of man any real power to put itself in antagonism to His Will, they have undermined the basis of Ethics, have turned Theism into Pantheism, and converted human individuality from being a real "other" than God into a mere finite phase of God's Eternal Life. Nevertheless, I believe that Hermann Lotze was much helped by a study of Idealism to that conception of a substantive Monism underlying the partial Dualism and Individualism which is presented in nature and in humanity, and was thus enabled to give to his philosophy of physics, ethics and religion that solid and rational foundation in the indestructible facts of consciousness upon which in the main it appears to me to securely rest.

There is another thought, at least as old as Aristotle, which Hegel and his followers deserve the credit of having emphasized and developed in a most suggestive and fruitful way, viz. the idea that in an organism a complete knowledge of any one of its parts, or of any stage in its process of growth, implies a knowledge of the whole; so that in studying the nature of a plant, or the evolution of the cosmos, the motto of the Hegelian is, as has been well said, *Respice finem;* and so with good reason they feel sure that Mr. Herbert Spencer's mode of explaining cosmical evolution cannot possibly turn out a complete success. On the merit of Hegelianism in this direction, Prof. W. James of Harvard says,[1] in his brilliant and humorous way, some words to the point:

"The principle of the contradictoriness of identity and the identity of contradictories is the essence of the Hegelian system. But what principally washes this principle down with most beginners is the combination in which its author works it with another principle, which is by no means characteristic of his system, and which for want of a better name might be called the 'principle of totality.' This principle says that you cannot adequately know even a part until you know of what it forms a part. As Aristotle writes, and Hegel loves to quote, an amputated hand is not even a hand; and as Tennyson says:

[1] *Mind*, April, 1882, p. 195.

'Little flower—but if I could understand
What you are, root and all, and all in all,
I should know what God and man is.'"

As Prof. James afterwards remarks, it is obvious "that until we have taken in all the relations, immediate or remote, into which the things actually enter, or potentially may enter, we do not know all *about* the thing." But when Hegelians jump from this sound Aristotelian doctrine to the wholly different doctrine that the *relations* constitute the *reality* of the thing, they perform a very questionable feat of intellectual gymnastics.

Having thus endeavoured to appraise, as fairly as I can, the permanent good which Hegelian speculation has, directly or indirectly, conferred on philosophy, I will now recal your attention to what appears to me to be the fatal defect in the system. Its chief defect I take to be this, that in representing both nature and man as merely moments in the self-evolution of the Idea, or self-existent thought-principle, it deprives both physical and psychical existences of that degree of selfhood or independent reality which is, on the one hand, needful for any satisfactory science of the cosmos, and, what is far more important, is quite indispensable for a satisfactory *rationale* of man's ethical and religious consciousness.

The limits of these Lectures do not allow of my criticizing the grounds on which Green and others maintain that all that we call reality in nature has no other meaning than is implied in the fact that physical things are thought by some self-consciousness. In a previous Lecture I have glanced at this subject and pointed out that Green's theory of "reality" is quite incapable of giving any intelligible explanation of the reality of pains and pleasures to irrational animals themselves. Practically the further discussion of this subject is hardly, I think, called for, seeing that the popular theories of evolution have, for the nonce at all events, taken all life out of the pretensions of idealism, whether it be the sensational idealism of Mill, or the rational idealism of Green, to resolve the dynamic sequences of the cosmos into a necessary succession of relations in the human or Divine consciousness. You will no more persuade the evolutionist of the present day that the formation of solar systems, and the successive stages of geological and biological evolution, have no other reality than that they are necessary stages in the thought of the Eternal, than, in that wonderful story, "Through the Looking-glass," Tweedledum and Tweedledee were able to convince Alice that she was nothing more than "a sort of thing in the Red King's dream."[1] Tell the scientist that the facts of cosmical evolution are the successive manifestations of the *Will*, or energizing of God, as well as of His Thought, and you may, perhaps, carry him with you. What science imperatively demands, and will never cease to demand, is a real *dynamic* ground and cause for the eternal sequences of natural phenomena, and no subtile manipulation of the *idea* of Force will ever succeed in supplying the place of the *real force* with whose presence and activity neither common sense, nor science, nor sound philosophy, can possibly dispense. At any rate, everybody knows that his own will does not derive its reality

[1] See the late Prof. W. K. Clifford's *Lectures and Essays*, Vol. II. p. 143.

simply from being an object of the Eternal Subject, and by necessary analogy he cannot help concluding that both the energies of nature and the souls of animals have some other hold on reality than is expressed by referring them to the objective side of the Eternal Self-consciousness.

However, in this course of Lectures we are not so much concerned with the question of the kind and degree of reality which Absolute Idealism allows to the centres of force in nature or to the souls of animals. The crucial question with us at present is: What kind of reality, and what degree of real causality, does Hegelianism allow to the human individuality, to this Personal Self with whose character and responsibility both Ethics and Religion are so vitally concerned? I hope I have made it clear to you that in regard to the *universal* features of our consciousness, in regard to our reason and to the essence of our ideals, there is no real dualism between man and God; but the common consciousness of mankind declares that in the case of the *Will* which constitutes the essence of each man's individuality there is a real dualism, and therefore a possible antagonism, between the will of the dependent spirit, man, and the Will of the Absolute and Universal Spirit, God. I also maintain that such real duality of will, and not the *appearance* of duality, as Mr. F. H. Bradley puts it, is the essential condition, not only of all true ethical relations between man and God, but also of those personal relations between our finite minds and the immanent Eternal in which consists the highest blessedness of man, and, if the deepest intuitions of man's spiritual experience tell true, the highest blessedness of God likewise. It is on this field of thought that the great battle of the religious philosophies—the battle between the Ethical Theism of such thinkers as Lotze, Ritschl and Dr. Martineau, and the Absolute Idealism of Hegel and his disciples—will have to be fought out.

Goethe, in one of his poems, says:

> "Freundlos war der grosse Weltenmeister,
> Fühlte Mangel, darum schaf Er Geister."

Let us, accordingly, consider whether the Hegelian account of these "*Geister*"—which, in Goethe's view, the great World-master projects, in some way incomprehensible to us, out of His own substance that they may be a real "other" to Himself, so that He and they may enter into responsive and reciprocal personal relations—let us consider, I say, whether the sort of individuality which in Hegel's view is conferred on man by God is really such as, on the one hand, to allow of true *ethical* relations between man and God, and, on the other hand, to meet that eternal need, or, I should rather say, that Eternal Love in God, in which the manifested universe, with man as its culmination, has its perpetual ground and source. If Divine Love has called into existence these human individualities that they may be able in a measure to understand His essential character, and so of responding in an ever-increasing degree to His infinite Perfection, then surely these individualities, these *Geister*, are ends in themselves of God's Eternal energizing, and the preservation of their separate reality must be a matter of quite infinite importance in the cosmical economy. Hence the quite limitless value set upon each human soul in the world's highest and most influential religious literature; and quite in accord with this is Kant's assertion that the only thing which possesses absolute value in the universe is a "Good Will."

As I before mentioned, there are solid grounds for concluding that this high estimate of the value of the individual soul is mainly the outcome of Hebrew and Christian influences, and that the germ of this great truth may be traced back to the special prominence which the higher minds among the Hebrews gave to moral conduct and to the ethical consciousness. To recal what I said in the last Lecture: just as the belief in an external world has arisen out of the experience of resistance to our volitional efforts, so whenever the ethical experiences of life receive steady attention, it is found that in these experiences man encounters an authority which is felt to be entirely distinct from any product of his own finite individuality, or of the collective individualities of the society of which he forms a part. Two indestructible facts of consciousness will always save mankind from being permanently the slave of Pantheistic illusions; first, the rational consciousness that our finite selves are not primitive or self-existent, but are dependent on a deeper and Absolute Reality; and secondly, the ethical consciousness that our personal wills are capable of being resisted by the inner self-revelation of a higher and Absolute Will. When an ideal of conduct whose worth we recognize clashes with our own personal desires, we cannot give any more satisfactory interpretation of what we feel than in saying that an infinite source of authority reveals its presence in our self-consciousness, enjoining this, forbidding that; and all other interests in life are felt to be really subordinate in importance to man's harmonious or antagonistic relation to this felt inner authority. Out of this experience springs a very clear conception of a real distinction of Causality in God and man; and when this distinction is attended to and fairly estimated, it wholly prevents the possibility of regarding man as a mere phase or mode of manifestation of the Eternal Unity or Self.

Let me now refer to some of the grounds which, in my view, justify the charge that Hegelianism ignores or undervalues individual personality, and tends to explain away and dissipate that real and vital distinction between the will of the individual man and the Will of God on which all genuine conviction of moral responsibility ultimately rests. I will begin with a passage out of Hegel's *Encyclopædie*,[1] in which he briefly describes the relation of God to man and nature.

"The good," he says, " the absolute good eternally accomplishes itself in the world, with the result that it is already accomplished in and for itself and does not require to wait for us. That it does so wait is the illusion in which we live, and which is the sole active principle upon which interest in the world rests. The idea, in its process, causes this illusion to itself, sets another over against itself, and its whole action consists in cancelling this illusion. Only from this error does the truth spring, and herein alone lies the reconciliation with error and finitude: otherness or error as cancelled is itself a necessary moment of truth which *is* only in so far as it makes itself its own result."

---

[1] *Works*, Vol. VI. p. 15. Some excellent critical remarks by Rosmini on this passage will be found in Prof. Thomas Davidson's *Philosophical System of Rosmini-Serbati*, p. 145.

From Hegel's way of viewing human life, then, it follows that both the finite individual himself, and all that we find most interesting in the individual, his moral struggles, his gradual growth of character, are, when looked at from the high philosophical standpoint, or, as Spinoza would say, *sub specie æternitatis*, part of an endless series of transient illusions. Goethe's *Weltenmeister* would surely find little relief from the sense of friendlessness in the timeless consciousness of this alternate positing and cancelling of illusions.

And here a few words seem called for on this doctrine that the Eternal Self-consciousness is *timeless*. Green, in the First Book of his "Prolegomena to Ethics," says that every act of knowledge in the case of man is a timeless act. In comparing the different aspects of the stream of successive phenomena the mind must, he says, be itself out of time. I cannot myself feel the force of his reasoning. Surely all that is needed for such knowledge is that the self that knows should remain really identical with itself through all the successive changes in its conscious states. And though we are entering a purely speculative region when we ask whether Time is an essential condition in the very nature of God, I cannot for my own part see any sound reason for the conclusion that the eternal series of physical and mental phenomena, which to us are past, present and future, are all equally present at once to the self-consciousness of God. Not only is such a statement one which conveys no positive idea to the human mind, and which if true would make man's moral freedom a self-contradiction, but it appears to me to deny to the Supreme

Being all those aspects of consciousness which lend interest to our own life. If the consciousness of the Eternal is timeless, then, as Hegel says, to Him our individual selves and our development of character must appear as illusions; but if He waits to see the issue of that moral freedom which He has conferred on us, and at every moment out of the reserved possibilities which He keeps in His own hands neutralizes as effectually as possible the temporary disorder that our misused freedom may occasion, then the relation between the individual soul and God is of perpetual and ever new interest to the Eternal as well as to man; and instead of the Hegelian idea of God's self-consciousness as an eternal cancelling of illusions, we have the Christian idea of God as taking an infinitely varied interest in the history of the plurality of real individuals whom His creative love calls into existence.[1]

The essential inability of Absolute Idealism to extri-

[1] On this difficult question of God's relation to Time, Prof. James of Harvard, in a very able article on "The Dilemma of Determinism," in the *Unitarian Review* for Sept. 1884, writes : " Is not, however, the "timeless mind" rather a gratuitous fiction ? and is not the notion of eternity being given at a stroke to omniscience only just another way of whacking upon us the block-universe, and of denying that possibilities exist ?—just the point to be proved. To say that Time is an illusory appearance is only a roundabout way of saying that there is no real plurality and that the frame of things is an absolute Unit. Admit plurality, and time may be its form. To me, starting from the appearance of plurality, speculations about a timeless world in which it cannot exist are about as idle as speculations about a space of more than three dimensions—good intellectual gymnastics, perhaps, but at bottom trifles, *nugæ difficiles*." See also Lotze's *Metaphysics*, p. 268ff., where, in opposition to Kant, Lotze emphatically contends for the transcendental validity of Time.

cate itself from fatalistic and Pantheistic conceptions of human nature is most clearly exhibited in Green's "Prolegomena to Ethics." And it is most clearly seen here because the ethical intensity of Green's own mind always prompted him to take an estimate of personality antithetic to that which the idealist philosophy allows. In fact, he uses language at times which is altogether Kantian and not Hegelian. Thus he says: "In virtue of his character as knowing, we are entitled to say that man is, according to a certain well-defined meaning, a Free Cause." The reading of the "Prolegomena to Ethics" does not enable me to see how man can be supposed, on Green's theory, to have either original causality or freedom. For what does Green mean by an individual man? His account of man's origin and nature is as follows: when, in the course of the development of the objective side of God's thought, a particular organization, the human body, appears, then God's eternal self-consciousness *reproduces* itself in connection with this body. To use his own words:

"Our consciousness may mean either of two things; either a function of the animal organism which is being made gradually and with interruptions a vehicle of the eternal consciousness; or that eternal consciousness itself as making the animal organism its vehicle, and subject to certain limitations in so doing, but retaining its essential characteristic as independent of time, as the determinant of becoming which has not and does not itself become."[1]

It thus appears that man is regarded by Green under two aspects, first, as a mere individual having a beginning

[1] *Prolegomena to Ethics*, p. 72.

and a history; and, second, as the eternal or timeless consciousness under certain limitations. Unfortunately, it is a great source of confusion in Green's reasoning that he uses the term "consciousness" in a double sense, at one time meaning the self-consciousness of the individual man, at another the Eternal Self-consciousness; for, indeed, he cannot consistently with his first principles distinguish the two.

Let us see, then, if in either of these aspects of human nature we can find any point where man as an individual exercises any free, self-determining choice. Green's main contention is that what is properly called Determinism means natural causation, as when a moving body moves other bodies, or when an animal acts under the influence of its strongest appetite; and he maintains that man's moral choices do not fall under this category. Green believes that he can avoid determinism by maintaining that a man's motives, when he makes a moral choice, are not influences outside of a man's self, but are an integral part of his own nature or character; and therefore to say that a man is determined by motives is to say that he is self-determined, that is, free. In order to make this intelligible, Green entirely alters the usual meaning of the word "motive." The contention of the believer in Free-will is that man, in the critical moments of temptation, is not merely a theatre on which conflicting motives contend, but is himself able, by having his power of attention at his own free disposal, to so act upon his own ideas or emotional states as to make one or the other the dominant one. Now Green departs altogether from past philosophical usage; he calls the above competing influences, so long as a man's mind is not made up as to which of them he will chose, not "motives," but mere "solicitations of desire"; they do not become motives, he tells us, till the self-consciousness has identified itself with one or the other; then they are changed into motives, or elements in the self, which, under their collective influence, presents some one line of action to itself as its greatest good.

Whether Green has done any service to psychology by this change in the meaning of the word "motive" is doubtful, but at any rate it does not affect the point at issue between him and the believer in free-will, but only alters the phraseology employed. Green says the self makes its motives by identifying itself with one solicitation of desire rather than with another. Here, then, is the point at which, if anywhere, free-will is exercised. The libertarian, accordingly, wishes to know from the idealist whether the self has *any power of alternative choice* in thus identifying itself with one solicitation of desire rather than with another. It is of no avail that Green tells us that the very fact of our being able to know that we have these several solicitations of desire shows that we are the vehicles of an eternal or timeless self. That may or may not be, but the question at issue is: Have we as individual selves, selves with a history and a character developing in the direction of good or ill—have we a power of preference, a choice of alternatives, in the act of identifying ourselves with a certain solicitation of desire? Here is the important point; and here it is that, evidently against his own natural impulse, the necessities of the philosophy he has adopted compel Green to give such an account of the human personality as virtually makes each individual's history and the growth of that individual's character as much a matter of natural or necessary causation as is the development of a tree or of any one of the lower animals. What is the individual man according to Green? A particular form of character. And what is his will? This same character expressing itself in action.

"A man's character," he says, "is himself. His character necessarily shows itself in his will; man being what he is and the circumstances being what they are at any particular conjuncture, the determination of the will is already given, just as an effect is given in the sum of its conditions. The determination of the will might be different, but only through the man being different."[1]

It is clear, then, that there is not the slightest opportunity for the exercise of true freedom of will in human nature as Green depicts it.

In truth, there is no real individual self in Green's view. That which *knows* in our nature is not our individual self, but God's timeless Self using us as its vehicle. If we look into our consciousness in moments of temptation, we become aware, I believe, that our own true Self causally acts by way of attention upon our mental states, and according to the mode in which we employ this faculty of attention is our final choice morally good or morally bad. As Dr. Martineau pertinently asks: "Is there not a *Causal Self*, over and above the *caused self*, or rather the *caused state and contents* of the self,

[1] Green's *Works*, Vol. II. p. 318.

left as a deposit from previous behaviour?"[1] Now the characteristic feature of Absolute Idealism is that it will not recognize the existence of this Causal Self, though I believe every person is distinctly conscious of his own activity as such a Causal Self every hour in his life. But the Absolute Idealist resolutely ignores its existence. And, indeed, Mr. F. H. Bradley, in a long paper in *Mind* for July, 1886, entitled, "Is there any Special Faculty of Attention?" takes sides with J. S. Mill in holding that when we say we voluntarily attend to an idea, this only means that the idea in question happens to be more vivid or interesting than any of the immediately preceding or attendant ideas. It would be difficult, I think, to find a more flagrant case in which the clear deliverance of consciousness has unconsciously been perverted to meet the exigencies of a preconceived philosophical theory.

Of course, if the individual self has no causal power it has no real existence; on such a theory of human nature, all that our self-consciousness is capable of is simply *knowing*, and in knowing it is, in Green's view, nothing but a vehicle or phase of the timeless self-consciousness of the Eternal. Having thus handed over all that specially belongs to us as individuals to the action of natural or necessary causation, it is a mystery how Green could have imagined that he had left to the spirit of man any real freedom or genuine responsibility. And that Green's idea that moral freedom is possible to man in the absence of the recognition of any true individual self, capable of choosing between

[1] *A Study of Religion*, Vol. II. p. 227.

alternative possibilities and of exercising its causality in attention and volition, was simply a self-delusion, is strongly confirmed by the fact that one of the ablest and most earnest of the disciples of Green's school, Mr. Samuel Alexander (now Professor of Philosophy in Owens College, Manchester), has felt himself logically compelled to depart altogether from Green's conclusions on this question. In his work on "Moral Order and Progress,"[1] he writes:

"We cannot distinguish human action from other kinds of causation as being self-determined in the sense that the process of willing goes on wholly within the human mind—that nothing can affect the mind's action except so far as it becomes a motive, and that a man acts thus from his own nature. For the same thing stated generally is true of all action even in the inanimate world. All action is a *joint* result of the nature of the thing affected and of that which affects it. All action in this sense is equally self-determination and equally compulsion. The difference between human and other action lies not in some special character of the mind's unity, but in the higher development of the mental states; the mind in willing is aware of what affects it, the wall is not. But this difference does not invalidate causation; it only shows that we have causation working in a different subject. The consciousness which makes such a difference to human action, and on account of which human action is justly described as self-determination, is something merely phenomenal, not something which puts an absolute barrier between it and other action."

Prof. Alexander does good service to philosophical thought in thus working out the necessary logical consequences of the idealist's denial of true causality to the individual self. Take away this causality, and, as Prof.

[1] P. 337.

Alexander virtually admits, man becomes, so far as real responsibility is concerned, on a par with the tree or the stone. His moral character is, on this theory, an inevitable growth; heredity and circumstances are the sole arbiters of his ethical destiny.

How, then, about the moral sentiments—the sentiments of praise and blame? Can consistent followers of Hegel still continue using the terms "moral responsibility," and "remorse" for wilful wrong-doing, in the same sense which these words bear when spoken by those who believe that in temptation alternative possibilities of moral decision are open to a man? Green evidently supposed that his disciples could continue to employ this phraseology, for he argues that Esau might very well have felt remorse for his conduct, because, though the action which expressed his nature was the joint outcome of his circumstances and character, yet as the process of personal development involves the reaction upon circumstances of the self-presenting and self-seeking Ego, Esau was bound to regard the act as in a true sense his own, and therefore to reproach himself for it.[1] To this the reply is, that if the self-presenting Ego had possessed any faculty for doing anything beyond simply *knowing* the successive changes in its own character, Green's contention might have some basis; but how any one who sees in the whole course of his mental and moral development nothing but a process, every stage of which was inevitable and admitted of no possible alternative, can consistently feel *remorse* for his past deeds, is to me wholly inexplicable. *Regret* and æsthetic senti-

[1] *Prolegomena to Ethics*, pp. 99 ff.

ments of repugnance, at certain phases of his career and past character, he may very well feel; but if he feels what is commonly called *remorse*, it must be because his philosophical convictions have not yet had time to duly modify his sentiments.

On this point, Spinozism and Hegelianism, if consistently thought out, come precisely to the same thing, and Spinoza's words in the *Ethica* must, I believe, find an echo in every thinker who, like Professor Alexander, has mentally carried out Oxford Hegelianism to its inevitable issues. Repentance and Remorse are sentiments which, in Spinoza's view, have no rational justification, though for the good of society it is desirable that vulgar minds should not be prematurely enlightened in regard to this matter; and this is what Spinoza's words come to, for he says in his fourth Book:

"Repentance is not a virtue; that is to say, it does not spring from reason; on the contrary, the man who repents of what he has done is doubly wretched or impotent..... It is not to be wondered at, however, that prophets, thinking rather of the good of the community than of a few, should have commended so greatly humility, repentance and reverence. Indeed, those who are subject to these sentiments can be led much more easily than others, so that at last they come to live according to the guidance of reason, that is to say, become free men and enjoy the life of the blessed."

No doubt T. H. Green would have repudiated this distinction between a philosopher's esoteric and exoteric teaching, but I doubt whether, if you come to the conclusion that there is in man no causal self, and no conceivable or possible alternative in any case of human self-determination, it would be possible for a true lover of his fellow-men to find any legitimate stopping-place short of Spinoza's position. Still, the very fact that you feel doubtful whether it is for the good of mankind that you should indiscriminately disclose a supposed truth, inevitably suggests the doubt whether your philosophical doctrine has a sure foundation. It appears to me self-evident that the emotion expressed by the word "remorse" is wholly irrational if Green's view of the mode of the development of character is correct. As Coleridge says in his "Aids to Reflection:" "With a deterministic system of human nature, not all the wit of man, not all the Theodicies ever framed by human ingenuity before and since the attempt of the celebrated Leibnitz, can reconcile the sense of *Responsibility*, nor the fact of the difference in *Kind* between *Regret* and *Remorse*." If, then, the followers of Hegel disallow the existence of any alternative possibility in man's moral self-determinations, and yet continue to use the words "ought," "responsibility," "desert," "merit," "sin," &c., they use them, as Professor Sidgwick remarks,[1] "with quite new significations," for the view taken concerning the possession by man of true freedom of choice "is the pivot on which our moral sentiments naturally turn."

I cannot within the limits of a Lecture do more than glance at the objections to the Libertarian view of man's moral conduct. There can be no doubt that just at present the doctrine of Free-will is very unpalatable to a large proportion of scientists and philosophers; still, whoever reads the chief philosophical periodicals of England,

[1] *The Methods of Ethics*, chapter on "Free-will."

VIII. ABSOLUTE IDEALISM.

America, France and Germany, will be aware that there are not the smallest signs of any falling off of interest and vigour on the Libertarian side of this controversy; indeed, within the last two or three years that side has been supported by an increased number of able advocates.[1] In Prof. Alexander's work on "Moral Order and Progress," occurs the strange statement that only two writers of note now take the Free-will side, these two

[1] It is true that some of the idealist thinkers have of late taken to speaking very disdainfully of all who take the Free-will side; and it looks as if ere long it will require some little moral courage to profess yourself a Libertarian in certain select circles of Oxford culture. Mr. F. H. Bradley, for instance, in his recent thoughtful work on *Appearance and Reality* (p. 435), writes: "Considered either theoretically or practically, 'Free-will' is, in short, a mere lingering chimera. Certainly no writer who respects himself can be called on any longer to treat it seriously." It appears, then, that whoever thinks it worth while to discuss the reasons which have made Lotze, Martineau, Edward Zeller, Renouvier, &c., firm believers in Free-will, and have led Kant to assert that a sinful act "could have been left undone," runs at present the risk of being considered somewhat wanting in "self-respect." I cannot but think that Mr. Bradley hardly appreciates the very deep foundations in our moral consciousness on which the belief in our moral freedom rests. Even those who theoretically reject it practically accept it at times in passing judgment on certain acts of themselves and others. It is one of those beliefs to which the familiar line, *Expellas naturam furca tamen usque recurret*, is eminently applicable. The keenest criticism never wholly kills it; and if it is contemptuously pitchforked out of academic lecture-halls and college common-rooms, it picks itself up very speedily, and soon puts in an appearance again. Indeed, I have little doubt that could we, like Rip van Winkle, take a long nap and waken up in the year 5000 or 10000 A.D., it would confront us amid the most highly evolved social and intellectual conditions, and the old controversy would be going on, with the Libertarians as numerous and as sanguine as ever.

being Lotze and Dr. Martineau. We are all more or less apt to think the

> "cackle of our bourg,
> The murmur of the world,"

and no doubt in the philosophical circle in which Prof. Alexander's great ability gives him a distinguisted place, the current idea is that highly educated Libertarians are now an almost extinct race of which only one or two fine specimens still linger in existence. The Libertarian cause is, however, by no means so hopeless and helpless as Prof. Alexander imagines. When we glance over the list of recent distinguished thinkers, and find on the Libertarian side (in addition to the two eminent men whom Prof. Alexander specifies) such thinkers as Renouvier and Fonsegrive in France, Edward Zeller, Kuno Fischer, Dr. Schaarschmidt in Germany, Prof. W. James and many others in America, we cannot doubt that there exists reasonable ground for the expectation that Free-will will not only, as heretofore, have the support of at least nine hundred and ninety-nine out of a thousand of ordinary mortals, but also that it will by no means fail of adequate representation even in the highest ranks of philosophical culture.

In one important respect Green has quite failed to realize the true position of the believers in the freedom of the Will. He says that "on their theory a man may be something to-day irrespectively of what he was yesterday, and something to-morrow irrespectively of what he is to-day." This is not the case. The Libertarian never dreams of supposing that a man can act without motives, and what his motives are is strictly determined by what his character is at the time. What is a temptation to a man in one stage of moral development may cease to be a temptation in the next stage; and the acts of self-determination which modify a man's character to-day alter the character of the temptations or moral problems with which he may have to deal to-morrow. In every temptation a man feels the influence of at least two motives; and when he has decided, you may always in one or other of these motives see an apparently adequate explanation of the choice: it is only in our self-consciousness that the evidence lies that our own self's free causal activity in the way of attention counted for something in making one of the motives the prevailing one.

Following in the steps of Green, Mr. F. H. Bradley declares that Free-will is synonymous with "Chance."

"We must insist," he says, "that every act is a resultant from psychical conditions. This would be denied by what is vulgarly called Free-will. That attempts to make the self or will, in abstraction from concrete conditions, the responsible source of conduct. As, however, taken in that abstraction, the self or will is nothing, 'Free-will' can merely mean Chance."[1]

As I have before pointed out, our personal consciousness appears to me to emphatically endorse Dr. Martineau's assertion that man is a *Causal Self*, that is, he not only *has* mental states, but can attend to, and act upon, his own ideas and motives. In a moment of temptation he not only discerns which is ethically higher among the various impulses which arise out of his character at the time, but he is able to freely select among these conflict-

[1] *Appearance and Reality*, p. 435.

ing springs of action, and by attending to and emphasizing one, to cause that one to take effect on conduct; and the contention of the believer in Free-will is, that if man does not possess this power over his springs of action, he cannot, in any true ethical sense, be called "responsible" for the growth of his character. Accordingly, Mr. Bradley's charge that Free-will means Chance comes to no more than this, that some of man's self-determinations are intrinsically incapable of being predicted. Now the obvious answer to this is, that in a universe which is to subserve the highest moral and spiritual ends, a limited area of this contingency, which Mr. Bradley terms "chance" (but which I should term the sphere of man's free causality), is an indispensable constituent. Were that which Mr. Bradley calls "chance" wholly eliminated from the universe, and man so constituted that adequate psychological insight would give an exhaustive explanation in every case why one man becomes a saint or a hero and another man a hypocrite or a scoundrel, I venture to maintain that not only would all ethical terms have to be emptied of their now recognized meaning, but the drama of individual life and of human history would be deprived of all that makes it most interesting to the mind of man, and, so far as we are able to see, to the mind of God also.

It will be evident from what I have said that man's moral freedom can cause deviation from the uniform order of psychical sequence only within very narrow limits; still within these limits there is a sufficient basis for responsibility. The vast majority of every man's self-determinations involve no temptation, that is, no inner moral struggle; they are the inevitable expression of his formed character, and might be fully explained by any one who had full insight into the dynamics of his inner life. The only features of the moral life which are intrinsically beyond the reach of prevision are those in which *temptation* comes in. In such cases, the agent is not merely giving expression to his already formed character, but is by his voluntary self-determination *changing that character* for good or ill. Only, then, in the comparatively rare instances in which the soul is called upon to decide between the cravings of its lower self and the invitations and injunctions of the ideal, or between its previous moral ideal and some newer and higher ideal which puts in its authoritative claim, do we come upon the critical points in a man's changing moral history, in the case of which true freedom of choice is exercised, and therefore certain foresight of the result is impossible. Though such critical choices are comparatively infrequent in most men's lives, it is to the behaviour of the true self in such moments of ethical trial that the moral worth or worthlessness of a man's character is mainly due. Still, even when the character is undergoing a decisive moral change, this change ordinarily makes but a very gradual alteration in the man's outward actions, so that it is not at all surprising that, notwithstanding free-will, moral statistics preserve much general uniformity, and that we can in the very large majority of cases safely predict how a person whom we know well will act. Free-will is by no means that serious disturber of uniformity of law and possibility of prevision which its opponents are wont to assert it to be. It is indispensable as a rational ground for moral responsibility, for the existence of real merit and demerit, for the judgment of approbation and disapprobation; but what is necessary for the securing of these all-important ends is quite compatible with a modest science of ethics and with a philosophy of history which does not lay claim to a near approach to omniscience.

To sum up, then, the chief results of our inquiry: it appears to me that the Hegelian philosophy of nature, ethics and religion, lacks a solid foundation in the ultimate and indestructible facts of our self-consciousness. As Idealism cannot allow to the individual man the possession of a real and permanent Self, to whom a certain independent causality and freedom of action is delegated by the Eternal, it is compelled, however reluctantly, to represent individual human spirits and their moral history as merely transient phases in an eternal process of thought-evolution—a process which appears to the human mind under an illusory temporal and successively developing form, but which is related as a completed whole to the timeless *Idee*.

This denial of any real and permanent individuality and causality to man as distinct from God has for its necessary counterpart the effacement of any effective distinction between God and the world of matter and mind. God, when thought of by abstraction as distinct from nature and humanity, becomes merely the Logical Subject which serves to unify the collective groups and series of cosmical phenomena. The existence and laws of succession of all physical and mental changes involve their indivisible association with, and relation to, a timeless principle of thought. But as this timeless principle exhaustively manifests itself in phenomena, and these phenomena find their sole and sufficient explanation in the relations among themselves which science and philosophical reflection gradually discover, God, being equally a factor in all phenomena and serving simply for their logical unification, may, as a late student of Balliol acutely remarks,[1] be safely treated by the consistent idealist, both in the study of nature and in the study of mind, as what the mathematicians call *une quantité négligeable*.[2] And that this complete merging of all theological interest in a purely scientific and philosophical interest is the inevitable outcome of the system, is confirmed by the fact that it is not with Theology, nor with anything directly connected with Theology and Worship, that the majority of the more gifted and high-minded young Idealists are now chiefly concerned. Ethics and Sociology have in their case practically supplanted and replaced to a very large extent the interest which was formerly felt in religion and in the worship of the Eternal. Notwithstanding Green's and Principal Caird's

[1] *Riddles of the Sphinx: a Study in the Philosophy of Evolution*, by a Troglodyte, p. 327.

[2] Some Hegelians, such as Prof. Royce of Harvard, maintain that the Eternal One *knows* all physical and psychical changes; others refuse to predicate self-consciousness of the absolute principle of unifying Thought; but all, I believe, are at one in declining to appeal to the direct *volitional causality* of God; and hence it is that Mr. Bradley and his *confrères* are so anxious to show that the volitional causality in attention, which is commonly attributed to man's true self, is a psychological illusion.

cherished idea that their philosophical views furnish the only satisfactory *rationale* of what is deepest in Christian thought and sentiment, the fact remains that idealist interest and enthusiasm increasingly tend to find exclusive expression in the study of ethical theory and in noble efforts to apply and realize ethical ideals in social and political life.

There is another very serious difficulty, to which my limits only allow me to give a passing mention, which helps to still further weaken the Idealist's interest in Theology—I refer to the only too prominent presence in the world of Moral Evil. This is a serious problem for Ethical Theist and Absolute Idealist alike, and how the former seeks a partial solution of it I have tried to show in the preceding Lecture. But formidable as is the difficulty for the Ethical Theist, for the Absolute Idealist it is far more so. The Ethical Theist holds that God, as an essential pre-condition of ultimately conferring on man the highest possible good and blessedness, has delegated to him a degree of freedom of will, and so rendered it possible for him to make a bad use of this privilege, and thus to mar and retard within certain limits the realization of the Ideal and the Divine in individual and in social life. Hence in his view this sin and wickedness is an absolute evil, but it is an evil which is permitted to exist by the Eternal, because the effacement of it would mean at the same time the effacement both for God and for man of the possibility of reaching the highest spiritual good; and though it is permitted to exist, the limitation of it is ensured by the reserve of possibilities which are still open before the Divine Causality. But by the Absolute Idealist no portion of this Moral Evil can be ascribed to the antagonistic causality of man. In his view every feature in the process, the basest and cruelest, as well as the noblest and the most beneficent, are equally indispensable features in that process of self-evolving Thought which constitutes the universe. Every personal self-determination or choice, be it moral or be it immoral, is, from the highest point of view of the Hegelian, a perfect choice, seeing that it is "a function of the Perfect Whole."[1] This being the case, it is impossible, I contend, to see any valid reason why the principle of Eternal Thought and Eternal Love should, in its process of self-manifestation, take its way through all the actual depravity and suffering in the world, for in the view of the Idealist the Causality of God is wholly unconditioned and unimpeded by any possible counteracting causality on the side of the human will. And if it be hard to see why there should be so much that is morally repulsive in society, if the character of each human being is precisely that which it must be and, therefore, ought to be, it is still harder to reconcile with Eternal Love the fate of the many who appear to be unfortunate victims of this evolutionary process. If it were the tendency of Absolute Idealism to engender and support a faith in personal Immortality, we might find in this faith some clue to the solution of this dark problem; but, if we may judge from the latest utterance of one of the profoundest of the living thinkers that Oxford Idealism has produced, the hope of a Future

---

[1] See Mr. Bradley's *Appearance and Reality*, p. 508.

Life is likely to receive from this school of thought but very meagre encouragement.[1]

Here, then, I believe is an additional reason why the best aspirations and interests of many of the younger Hegelians are largely diverted from theological study and from united worship to what they feel is, at all events, a work about whose essential divineness there can be no doubt or question—the aiding to dissipate ignorance, to elevate social ideals, and to eliminate as far as possible all that makes for selfishness and vice.

All honour to them for their noble, self-forgetful aims! My only fear is (as I have explained in the previous

---

[1] Mr. Bradley thus summarizes the results of his reflection on this subject: "And the general result to my mind is briefly this. When you add together the chances of a life after death—a life taken as bodiless, and again as diversely embodied—the amount is not great. The balance of hostile probability seems so large that the fraction on the other side to my mind is not considerable. And we may repeat, and may sum up our conclusion thus. If we appeal to blank ignorance, then a future life may even have no meaning, and may fail wholly to be possible. Or if we avoid this worst extreme, a future life may be but barely possible. But a possibility, in this sense, stands unsupported face to face with an indefinite universe. And its value so far can hardly be called worth counting. If, on the other hand, we allow ourselves to use what knowledge we possess, and if we judge fairly of future life by all the grounds we have for judging, the result is not much modified. Among those grounds we certainly find a part which favours continuance; but, taken at its highest, that part appears to be small. Hence a future life must be taken as decidedly improbable:" loc. cit. p. 505. For a lucid exposure of the ambiguous use of the word "Self," which pervades and vitiates Hegel's treatment of the doctrine of Immortality, see Prof. Seth's *Hegelianism and Personality:* "Even if we take Hegel's argument at his own valuation it is only the immortality of the Absolute Self which it proves:" p. 226.

Lecture) that this social interest and enthusiasm is intrinsically incapable of permanently sustaining itself at a high level, apart from a truer doctrine of man's moral freedom and responsibility, and of his personal and ethical relationship to that supreme Self-consciousness on whom all human spirits eternally depend.

Lecture IX.
ETHICAL THEISM.

The philosophies of religion between which the thoughtful mind is called upon to choose in the present day may be divided into Theism and Pantheism. Deism is an accidental, and now probably almost extinct, form of Theism which grew out of a particular phase of intellectual culture. In the seventeenth century the great achievements of science were in the direction of mathematical and experimental physics. Hence, as Dr. Martineau admirably describes it:[1]

"The imagination of men ran easily into mechanical grooves, and nothing seemed perfectly clear till it could be brought into the likeness of *a machine;* every regular *consecution* of things was apt to be described as *wheel upon wheel;* every transmission of force, as the operation of a weight or spring upon clockwork, and those who denied the free-will of man pronounced him a *machine,* or with the prophet compared him to clay upon the potter's lathe."

Religious ideas, accordingly, were conceived in analogy with the prevailing scientific conceptions; God was supposed to have constructed nature, and, according to some few Deists, to have then left it to work according

[1] *A Study of Religion,* Vol. II. p. 188.

to the laws he had imposed upon it. Many Deists, however, admitted that God was ever present and active in general law; but still, even in this case, the law is regarded as a kind of external force compelling matter to take a particular shape and direction. And this mechanical way of conceiving of God's action was not confined to the Deists, or adherents of what was called natural religion; it pervaded the minds of believers in what was called revealed religion also, for revelation was regarded as simply a particular kind of external divine action, by which certain ideas were imparted into the minds of the prophets, and their authenticity as coming from God satisfactorily proved by the working of miracles and the fulfilment of prophecy. Hence all knowledge of God, when Deistic ways of thought were prevalent, was supposed to have its origin from without the soul, either in the observation of design in nature, or in the study of the supernatural revelations communicated by God through the intermediation of prophets. As this Deistic way of thinking was brought about in modern thought largely by the influence of science, so it began to pass away so soon as the main interest of science passed from merely physical and material phenomena to the study of biology.

As Aristotle had long before pointed out, in the case of an organism we have to do with the product, not of an external force, but of an immanent idea—of a final cause which seems to pervade the whole body, and dominate every stage of the process of growth. The application of this idea to theology caused in Europe a revival of the idea of God common to many of the early Christians and to the Pantheistic thinkers of India and Greece, that God is not an external creative energy, but the immanent life of both nature and the human soul. The energies in nature are now conceived of, not as imposed on nature from without, but rather as being the modes of action of an indwelling life or soul. This idea of the immanence of God in nature and in the spirit of man is common, then, both to Theism and Pantheism. It has taken possession, in some degree, of all forms of religious thought, and has given a new impulse to philosophy, to poetry and to art. Herein lies the explanation of the statement which we now frequently hear, that all religion of the inner and deeper sort must be in some measure Pantheistic. For this assertion is certainly true, if by "Pantheistic" we mean that the life and evolution of every object of nature and of every rational soul implies the indwelling presence and immanent activity of the life which animates and unifies the whole. But this conception of God as immanent in nature and the soul is not peculiar to what is technically called Pantheism; it is common to Theism also, and distinguishes both Pantheism and Theism from what was formerly called Deism. Pantheism assumes two chief forms, according as, on the one hand, the idea of God is first derived by abstraction from the universal elements of thought implicit in the human consciousness, or, on the other hand, is arrived at from the study of the phenomena of nature, through the apprehension of a common principle of which all the objects and forces of nature appear to be modes of manifestation. The latter Pantheism (now often called Agnosticism) may be distinguished as the lower or scientific Pantheism; the former, which is exemplified in such systems as those of Spinoza and Hegel, may be characterized as the higher, or metaphysical, Pantheism. This latter Pantheism, inasmuch as it regards God as a principle of thought, and sometimes as a self-consciousness, is often by its adherents, and by historians of philosophy, termed a species of Theism. In order, therefore, in the present Lecture to distinguish my own position from the position occupied by the Hegelians, or Absolute Idealists, it will be convenient to borrow from Dr. Martineau, as a name for the form of cosmical theory which, in my view, best explains the facts of man's moral and religious experience, the name, *Ethical Theism.*

From what I have previously said it will follow that there is much in common between the higher Pantheism and that Ethical Theism to which I now wish to direct your attention. Both Theist and Pantheist may feel in their minds and hearts the inspiriting sense of relationship with the Universe; both may be lifted above the common cares and interests of life by ideal imaginings and transfiguring hopes; both may feel the conflict between their personal life, with its self-seeking appetites and ambitions, and that universal life which is seeking unimpeded expression through their individuality. Both may feel all this; but they part company when they come to reflect on the real nature of the relation between themselves as individuals and that Universal Soul, that dominant Self of the Universe, as Dr. Martineau terms it, which reveals itself in the human spirit in the form of its purest and highest ideals. As I said in a previous

Lecture, I believe that the true relation of our individual self to this cosmical Self, or God, is more truly apprehended when regarded, as it was particularly by the Hebrews, from the point of view of our moral consciousness. And if we compare this Hebraic or ethical view of our relation to God with that feature in Pantheism which represents the human soul as an efflux from, and reproduction of, the life which animates and unifies the whole, we arrive at a clear distinction between the attitude of the Pantheist and the Ethical Theist in regard to the relation of man to that Eternal Life out of which he emerges. The Pantheist sees in his own inner life but phases or modes of the life of the Cosmos manifesting itself under such limiting conditions as the particular stages of biological, intellectual and sociological development necessitate; and though, as he contemplates his own past career, he may see much that is repulsive to his ideal of beauty and perfection in the sensual and selfish passions which at times in his case realize themselves in his character and conduct, yet he cannot consistently, as Spinoza admits, feel repentance or remorse for such phases of his existence, since from the Pantheistic standpoint they are all necessary temporal stages in the evolution of the Eternal Thought. To the Ethical Theist, on the other hand, the ideals which visit his soul and claim his allegiance are not simply influences from the Universal Soul which necessarily find a definite expression in accordance with the particular character of the individual soul which feels them; they are invitations and injunctions arising in the dependent soul by the immanent action of the Universal Soul, and the former is, to a certain very real extent, left free to determine itself in favour of or against these divine influences. The essential difference between the Pantheistic and Theistic attitude of mind may be realized as follows. Theist and Pantheist alike may with Wordsworth conceive of God as One—

> "Whose dwelling is the light of setting suns,
> And the round ocean and the living air,
> And the blue sky, and in the mind of man :
> A motion and a spirit which impels
> All thinking things, all objects of all thought
> And rolls through all things."

But only an Ethical Theist could, with Wordsworth, address "Duty" as "Stern daughter of the voice of God"; only an Ethical Theist could consistently say, with Browning, that God's plan was—

> "To create man and then leave him
> Able, His own word saith, to grieve him."

Or, with Tennyson:

> "Our wills are ours, we know not how;
> Our wills are ours, to make them thine."

So, too, it is only an Ethical Theist who could exclaim with Marco Lombardo in Dante's *Purgatorio:*

> "Ye who are living every cause refer
> Still upwards to the heavens, as if all things
> They of necessity moved with themselves.
> If this were so in you would be destroyed
> Free-will, nor any justice would there be
> In having joy for good, or grief for evil."

The Ethical Theist, then, does not believe that the highest aim of God in the case of human spirits is the mere development of reproductions of Himself under temporal limiting conditions, but rather that His own infinite love can only find adequate expression and response in giving existence to rational beings with some real power of free self-determination; and that in order to bring about the infinitely precious result that human mind and hearts should freely respond to the divine appeal, God vacates, in the case of man's moral decisions, to some real extent the exercise of His own determining causality; or, as Browning expresses it:

> "God, whose pleasure brought
> Man into being, stands away,
> As it were, a hand-breadth off, to give
> Room for the newly-made to live,
> And look at Him from a place apart,
> And use his gifts of brain and heart."

Now out of this distinctly personal relationship in which the Ethical Theist feels himself placed in respect to the Universal Soul, there arises that sense of union and communion with the Eternal One, which (to again quote Dr. A. Réville's words) "is a source of secret (though it may be undefinable) comfort, of which those only can deny the reality who have never known it."

In Professor Seeley's treatise on "Natural Religion," he represents what I have called Ethical Theism as only one form of Religion, and defines it as the religion of goodness, while he maintains that there are two other forms of religion which in the present day have also their sincere votaries. Besides the worship of Goodness, there is, in his view, the worship of Beauty, which often constitutes the only religion of the artist; and there is the worship of Truth, or of the natural laws in which the unity of the Cosmos reveals itself, and the search of, and reverence for, truth often becomes the only form of devotion to which the savant surrenders himself. As we have before seen, there is an ideal of truth and reality in which the scientific man believes, and to the attainment of which he may consecrate his powers; there is an ideal of beauty which the artist discovers with increasing clearness, and to which he seeks to give more adequate expression; there is an ideal of social perfection of which every great social reformer believes he has a perception, and which he seeks to realize; but, as was shown in the passage I before quoted from Prof. Rauwenhoff, the man who wholly concentrates his attention on one of these aspects of the Universal Soul, which reveals itself in him, and thinks of and cares for nothing else, is in the position of a somnambulist who is under the mastery of one fixed idea. The artist who is an artist and nothing more has not yet realized his own human nature, and the same is the case with the scientist on whose soul nothing but science makes a recognized claim. But when the whole of a man's nature comes clearly before his consciousness (as it must sooner or later), then he perceives that these separate ideals have no absolute claim upon him—that the moral consciousness may at times require from the artist to forego his art, from the savant to waive for a while the pursuit of science, whenever moral reverence or the love of humanity demands the sacrifice. Dr. Martineau, in his "Types of Ethical Theory,"[1] has clearly shown that as the moral nature of man develops it reveals to him the relative

[1] Vol. II. chaps. vi. and vii.

worth of the several springs of action within him; and the truly moral and religious man is always conscious of a higher claim upon him than his science, or his art, or his poetry, which on occasion may require him to leave his favourite pursuit and to obey the ethical summons which proceeds from the Supreme Source of all ideals. The so-called Religion of Science, if it is abstractly cultivated, constantly tends to pass into depressing Agnosticism; and the votary of Beauty can only reach the highest and truest loveliness in conjunction with that moral reverence, that spiritual sense of relationship with the source of all perfection, which Ethical Theism recognizes and intensifies. Hence it will be found, I believe, that while a cold and narrow Deism is unfavourable to a warm interest in science, in art, and in the highest branches of literature, and while Pantheism has always a tendency to subordinate the moral to the merely scientific, artistic or literary, Ethical Theism proves at once eminently favourable to an interest in science, in art, and in all social reforms, inasmuch as it regards all these ideals as having their source in that Universal Soul who is at the very centre of man's personality, and recognizes in man's moral perceptions a true insight into the nature of the Eternal, an authoritative guidance in all the vocations of life. There are not, then, I contend, three possible religions, as Prof. Seeley appears to think there are; for religion proper does not clearly show itself in human nature till reverence for an authority, manifested in the conscience, presents the soul with a supreme ideal, in which the presence and the authority of the Eternal One are felt to be revealed.

IX. ETHICAL THEISM.

As the soul, in its ethical and spiritual experiences, thus realizes the presence and the absolute worth of an Ethical Ideal, it spontaneously conceives the source of this inspiration, and of the spiritual support which accompanies self-surrender to this inner authority, under the form of Personality. And though reflection at once suggests that there are essential limits in our human personality which can have no possible application in the case of God, yet there are substantial reasons for concluding that these limitations may be dropped without affecting the essence of the idea, and that, in truth, our finite human personality suggests a deeper personality which is not, as ours is, dependent on another cause to create it, and on an external world to awaken and develop it.

Pantheistic systems, in as much as they represent the personality of man as merely a limited phase of the infinite and eternal Being, cannot conceive or admit of any true analogy between the personality of man and the nature of God. Thus Spinoza says that the human intelligence has no more in common with the divine intelligence than the animal we call "dog" has with the constellation in the heavens to which we give the same name. If, however, the human and divine intelligence were so utterly dissimilar, it would be quite unintelligible how it comes about that the human mind is capable of gradually interpreting that "materialized logical process" of evolution in which the Eternal Intelligence manifests itself. Hegel, in like manner, says:

"It is absurd to predicate personality or selfhood of the Infinite, which by its very nature is the negation of personality or selfhood; the *Infinite*, being that which combines and contains all, and which, therefore, excludes nothing."

To this Mr. W. S. Lilly[1] (following Lotze) pertinently replies:

"This would be true if Personality were a limitation. But it is not. In the proper sense of the word, Personality (*für sich sein*) can be predicated only of the Infinite. Perfect selfhood means *self-existence*. What we call personality or selfhood in man, is but the finite effluence from the Source of Being, in whom alone is Perfect Reason, Perfect Will. This ultimate reality contains within itself the conditions of its own existence. Man *does not*, for he needs the stimulus of the not-self to be conscious of his own selfhood. He does not need that stimulus to *become a person*; for the not-self does not *create* consciousness; it is merely the occasion of its manifestation. The idea of personality, like all ideas, is fully realized only in the Self-existent one; the original of all existence—which transcends all our ideas, yet in transcending includes them."

This Absolute and Eternal Being is manifested in the human consciousness as the originator of the soul's dependent existence, and of that supreme ethical law which man's developing moral insight ever more and more clearly apprehends. In this ultimate reality religion sees the Supreme Good in whom all ideals are realized; the Ultimate Ground and Cause of the Universe; the Self-existent One, out of whom all finite personalities proceed, and in whom alone Perfect Personality is realized. If this view of the Supreme Being taken by Ethical Theism be the correct one, it follows that the Pantheistic conception of God as simply immanent in the phenomena of the Cosmos is inadequate.

---

[1] *The Great Enigma*, p. 241.

Pantheism and Theism are sometimes represented as maintaining, the one the *immanency*, the other the *transcendency*, of God. Theism, however, as now generally understood, no less than Pantheism, teaches the immanency of God in nature and humanity: but while Pantheism holds that God's nature is exhaustively manifested in the cosmos, Theism maintains that the inner nature of God transcends all phenomenal manifestations.

"The Pantheist," writes Dr. Martineau, "can say nothing affirmative of God's agency which the Theist may not repeat. The conflict begins with the Pantheist's *negative* proposition, that beyond the natural order of things, and prior to it, no divine life or agency can be. It is this *limitation* of the supreme existence, the *denial* of a supra-mundane cause, which alone the Theist is concerned to resist..... It is simple ignorance both of the principle and history of his doctrine to charge him with planting all divine agency outside of nature except at her birth-hour, at an indefinite distance from its self-realizing purpose in the constitution of living beings. It is sufficient for him if God be *somewhere more than the contents of nature*, and *overpass them* in his being, action and perfection. Let this condition only be saved, there is no limit to the admissible identification of what are called 'natural powers' with him, or of organic purpose with his design."[1]

As Dr. Martineau has further shown, the very fact that the universe is the manifestation of a Divine Idea, implies that the idea must transcend its phenomenal expression. And not only so, but the facts of man's moral and spiritual consciousness remain unintelligible if the essence of the Supreme Being is supposed to be wholly exhausted in the natural order of phenomena which he calls into existence. All real religious experience proves that the Abso-

[1] *A Study of Religion*, Vol. II. p. 150.

lute Being who eternally manifests His energy in the creation of the world of matter and of mind, still out of the unpledged freedom of His own essential being enters into personal communion with His rational creatures. It is, indeed, in virtue of this transcendent freedom of God as a Spirit that real union and communion between Him and the human soul, which to many persons is a rich source of peace and joy and strength, becomes possible. As Dr. Charles Beard finely says, in his Hibbert Lectures:

"Many scientific men now tell us that we are everywhere in the grip of law; there is nothing in our life which is not accounted for by our inheritance and our environment; if God exists, He neither can nor will break asunder the bonds of fate which tie us down; we cannot feel the touch of His hand upon our personal life, and the best that is left to us is the faith that somehow in a general way, in which we too shall have our share, 'good will be the final goal of ill.' And the only escape from this spiritual imprisonment lies in keeping open a region of free and intimate intercourse between God and the human soul. There is the less difficulty in this, as the existence of such a region, the reality of such an intercourse, are precisely the message which religious men in all ages bring, out of the depths of their own experience, to those who have less insight than themselves. This they announce as 'the fountain-light of all their day, the master-light of all their seeing;' and not their light only, but their strength and consolation. And as this experience involves a series of facts as real and as little to be pushed aside as the embryonic changes and the aborted organs which are rightly regarded as so full of meaning, Religion yet retains the right of reserving to herself a space in which spirit may meet with spirit, on the one side in impulse and support, on the other in aspiration and self-surrender."[1]

[1] *The Reformation*, p. 397.

IX. ETHICAL THEISM. 341

These profound utterances by Dr. Martineau and Dr. Beard bring out into clear relief the fact of free spiritual intercourse between the Soul of souls and the individual soul. This religious experience, which few persons are wholly destitute of, while to some it is felt to be the most precious and significant feature in their lives, firmly establishes the Theistic position, that while the *immanent* presence and activity of God is manifested in the orderly physical and mental phenomena of which science takes cognizance, the *transcendent* action of God in human souls is no less evident in the authority of the conscience, and in the more or less vivid consciousness of infinite Divine sympathy and support through which the Eternal Self responds to the spirit's self-surrender to the divine voice within.

Most closely connected with this religious experience of communion between the finite Spirit and the Father within it, is the question as to the *continuance* of that communion. Is this communion conditioned and limited by the life-time of man's physical organism? or is this present life but one stage in a progressive intimacy with that Eternal Being, whence man derives his self-consciousness, his moral freedom, his capacity for limitless thought and infinite affection? If in calling into existence spirits capable of increasing response to His Self-revelation, the Supreme Being summons them to a destiny of which this present life is but the prelude, it may at the first glance seem most irrational that the same Love which purposed this Immortality should not have made it unmistakably clear that such a career of unending development lies before each rational soul. We should remember, however, that if Ethical Theism be a sound philosophy of religion, it would be an indispensable feature in the creation of human spirits who should *voluntarily* (and not by compulsion or bribe) draw near to the Eternal that the conditions of free moral choice should be completely secured to mankind. But could real freedom of choice be possible if it were a strictly demonstrable certainty that the character which we fashion for ourselves here by our daily moral self-determinations would inevitably affect our destiny through eternity? If earth is to be really a place for the growth of disinterested virtue and goodness, then *scientifically demonstrable knowledge as to the eternal consequences of moral conduct must be withheld.* As our great poet Browning says, in his profound philosophical poem, "La Saisiaz":

> "Once lay down the law, with Nature's simple 'Such effects succeed
> Causes such, and heaven or hell depends upon man's earthly deed
> Just as surely as depends the straight or else the crooked line
> On his making point meet point, or with, or else without incline,'
> Thenceforth neither good nor evil does man, doing what he must.
> Lay but down that law as stringent, 'Wouldst thou live again, be just,'
> As this other, 'Wouldst thou live now, regularly draw thy breath!
> For suspend the operation, straight law's breach results in death—'
> And (provided always, man addressed this mode be sound and sane)
> Prompt and absolute obedience, never doubt, will law obtain!"

And not only would this definite and absolutely certain knowledge of a retributive hereafter largely deprive our moral choices of true ethical worth by making self-love and virtue practically coincident, but as we now see, in the case of persons who become absorbed in real or supposed spiritualistic phenomena, the interest in the affairs of the after-world would be very detrimental to the achievement of the one thing needful here, viz. to the building up of a high moral character by virtue of earnest devotion to the realization of a lofty ideal under the social conditions of this present world.

If, then, we are right in supposing that the goal to which evolution tends is the development of free, self-conscious, rational beings, who by their own voluntary choice obey the injunctions and respond to the invitations of the immanent Universal Soul, we see that it is quite in accordance with this supreme end of the universe that the soul's highest relations to the Eternal Self, and therefore to the Future Life, should not rest upon that basis of demonstrable certainty which characterizes the mathematical and physical sciences, but should be of the nature of Belief or Faith, which admits of degrees, and the amount of assurance of which is largely dependent on the measure in which we freely surrender ourselves to the claims of our higher nature—pass, that is, into practical sympathy and co-operation with that indwelling Father who is only truly known as He is loyally followed and supremely loved.

But if demonstrative certainty with regard to the reality and conditions of man's life hereafter is neither possible nor compatible with the highest end of this present life, it is none the less true that it is indispensable, both for man's happiness and for his persistent moral endeavour, that a *faith* in immortality (a faith which at times quite reaches to moral certainty) shall be accessible to the human mind and heart. Such a belief, a thoughtful study of the cosmos, and of the highest phases of human faculty and character as culminating features of cosmical development, tends, I maintain, to engender and to increasingly strengthen. It is in the contemplation of the eternity and infinity which our highest powers and affections imply and require for their complete exercise and satisfaction, and in the consciousness of sympathy and ethical communion between the finite soul and the Universal Soul, that the belief in the continuity and indestructibility of the personal relation between the human soul and the Soul of souls reaches its maximum of intensity. But even apart from these higher spiritual experiences, the insight into the history and tendency of the physical and psychical universe, which our present scientific knowledge gives, affords of itself a strong presumption that both the resources of the cosmos and the destiny of humanity extend indefinitely beyond the limits where our finite powers of sensible perception reach the end of their range. For if we take man as the manifestly highest production of the long process of biological development, and study his powers and aspirations, we find that if we suppose physical death to be the end of the individual man's existence, the fitness of means to ends, the symmetry and rationality which appear to characterize all the lower forms of organic life are in the case of man conspicuously missing.

If we consider the upward trend of the brute creation, we observe that the insentient organic life of the vegetable is the necessary preparation for the emergence of the higher sentient forms with power of locomotion; and in sentient beings the nervous system, which at first merely subserves sensation, motion and reproduction, begins at length by imperceptible degrees to prepare the way for intellectual life. A new differentiation in the brain, which commences almost imperceptibly and is for a long time quite subordinate to the nervous centres of mere feeling and movement, gradually assumes structural and functional prominence; till at length the cerebrum, the organ which subserves intelligence, which in the lower vertebrate animals is hardly the size of a pea, becomes in man by far the most important portion of the brain substance. In the human being, the development of physical size and shape appears to reach its acme and stops, the process of evolution now concentrating itself on the development of the intellect and the higher affections, and on the more elaborate structure of the physical organ which appears to minister to these higher functions of life. The struggle for existence which has characterized the lower processes of evolution is gradually replaced by intellectual competition which results in the increasing development of man's mental powers. But even intellectual competition is evidently subservient to something higher. Beneath all this rivalry which arises from man's inheritance of animal passions, and from the application of intellect to furthering man's craving for self-preservation and self-gratification, there gradually arise and come to the front in human nature new principles which do not lead to competition and to the development of exclusive individualism, but, on the contrary, completely transcend all individual interests.[1]

Though the occasion of the emergence of these higher

[1] See, for a more elaborate and forcible presentation of the above argument, Prof. J. Fiske's admirable little treatise on *Man's Destiny.*

springs of action in human life is the growth of the sympathetic feelings which have developed out of the gregarious instincts of animals, yet by virtue of the dawn and development of the rational principle in human nature, ideas and sentiments arise of a quite universal character; and these new principles carry with them an authority to hold in check, and if necessary to overrule, the lower principles of competition and self-preservation. Hence arise in the mind living interests which cannot find adequate satisfaction within the range of this present existence—a desire to know which has no limits, a capacity for love which demands eternity, an ideal of moral rectitude and of beauty which advances to loftier heights as its lower forms attain realization, and so allows of no finite goal to man's rational, moral and æsthetic pilgrimage. In the lower stages of animal life, the appetites and instincts all subserve the well-being and reproduction of the animal's physical structure; but in man, springs of action, aspirations and ideals arise which altogether transcend the physical frame, which dominate the organism, use it for their own purposes, and, if occasion should arise, make man ready and willing to sacrifice even his own physical organism for the attainment of some higher end.

As Dr. Martineau eloquently writes:

"We here see the very impulses which begin as purveyors for the body ending with a conquest over its importunities, and a subjugation of it to rational, if not unselfish, aims. And, the moment we enter the inner circle of human characteristics, the interpretation of these characteristics as instruments for working the organism utterly fails us. Who would ever think of referring the sentiment of *Wonder* to its physiological use? It neither helps the digestion nor regulates the temperature; it succours no weakness, it repels no foe; the labour to which it incites, the enthusiasm which it kindles, often detract from the animal perfection and consume the organic powers that serve it, and only elevate the level and widen the relations of life opening to it intellectual interests and possibilities unlimited in extent and inexhaustible in duration.... It is not physically that we are nobler and more complete for our libraries, or theatres, or 'Schools of Athens.' Compassion, sympathy, attachment, also serve in us, no doubt, the same ends for which they more or less exist in other creatures. But how soon and far do they transcend this useful function, and claim a good upon their own account!... If you judged these features of humanity by a *prospective* instead of a *retrospective* measure, and asked yourself *whither* they look instead of *whence they come*, could you hesitate to say: 'It is for these that we are made; these it is to which we must yoke our physical power in humble service, by which we are to rise above it, and pass into a life of larger dimensions.'"[1]

As we reflect upon considerations such as these, we are spontaneously led to the conclusion, that as there is a striking harmony in the lower stages of the animal creation between the animal's appetites and instincts and its actual life, the same must hold good in the case of man also; and that, consequently, as in human nature there arise ideas and aspirations for which the limits of this earthly existence afford no satisfaction, the explanation of this apparent anomaly must be found in the belief that the soul's connection with its present physical organ is not the whole, but only the preliminary stage, of that career in the course of which its unlimited capacities and aspirations will find increasing exercise and satisfaction.

Whether or not our true self first begins to exist with

[1] *A Study of Religion*, Vol. II. p. 343.

our advent at physical birth we cannot say, but we have in consciousness clear evidence that this personality of ours preserves its identity amid the incessant changes of our physical frame. And if it be urged by the Pantheist that, though we are eternal in the sense of being a phase of the self-existent Absolute, our individuality is finite and transient, and that at death the efflux from the Eternal Self, which appears for a short season as a personal Ego, will flow back into the ultimate Unity out of which it arose, the Theist may well reply, that the rational presumption is, that personalities, characters built up by long years of patient loyalty to the Ideal, of self-surrender to Divine guidance, are infinitely too precious both in the view of each other and in the view of the Eternal to be allowed to perish. Dr. Martineau, in the second volume of "A Study of Religion,"[1] translates from "Schleiermacher's Life" a touching correspondence between Schleiermacher and one of his pupils, a young widow from whom a dearly beloved husband had been snatched away by sudden illness. This correspondence vividly shows how wholly unsatisfactory to the pure and loving heart is the Pantheistic doctrine of the state of the soul after death.

"I implore you," writes the bereaved one to her old friend and teacher, "I implore you, Schleier, by all that is dear to God and sacred, give me, if you can, the certain assurance of finding and knowing him again. Tell me your inmost faith in this,

[1] P. 360. The whole of this deeply interesting correspondence, with Dr. Martineau's comments thereon, is most valuable as exhibiting in the clearest light the intrinsic incompetence of Pantheism (be it the Pantheism of Schleiermacher or that of Hegel) to respond to the reasonable claims of the soul's highest and noblest affections.

dear Schleier: oh! if it fails, I am undone. Speak to my poor heart: tell me what you believe. You say, his soul is resolved back—quite melted away in the great All; the old is quite gone by, it will never come to recognition again; oh, Schleier, this I cannot bear!"

But Schleiermacher can only reply:

"How can I dissipate your doubt, dear Jette? It is only the images of fancy in her hour of travail that you want me to confirm. If he now is living in God, and you love him eternally in God, as you knew and loved God in him, can you think of anything more glorious?"

Nothing can be more pathetic than Schleiermacher's strenuous but ineffectual efforts to bring consolation to this stricken heart while remaining faithful to his own Pantheistic principles.

"True it is," he says, "that in the personal life the spirit does not find its essence, but only makes its apparition,—to be renewed, we know not how: all here is beyond our knowledge: we can only imagine."

"Ah, then," she thinks, "the apparition has vanished for ever,—that dear personal life which is all that I know; he is Ehrenfried no more: gone to God, not to be kept safe, but to be eternally lost in Him."

Most reasonable is this protest of her loving heart, for, as Dr. Martineau truly says, "Love—knowledge—where *persons* are not: can there be a greater contradiction?"[1]

---

[1] In regard to these deeper problems of the spirit, the insight of the higher affections is keener than that of the intellect; and the poet is often a better guide than the savant or the philosopher. Hence such poems as Browning's "Evelyn Hope" are not mere imaginations, but have in them an element of real inspiration:

But the doubt suggests itself, Where, then, is the departed spirit? and where is the body whereby it is placed in organic and conscious relation with the cosmos and with other spirits? Reflection reminds us that while recent science makes it evident that our actual knowledge of the universe is but slight and superficial, it at the same time suggests and renders probable the existence of far deeper cosmical resources of whose nature we have at present but a faint inkling. Our bodily senses do but admit to a perception of the outermost film of the unfathomable reality. With acuter senses, a richer world would at once open before our astonished vision; and it is not at all improbable that there exist different aspects of reality from those which we now perceive, to which new senses of a more subtile nature may give our spirits access. Even the scientific imagination, though it can penetrate far deeper than the senses, and reach that mysterious all-pervading ether which altogether evades our sensible perception, still starts profounder questions than any that

"For God above
Is great to grant as mighty to make,
And creates the love to reward the love;
I claim you still for my own love's sake!
Delayed it may be for more lives yet,
Through worlds I shall traverse, not a few;
Much is to learn and much to forget
Ere the time be come for taking you."

Of a like character is that grand Threnody which the death of his beloved and gifted child wrung out of the heart of Emerson, in which occur the lines:

"What is excellent
As God lives is permanent:
Hearts are dust, hearts' loves remain;
Heart's love will meet thee again."

it solves. The dissipation of force, and the as yet wholly unrevealed secret why, in spite of that continual dissipation, a past eternity has not brought the dynamic activity of the cosmos to a standstill, suggests a transcendent source of new cosmical life and energy, and warns us that human science is by its very nature intrinsically incapable of reaching an exhaustive and fundamental exposition of the inner life and nature of the universe. And as to the question of a bodily investment for the liberated spirit, it is by no means improbable that, as Swedenborg thought, each soul in this present life, as its character forms, is fashioning its own spiritual body—a body either lovely with the beauty of virtue, or disfigured by the impress of selfishness and vice. We need not go in imagination into remote regions of space to find our heaven or hell; there are depths of being immediately around and within us which open limitless possibilities as to the "where" and "how" of the departed spirit's existence. Nay, I am inclined to think, with Kant and Lotze, that Space[1] itself is but the mode or symbol under which finite minds, by the necessity of their constitution, picture the invisible relations of metaphysical reality; and while this beneficent constitution of our perceptive faculty is the condition of clear scientific insight and discrimination, it at the same time gives an appearance of isolated separateness to things, and hides that deeper metaphysi-

[1] If Space be an *objective reality*, it must be conceived either as an attribute of God, or as independent of God, and co-eternal with Him. To both of these alternatives there appear to me to be formidable objections which I am unable to surmount. In regard to Time, on the other hand, I have in the previous Lecture given my reasons for dissenting from Kant's view.

cal connection whereby all things, in spite of their partially independent existence, are yet on the inner side of their being inseparably connected with one underlying and undivided Unity.

If, then, neither physics nor metaphysics are capable of finally closing the door of negation against the possible realization of our infinite spiritual aspirations and quenchless loves, does not our *moral* nature also furnish solid ground for the positive assurance that of the seeds of character which in virtue of our free ethical activity we sow in this life we shall assuredly reap the harvest either here or hereafter? It is not *immediately* that either sinful or virtuous conduct works out its inevitable retributions. Sin and suffering are inseparably connected, and the suffering is at once the expression of Divine Justice and of Divine Love, for only suffering heals the spiritual hurt which Sin has wrought. As Dr. Martineau forcibly puts it:

"Our moral nature cannot run through its own cycle in our experience here. It announces a righteous rule which again and again it brings to mind and will not suffer to be forgotten, but of which it does not secure the execution. It is a prophecy carrying its own credentials in an incipient foretaste of the end, but holding its realization in reserve; and if Death gives a final discharge alike to the sinner and the saint, we are warranted in saying that Conscience has told more lies than it has ever called to their account."[1]

Further, is it conceivable that that wonderful thing called *Character*,[2] which grows stronger and stronger in

[1] *A Study of Religion*, Vol. II. p. 388.

[2] "Strange to say, it is in old age, when we are told all is decay, that the sinews of the spirit are more knit for climbing than the sinews

a good man's life, which is mighty enough to bear up patiently under all disease and trial, which no temptation, however mighty, can divert from its course, and *which grows firmer and solider as the body ages and grows weaker*—is it conceivable, I ask, that this spiritual nature, whose life and growth is by no means parallel with that of our mere physical structure, should at the same time be vitally implicated in the act of physical dissolution? Is it conceivable that the prophet, or great social reformer, whose personality was powerful enough to initiate a movement the influence of which extends over many centuries, whose will possessed such spiritual force that no inducement could make it swerve a jot from its allegiance to Eternal Duty and Eternal Love, should break up and be chemically dissolved and dissipated at the stroke of an executioner's axe, or because a few nails are driven into its physical organ and vehicle?

Nor can I regard it as credible that the world's greatest thinkers, artists and poets, of many of whom the genius was only fully recognized after they had departed this life, should wholly vanish from the sphere of conscious being, and never become aware of the sincere homage of admiration and love which a grateful posterity delights to offer at their shrine. We read with joyfulness of spirit George Eliot's grand utterance:

of the body were in youth, and the inner man is renewed day by day as by an elixir of life for the effort age has to make. As we grow older, even as the *intellect* gets weaker and weaker, *spiritual things*—love, joy, peace, quietude, temperance—grow stronger! All the strength of the past lingers in our spiritual life as *spiritual power*."—From a newspaper report of a recent sermon by the Rev. Stopford Brooke.

IX. ETHICAL THEISM.

> "O may I join the choir invisible
> Of those immortal dead who live again
> In minds made better by their presence!"

but how certainly and suddenly would the mighty charm of these noble words fade away if for the "choir *invisible*" we were to read the "choir *unconscious*." Surely it is because, though invisible, they are felt to be still living with God, that the thought of them is so full of inspiration and of poetic power.

But in addition to man's intellectual and moral nature, there is our specially *spiritual* or religious nature (which lies at the deepest heart and core of our being); and the spiritual consciousness of communion with, and sympathy from, the immanent Eternal is with many persons the firmest basis for their faith in Immortality. The more the sense of personal relationship to God deepens, the more religion takes a strong and vital hold upon us, and we realize more fully our personal union with that Eternal Self, the Father within us, out of whose living presence arise all our aspirations for truth, all our ideals of perfection, all those yearnings of divine love which raise us above our finite selves, the more assured and confident we become that ideas of death and final separation are wholly inapplicable to this felt spiritual relationship with the eternal Cause and Ground of all existence. We feel with Jesus, "He is not the God of the dead, but of the living."[1]

---

[1] This instinctive faith, that Death cannot break the link of Love which unites the finite mind with the Universal Mind, is well expressed in the lines which Emerson, in his Essay on the *Over-soul*, quotes from Henry More, the thoughtful Platonist of the seventeenth century:

It is not merely or chiefly for his own individual satisfaction that man hopes for and believes in a Hereafter; it is not from egoistic motives that many noble souls cling with such tenacity to the idea of Immortality: it is rather because they feel that the Divinity which is immanent in their own consciousness would be baffled, confounded and disappointed, if this short life were all. All through the process of Evolution, Matter and Mechanism have appeared to be subservient to the advent of human self-consciousness—of a being of " wise discourse, looking before and after," and capable of ever-increasing participation in Divine Thought and Divine Love. Shall, then, this self-revelation of God in the human consciousness, to which all the earlier stages of biological development have slowly but surely led up, suddenly and irrationally break off just when the finite mind has awakened to a clear sense of its essential relationship to the Universal Mind, and is standing, with yearning gaze, on the threshold of the infinite possibilities and hopes which the felt immanence of the Eternal appears to at once disclose and guarantee? Shall the curtain of Death suddenly fall, and prematurely end for ever the opening drama of man's spiritual career, leaving it wholly incomprehensible why this gradual ascent in the scale of life, this emergence of capacities and affections which transcend all finitude, should abruptly terminate in this sorry

> "But souls that of his own good life partake,
> He loves as his own self; dear as his eye
> They are to him : he'll never them forsake :
> When they shall die, then God himself shall die;
> They live, they live in blest eternity."

fiasco, which leaves matter and mechanism after all the real masters of the situation,—the lords, and not, as heretofore, the servants of the spirit's higher life?

For myself, I cannot believe that Death will thus falsify the prophetic presentiments of the Intellect, the Conscience and the Heart, and I will bring my treatment of this subject to a close with the following sober and forcible words by Prof. J. Fiske which give clear expression to my own conclusion:

"The more thoroughly we comprehend that process of Evolution by which things have come to be what they are, the more we are likely to feel that to deny the everlasting persistence of the spiritual element in man is to rob the whole process of its meaning. It goes far towards putting us to permanent intellectual confusion, and I do not see that any one has as yet alleged, or is ever likely to allege, a sufficient reason for our accepting so dire an alternative. For my own part, therefore, I believe in the immortality of the soul, not in the sense in which I accept the demonstrable truths of science, but as a supreme act of faith in the reasonableness of God's work."[1]

The general result, then, to which the thoughts which I have sought to express in these Lectures lead, is this: that while our felt dependence on the Absolute, and the rational need of the eternal creative causality of the Absolute to explain, not only the existence of the infinite series of dynamic energies which make up the universe, but also their organic unity, compel the mind to a belief in the reality of One Self-existent Ground and Cause for the evolving universe, it is in the progressive discernment of the universal and authoritative ideals of

[1] *Man's Destiny*, p. 115.

truth, beauty and goodness, that the essential nature and character of the immanent God is revealed within us. We are differentiations of His Substance, and in the universal elements of our higher life His Being and our being are at one, for what is the Ideal in us is the eternally Real in Him. In our most exalted rational, ethical and spiritual experiences we immediately feel the presence, the sympathy, and the absolute worth and authority of the Divine and the Eternal.

The *raison d'être* of this eternal series of differentiations of God's substance appears to be, that, when the fitting stage of evolution is reached, rational spirits, who in their higher nature share His essential life, but as individuals have a delegated freedom of will, may of their own voluntary choice respond to the injunctions and invitations of the indwelling Eternal, and so enter into ever closer personal intimacy and co-operation with Him. Though in the lower stages of mechanical evolution the immanent energy of God compels the action of the monads of nature by what we call physical necessity, yet this mechanical character of the lowest forms of God's self-manifestation in the cosmos is simply the indispensable prior condition of a coming superstructure of rational and moral freedom. In the case of the self-conscious soul, the Eternal no longer wholly deals with it through necessity (either physical or psychical), but appeals to it, through its progressive Ideals, to throw in its lot with the essential being and aims of the Universal Spirit of the Cosmos. Hence arises a felt personal relationship between the dependent soul and the Father within it—a relationship based on the fact that man in his higher experiences attains some conscious apprehension of the Infinite, feels aspirations and affections which have nothing finite in their nature.

And so the faith inevitably tends to arise that God, who gives to man this moral freedom and this advancing insight into His Perfections, will open up for him an unlimited possibility of rising above the finite and the temporal, and of enjoying eternally in increasing measure that intimacy and sympathy with Himself to which man's life on earth is only the propædeutic stage. The infinite capacities and aspirations of man, as Fourrier said, predict his destiny; and we can well imagine that, in view of the highest good of conscious union with Himself, the Eternal has been willing to sacrifice to a large extent the lower good of unvaried personal ease and comfort, in order that through the indispensable path of trial, temptation, suffering and sorrow, man may at length, by his own voluntary choice and effort, attain to spiritual blessedness, to that harmonious inter-communion of the human and the Divine, which only the freely proffered Grace of God, and the free and persistent response of the human will can ultimately realize.

Permit me, in conclusion, to say a few words on that immediate consciousness of God which, in my view, is so important an element in religious faith. Believing, as I profoundly do, that all wholly satisfying and effective religious belief arises out of the immediate feeling of God's self-revealing presence in our consciousness, these Lectures will, in my view, have failed of their main purpose, if they have not had some slight flavour of that "Divine philosophy" which the poet Milton found so "charming"; that is, if they have not helped my hearers and myself to realize more vividly, and to believe in more unreservedly, that *ideal* side of our being in which God, as it were, lends a portion of His eternal life to us that we may by earnest thought and action make it at length our very own. If they have at all succeeded in rendering this "eternal" aspect of our higher thoughts and sentiments more truly real to us, I doubt not they will have conduced to a firmer belief in God and to a clearer insight into His character. If so, they will also have stimulated us to so use our moral freedom as to rise above the atmosphere of low personal desires and ambitions which clouds the spiritual insight of the soul, and to avoid of all things the hardening selfishness (the only real Devil and Hell in the cosmos) which incapacitates the finer fibres of our heart and mind for vibrating to the throbbing of that Eternal and Universal Love which is the life-pulse of the universe, whose unresisted influence in human souls makes the music of the world.

Spiritual Love is intuitively discerned to hold the highest place among the Ideals which testify to the immanence of the Eternal in the self-consciousness of man; and the bright and hopeful feature in modern civilization is the widespread practical recognition of the supreme divinity of this unifying sentiment which, in the view of the founder of Christianity, is synonymous with God. The power of this deep actuating principle is proving altogether too strong for the restraining bonds of religious Dogmatism, and is shattering all theological creeds which refuse to expand in accordance with its eternal and, therefore, authoritative claims. By many cultured persons at the present time this destruction of "orthodox" dogmas by the expansive force of broad humanitarian sympathies is supposed to involve the dissolution of Theistic faith, and the coming replacement of churches by schools of high art and by societies for ethical culture. But, unless I have in these Lectures gone altogether astray from the truth, this very recognition of the intrinsic supremacy of Love among the springs of human action, so far from being indicative of the disintegration and decay of Ethical Theism, is simply the outward sign that the living spirit of religious faith is liberating itself from the outworn formulas which now so often cramp and stifle its free expression. The theology which is based on external and miraculously-attested Revelation has reached an apologetic and tottering stage, and its downfall is evidently drawing near; but in its place is uprising a theology sublime and beautiful—a theology which rests upon the indestructible foundations of the felt immanence of the Eternal God in man's purest and noblest ideals, and on the consciousness of sympathetic response from the indwelling Father to all aspirations and efforts through which man seeks to realize in character and conduct that implicit divinity which at once links man to God and all men to each other in closest brotherhood.

To this Theistic faith of the future the present fruitful study of the great religions of the world is richly contributing; for as accurate scholarship and philosophic acumen penetrates to the central formative principles of each of these influential religions, this principle is found

IX. ETHICAL THEISM. 361

to spring from true spiritual insight in some deeply religious soul. These faiths, it is beginning to be clearly seen, derive their life and power from the recognizing and emphasizing of some important aspect of the self-revelation of the Eternal in the rational, ethical and spiritual self-consciousness of man;[1] and if the Theism

[1] In illustration of this truth, it is very interesting and significant to have the testimony of one of the most cultured and religious minds among the Hindoos, viz. of Mr. Protap Chunder Mozoomdar, the present leader of the Brahmo-Somaj or universal-religion movement in India, who, in the course of his Farewell Address, given on Dec. 5th, 1893, in the Arlington Street Church, Boston, U.S.A., on his way home from the Parliament of Religions in Chicago, says: "I maintain that this simple religion which I have tried to lay before you has the power of absorbing to itself all the resources of all the great religions. Believing in nothing more complex than that God is and that he is good, that he is near and that he is loving; believing in nothing more complex than that you are my sisters, my brothers, and my friends,—I have the spiritual wealth of all the great religions that ever flourished. What is there in the enthusiasm and energy of Islam that I cannot accept? What ails my liberal religion that I cannot assimilate that energy, that fidelity, that monotheistic influence, that obedience to the laws of God? What ails me that I cannot assimilate the marvellous benevolence of Buddhism,—its self-conquest, its kindness to man and beast alike, its tolerance, its equality of men and women, its poverty and simplicity? What is the matter with my simple theistic principles that I cannot absorb the wonderful insight of the Hindu into the spiritual constitution of the universe? Why should I not learn from him that introspection by which in his own soul he beholds the glorious manifestation of his supreme Brahma? Why should not I learn from him the law of self-renunciation, of absolute self-forgetfulness, and his devotion in life and death to the search for the glorious purposes of God and the carrying of them out? Why should I not sing the swelling Psalms of David, which have reverberated for so many centuries? And when we think of Christ and his beloved Father, is there anything that can keep me back from the love of Jesus, the Son of Man?.... All the treasures of all scriptures that teach the dealings of God are mine."

associated with the name of Jesus of Nazareth is destined, as I believe it is, to be the cosmopolitan faith in which all religious souls will finally concur, this will be for no other reason than that the profound ethical and spiritual experience of Jesus revealed to him that the essence of the indwelling Eternal, and, therefore, the highest ideal that man can seek to realize, is sympathetic, self-sacrificing Love.

And what makes the faith of Jesus, not simply a philosophical theory, but a soul-satisfying religion, is that this supreme immanent principle of Love is with him no merely abstract quality in which all good spirits share, but is a living concrete reality whose actuating presence in the soul carries with it a sense of personal relationship between the human spirit and the Eternal of so real and intimate a character, that the intimacy of finite souls with each other is but the finite reflex and image of this fundamental divine experience. It is, indeed, a truth which every deeply-feeling and deeply-thinking mind cannot fail to recognize, that no human love is of the truly spiritual and eternal sort if it does not contain, as an integral factor, the sense of a still deeper relationship to the Eternal Self, or, as Jesus expresses it, to the Father within us. As the poet Lovelace says, in the graceful love-song from which I have before quoted, he could not love his sweetheart so much "loved he not honour more," so all true friends feel, with more or less vividness, that their friendship would lack its most essential element, did it not involve a sense of deeper personal intimacy on the part of each with the Absolute Reality, the Eternal Friend.

IX. ETHICAL THEISM.

We experience the feeling of this Divine Presence at the very heart of our profoundest philosophic thinking, in each act of resolute devotion to moral principle, and with special intensity in every act of self-surrender to the promptings of Humanity and Love. If this Absolute Presence which meets us face to face in the most momentous of our life's experiences, which pours into our fainting wills the elixir of new life and strength, and into our wounded hearts the balm of a quite infinite sympathy, cannot fitly be called a Personal Presence, it is only because this word *personal* is too poor, and carries with it associations too human and too limited, to adequately express this profound God-consciousness. But we cannot spare the word "personal" in this connection, for we have no higher term; and if we part with it, our description must needs sink to a lower level. And as I have before endeavoured to show, it is quite possible to retain all the essential and positive elements which this word connotes apart from those negative and limiting features which necessarily appertain to our finite experiences, and thus to discern in the highest forms of human personality a true, though not exhaustive, revelation of the nature of the Perfect Personality of God.[1]

[1] In the Address by Mr. Mozoomdar from which I have quoted above, there occurs the following striking utterance on this relation between the prophet's personality and the personality of God: "The personality of God, without which spiritual religion is impossible, is a truth which is revealed by human personality. The personality of man is a unique thing, and that alone enables us to reach the higher Personality from which these little units that we are have come. Human personality unfolds the great personality of God. .... What would Christianity be without the central personality of Christ, and

From this point of view, Religion and Ethics are, as we saw in the Seventh Lecture, most intimately associated; and ethical endeavour loses, I believe, a most important source of its own vitality if it dissociates itself from that sense of personal relationship to, and co-operation with, the Soul of souls, which dissipates pessimistic gloom, and kindles in the heart of the social reformer an immortal trust and hope which no frowns of society, and no failures and disappointments, can wholly quench.[1]

the great apostles who worked out his wonderful teachings? It is these Godlike men, these incarnations of God, these embodiments of the Divine Personality, that have made religion to me a personal matter. Our sorrows are so real, our sufferings are so pressing, that we hasten to some personality where there is sympathy, where there is love for distress, blessing for misery, comfort for pain, and healing for disease; and these personalities, when they are godly, work in the name of the Supreme Person whose servants and whose representatives they are."

[1] I have given further reasons for this conclusion in an Address delivered at the opening of the Session of Manchester New College, October, 1892, on the question, "Are Ethics and Theology vitally connected?"

14, HENRIETTA STREET, COVENT GARDEN, LONDON;
20, SOUTH FREDERICK STREET, EDINBURGH.

CATALOGUE OF SOME WORKS

PUBLISHED BY

WILLIAMS & NORGATE.

Abbotsford Series of the Scottish Poets. Edited by GEORGE EYRE-TODD. I. Early Scottish Poetry; II. Mediæval Scottish Poetry; III. Scottish Poetry of the Sixteenth Century. Price of each part, 3s. 6d.; fine paper, 5s. nett. IV. Scottish Ballad Poetry. Price 5s.; fine paper, 7s. 6d. nett.

Ainsworth (Rev. W. M.) Memorial of. With Portrait. Crown 8vo, cloth. 6s.

Barrow (E. P., M.A.) Regni Evangelium. A Survey of the Teaching of Jesus Christ. Crown 8vo, cloth. 6s.

Baur (F. C.) Church History of the First Three Centuries. Translated from the Third German Edition. Edited by Rev. ALLAN MENZIES. 2 vols. 8vo, cloth. 21s.

Baur (F. C.) Paul, the Apostle of Jesus Christ, his Life and Work, his Epistles and Doctrine. A Contribution to a Critical History of Primitive Christianity. By Rev. A. MENZIES. Second Edition. 2 vols. 8vo, cloth. 21s.

Beard (Rev. Dr. C.) The Universal Christ, and other Sermons. Crown 8vo, cloth. 7s. 6d.

Beard (Rev. Dr. C.) Lectures on the Reformation of the Sixteenth Century in its Relation to Modern Thought and Knowledge. (Hibbert Lectures, 1883.) 8vo, cloth. (Cheap Edition, 4s. 6d.) 10s. 6d.

Beard (Rev. Dr. C.) Port Royal, a Contribution to the History of Religion and Literature in France. Cheaper Edition. 2 vols. Crown 8vo, cloth. 12s.

Bleek (F.) Lectures on the Apocalypse. Translated. Edited by the Rev. Dr. S. DAVIDSON. 8vo, cloth. 10s. 6d.

Booth (C.) Life and Labour of the People. Vol. I. The East End of London. Third Edition. 8vo, cloth. 10s. 6d.
—— —— Vol. II. London (continued), &c. With Appendix of coloured Maps. In 2 vols. 8vo, cloth. 21s.

2000/3/94/N.

Castorius' Map of the World, generally known as Peutinger's Tabula. Printed in colours, after the original in the Imperial Library, Vienna. 5s.

Cleland, Mackay, Young (Professors) Memoirs and Memoranda of Anatomy. Vol. I. 16 Plates. 8vo, cloth. 7s. 6d.

Collins (F. H.) An Epitome of the Synthetic Philosophy. With a Preface by HERBERT SPENCER. 8vo, cloth. 15s.

Conway (Moncure D.) Centenary History of the South Place Ethical Society. With numerous Portraits, a Facsimile of the Original Autograph MS. of the well-known Hymn, "Nearer, my God, to Thee," and Appendix containing an Original Poem by Mrs. ADAMS (1836), and an Address by WILLIAM JOHNSON FOX (1842). Crown 8vo, half vellum, paper sides. 5s.

Davids (T. W. Rhys) Lectures on some Points in the History of Indian Buddhism. (Hibbert Lectures, 1881.) Second Edition. 8vo, cloth. 10s. 6d.

Delitzsch (Professor F.) Assyrian Grammar, with Paradigms, Exercises, Glossary, and Bibliography, Translated by the Ven. Archdeacon R. S. KENNEDY. Crown 8vo, cloth. 15s.

Delitzsch (Professor F.) The Hebrew Language viewed in the light of Assyrian Research. Crown 8vo, cloth. 4s.

Drummond (Dr.) Philo Judæus; or, the Jewish Alexandrian Philosophy in its Development and Completion. By JAMES DRUMMOND, LL.D., Principal of Manchester College, Oxford. 2 vols. 8vo, cloth. 21s.

Enoch, The Book of, the Prophet. Translated from an Ethiopic MS. in the Bodleian Library, by the late RICHARD LAURENCE, LL.D., Archbishop of Cashel. The Text corrected from his latest Notes by CHARLES GILL. Re-issue, 8vo, cloth. 5s.

Erman's Egyptian Grammar, Translated under Professor Erman's supervision, by J. H. BREASTED, Professor of Egyptology in the University of Chicago. Crown 8vo, cloth. 18s.

Ewald's (Dr. H.) Commentary on the Prophets of the Old Testament. Translated by the Rev. J. F. SMITH. 5 vols. 8vo, cloth. Each 10s. 6d.

Ewald's (Dr. H.) Commentary on the Psalms. Translated by the Rev. E. JOHNSON, M.A. 2 vols. 8vo, cloth. Each 10s. 6d.

Ewald's (Dr. H.) Commentary on the Book of Job, with Translation. Translated from the German by the Rev. J. FREDERICK SMITH. 8vo, cloth. 10s. 6d.

Frankfurter (Dr. O.) Handbook of Pali ; being an Elementary
Grammar, a Chrestomathy, and a Glossary. 8vo, cloth. 16s.

Gould (Rev. S. Baring) Lost and Hostile Gospels. An Account
of the Toledoth Jesher, two Hebrew Gospels circulating in the Middle
Ages, and Extant Fragments of the Gospels of the first Three Centuries
of Petrine and Pauline Origin. Crown 8vo, cloth. 7s. 6d.

Harnack (Axel) Introduction to the Elements of the Differential
and Integral Calculus. From the German. Royal 8vo, cloth. 10s. 6d.

Hatch (Rev. Dr.) Lectures on the Influence of Greek Ideas and
Usages upon the Christian Church. Edited by Dr.FAIRBAIRN. (Hibbert
Lectures), 1888.) 8vo, cloth. 10s· 6d.

Hausrath (Prof. A.) History of the New Testament Times. The
Time of Jesus. Translated by the Revs. C. T. POYNTING and P. QUENZER.
2 vols. 8vo, cloth. 21s.

Hausrath (Prof. A.) History of the New Testament Times. The
Time of the Apostles. Translated by LEONARD HUXLEY. 2 vols. 8vo,
cloth. 21s.

Hemans (Chas. I.) Historic and Monumental Rome. A Handbook for the Students of Classical and Christian Antiquities in the Italian
Capital. Crown 8vo, cloth. 10s. 6d.

Hemans (Chas. I.) History of Mediæval Christianity and Sacred
Art in Italy (A.D. 900—1600). 2 vols. Crown 8vo, cloth. 18s.

Hiller (H. Croft) Against Dogma and Freewill, and for Weismannism. Second and greatly enlarged edition. Containing, *inter alia*,
beyond the Original Text, a Concise Statement of Weismann's Theory, a
Controversy on its Application to Sociology, and an Examination of the
Recent Criticism of Professor Romanes. Demy 8vo, cloth. 7s. 6d.

Keim's History of Jesus of Nazara. Considered in its connection
with the National Life of Israel, and related in detail. Translated from
the German by ARTHUR RANSOM. Complete in 6 vols. demy 8vo.
Each 10s. 6d. (or 6 vols. for 42s nett.)

Kennedy (Rev. Jas.) Introduction to Biblical Hebrew. 8vo, cloth.
12s.

Kiepert's New Atlas Antiquus. Twelve Maps of the Ancient
World, for Schools and Colleges. Eleventh Edition, with a complete Geographical Index. Folio, boards. 6s.

King (John H.) The Supernatural: its Origin, Nature and Evolution. 2 vols. demy 8vo, cloth. 15s.

King (John H.) Man an Organic Community; being an Exposition of the Law that the Human Personality in all its Phases in Evolution,
both Co-ordinate and Discordinate, is the Multiple of many Sub-personalities. 2 vols. demy 8vo, cloth. 15s.

The King and the Kingdom: a Study of the Four Gospels. Three Series, each complete in itself; with copious Indexes. Medium 8vo. Each 3s. 6d.

Kuenen (Dr. A.) The Religion of Israel to the Fall of the Jewish State. Translated from the Dutch by A. H. MAY. 3 vols. 8vo, cloth. 31s. 6d.

Kuenen (Dr. A.) Lectures on National Religions and Universal Religions. (The Hibbert Lectures, 1882.) 8vo, cloth. 10s. 6d.

Kuhne (Louis) The New Science of Healing, or the Doctrine of the Oneness of all Diseases. Forming the basis of a Uniform Method of Cure without Medicines and without Operations. Translated from the third greatly augmented German edition by Dr. TH. BAKER. 8vo, cloth. 7s.

Laurie (Professor Simon) Ethica: or the Ethics of Reason. By Scotus Novanticus. 2nd Edition. 8vo, cloth. 6s.

Laurie (Professor Simon) Metaphysica Nova et Vetusta: a Return to Dualism. 2nd Edition. Crown 8vo, cloth. 6s.

Lloyd (Walter) The Galilean: a Portrait of Jesus of Nazareth. Crown 8vo, cloth. 2s. 6d.

Lubbock (Sir John, F.R.S.) Pre-historic Times, as illustrated by Ancient Remains and the Manners and Customs of Modern Savages. With Wood-cut Illustrations and Plates. 5th Edition. 8vo, cloth. 18s.

Lyall (C. J., M.A., C.I.E.) Ancient Arabian Poetry, chiefly pre-Islamic; Translations, with an Introduction and Notes. Foolscap 4to, cloth. 10s. 6d.

Macan (R. W.) The Resurrection of Jesus Christ. An essay in three Chapters. 8vo, cloth. 5s.

Malan (Rev. Dr. S. C.) Original Notes on the Book of Proverbs. Mostly from Eastern sources. Vol. I. chap. i. to x., Vol. II. chap. xi. to xx., Vol. III. Chap. xxi. to xxxi. Each vol. demy 8vo, cloth. 12s.

Mind, a Quarterly Review of Psychology and Philosophy. Nos. 1—64. 1876-90. 8vo, each 3s. Vols. II.—XVI. in cloth. Each 13s.
—— New Series, Vols. I. and II. Each 13s.
—— Annual Subscription, post free. 12s.

Montefiore (C. G.) Origin and Growth of Religion as illustrated by the Religion of the Ancient Hebrews. (The Hibbert Lectures, 1892.) 2nd Edition. 8vo, cloth. 10s. 6d.

Müller (Professor Max) Lectures on the Origin and Growth of Religion, as illustrated by the Religions of India. (The Hibbert Lectures, 1878.) 8vo, cloth. 10s. 6d.

Nestle. Syriac Grammar. Bibliography, Chrestomathy and
Glossary. Translated by the Ven. Archdeacon R. S. KENNEDY, Professor
of Oriental Languages in the University of Aberdeen. Crown 8vo,
cloth. 9s.

O'Curry (Eug.) Lectures on the Social Life, Manners and
Civilization of the People of Ancient Erinn. Edited, with an Introduction,
by Dr. W. K. SULLIVAN. Numerous Wood Engravings of Arms,
Ornaments, &c. 3 vols. 8vo, cloth. 30s.

O'Grady (Standish H.) Silva Gadelica (I.—XXXI). A Collection
of Tales in Irish, with Extracts illustrating Persons and Places. Edited
from MSS. and translated. 2 vols. Royal 8vo, cloth. 42s.
—— Or separately, Vol. I., Irish Text; and Vol. II., Translation and Notes.
Each vol. 21s.

Oldenberg (Prof. H.) Buddha: his Life, his Doctrine, his Order.
By Dr. HERMANN OLDENBERG, Professor at the University of Berlin.
Translated by W. HOEY, M.A. 8vo, cloth gilt. 18s.

Pfleiderer (O.) Paulinism : a Contribution to the History of
Primitive Christian Theology. Translated by E. PETERS. Second
Edition. 2 vols. 8vo, cloth. 21s.

Pfleiderer (O.) Philosophy of Religion on the Basis of its History.
Vols. I. II. History of the Philosophy of Religion from Spinoza to the
Present Day; Vols. III. IV. Genetic-Speculative Philosophy of Religion.)
Translated by Professor ALAN MENZIES and the Rev. ALEX. STEWART.
Complete in 4 vols. 8vo, cloth. Each 10s. 6d.

Pfleiderer (O.) Lectures on the Influence of the Apostle Paul on
the Development of Christianity. Translated by the Rev. J. FREDERICK
SMITH. (Hibbert Lectures, 1885.) 8vo, cloth. 10s. 6d.

Poole (Reg. Lane) Illustrations of the History of Mediæval
Thought, in the Departments of Theology and Ecclesiastical Politics.
8vo, cloth. 10s. 6d.

Pratt (Dr. H.) Principia Nova Astronomica. With 37 full-page
plates. Crown 4to, cloth gilt. 10s. 6d.

Protestant Commentary on the New Testament; with general
and special Introductions. Edited by Professor P. W. SCHMIDT and F.
VON HOLZENDORFF. Translated from the third German Edition by the
Rev. F. H. JONES, B.A. 3 vols. 8vo, cloth. Each 10s. 6d.

Renan (E.) On the Influence of the Institutions, Thought and
Culture of Rome on Christianity and the Development of the Catholic
Church. Translated by the Rev. CHARLES BEARD. (Hibbert Lectures,
1880.) 8vo, cloth. (Cheap Edition, 2s. 6d.) 10s. 6d.

Renouf (P. le Page) On the Religion of Ancient Egypt. (Hibbert Lectures, 1879.) Second Edition. 8vo, cloth. 10s. 6d.

Reville (Dr. A.) Prolegomena of the History of Religions. With an Introduction by Professor F. MAX MÜLLER. 8vo, cloth. 10s. 6d.

Reville (Dr. A.) On the Native Religions of Mexico and Peru. Translated by the Rev. P. H. WICKSTEED. (Hibbert Lectures, 1884.) 8vo, cloth. 10s. 6d.

Rhys (Prof. J.) On the Origin and Growth of Religion as illustrated by Celtic Heathendom. (Hibbert Lectures, 1886.) 8vo, cloth. 10s. 6d.

Sayce (Prof. A. H.) On the Religion of Ancient Assyria and Babylonia. Third Edition. (Hibbert Lectures, 1887.) 8vo, cloth. 10s. 6d.

Schloss (D. F.) Methods of Industrial Remuneration. Second Edition. 8vo, cloth. 10s. 6d.

Schmidt (A.) Shakespeare Lexicon. A Complete Dictionary of all the English Words, Phrases, and Constructions in the Works of the Poet. Second Edition. 2 vols. Imperial 8vo, 28s.; cloth. 31s. 6d.

Schrader (Professor E.) The Cuneiform Inscriptions and the Old Testament. Translated from the second Enlarged Edition, with Additions by the Author, and an Introduction by the Rev. OWEN C. WHITEHOUSE, M.A. 2 vols. With a Map. 8vo, cloth. Each 10s. 6d.

Schurman (J. Gould) Kantian Ethics and the Ethics of Evolution. 1882. 8vo, cloth. 5s.

Schurman (J. Gould) The Ethical Import of Darwinism. Crown 8vo, cloth. 5s.

Sharpe (Samuel) The Bible, translated by SAMUEL SHARPE, being a Revision of the Authorized English Version. 6th Edition of the Old, 10th Edition of the New Testament. 8vo, roan. 5s.

Sharpe (Samuel) The New Testament. Translated from Griesbach's Text by S. SHARPE, Author of "The History of Egypt." 14th Thousand. Fcap. 8vo, cloth. 1s. 6d.

Socin (A.) Arabic Grammar. Paradigms, Literature, Chrestomathy, and Glossary. Crown 8vo, cloth. 7s. 6d.

Spencer (Herbert) Works. The Doctrine of Evolution. 8vo, cloth,
First Principles. 16s.
Principles of Biology. 2 vols. 34s.
Principles of Psychology. 2 vols. 36s.
Principles of Sociology. Vol. I. 21s.
—— Vol. II. 18s.
Ecclesiastical Institutions. 5s.

Spencer (Herbert) Works—*continued.*
Principles of Ethics. Vol. I.   15s.
——— Vol. II.   12s. 6d.
The Data of Ethics. (Separately.)   8s.
Justice. (Separately.)   8s.
The Study of Sociology.   10s. 6d.
Education.   6s.
——— Cheap Edition.   2s. 6d.
Essays. 3 vols.   30s. (or each vol. 10s.)
Social Statics and Man v. State.   10s.
Man v. State. (Separately, sewed.)   1s.

——— Collins (F. H.) An Epitome of the Synthetic Philosophy. By F. HOWARD COLLINS. With a Preface by HERBERT SPENCER. 8vo, cloth.   15s.

Spencer (W. G.) Inventional Geometry. With a Preface by HERBERT SPENCER. 8vo, cloth.   1s.

Spencer (W. G.) A System of Lucid Shorthand. Devised by WILLIAM GEORGE SPENCER. With a Prefatory Note by HERBERT SPENCER. 8vo, cloth.   1s.

Spinoza. Four Essays by Professors LAND, VAN VLOTEN, KUNO FISCHER, and by E. RENAN. Edited by Professor KNIGHT, of St. Andrews. Crown 8vo, cloth.   5s.

Stokes (G. J.) The Objectivity of Truth. 8vo, cloth.   5s.

Strack (H. L.) Hebrew Grammar. Paradigms, Literature, Chrestomathy, and Glossary. Crown 8vo, cloth.   4s. 6d.

Strauss (Dr. D. F.) Life of Jesus; for the People. The Authorized English Edition. 2 vols. 8vo, cloth.   10s. 6d.

Waldstein (C.) Excavations of the American School of Athens at the Heraion of Argos. To be completed in about 4 Parts. Part 1, 20 pp. and 7 Plates. 4to, sewed.   12s.

Weizsaecker (C.) The Apostolic Age. Translated by JAMES MILLAR, B.D. 2 vols. demy 8vo, cloth.   21s.

Wright (Rev. J.) Grounds and Principles of Religion. Crown 8vo, cloth.   3s.

Zeller (Dr. E.) The Contents and Origin of the Acts of the Apostles critically investigated. Preceded by Dr. Fr. Overbeck's Introduction to the Acts of the Apostles from De Wette's Handbook. Translated by JOSEPH DARE. 2 vols. 8vo, cloth.   21s.

Ziegler (Th.) Social Ethics. Outlines of a Doctrine of Morals. Translated from the German. Crown 8vo, cloth.   3s.

Theological Translation Fund. A Series of Translations by which the best results of recent Theological investigations on the Continent, conducted without reference to doctrinal considerations, and with the sole purpose of arriving at truth, are placed within reach of English Readers.

Demy 8vo, cloth. 10s 6d *per vol.*

** A selection of six or more vols. at 7s. nett per vol., instead of 10s. 6d.

1. Baur. Church History of the First three Centuries. 2 vols.
2. Baur. Paul, the Apostle of Jesus Christ, his Life and Work. 2 vols.
3. Bleek. Lectures on the Apocalypse. 1 vol.
4. Ewald. Commentary on the Prophets of the Old Testament. 5 vols.
5. Ewald. Commentary on the Psalms. 2 vols.
6. Ewald. Commentary on the Book of Job, with Translation. 1 vol.
7. Hausrath. History of the New Testament Times. The Time of Jesus. 2 vols.
8. Keim. History of Jesus of Nazara. 6 vols.
9. Kuenen. The Religion of Israel to the Fall of the Jewish State. 3 vols.
10. Pfleiderer. The Philosophy of Religion on the Basis of its History. 4 vols.
11. Pfleiderer. Paulinism. 2 vols.
12. Protestant Commentary on the New Testament. 3 vols.
13. Reville. Prolegomena of the History of Religion. 1 vol.
14. Schrader. The Cuneiform Inscriptions and the Old Testament. 2 vols.
15. Zeller (E.) The Acts of the Apostles Critically Examined. 2 vols.

Theological Translation Library. New Series. Edited by the Rev. T. K. CHEYNE, M.A., D.D., Oriel Professor of Interpretation in the University of Oxford, and Canon of Rochester; and the Rev. A. B. BRUCE, D.D., Professor of Apologetics, Free Church College, Glasgow.

Weizsaecker (C.) The Apostolic Age. Translated by the Rev. JAMES MILLAR, B.D. 2 vols. demy 8vo. cloth. 21s.

Harnack (A.) Dogmengeschichte. New Edition. Translated by the Rev. NEILL BUCHANAN. [In preparation.]

Kittel (R.) Geschichte der Hebräer. Translated by the Rev. J. TAYLOR, D.D. [In preparation.]

WILLIAMS AND NORGATE,

14, HENRIETTA STREET, COVENT GARDEN, LONDON; AND
20, SOUTH FREDERICK STREET, EDINBURGH.

www.ingramcontent.com/pod-product-compliance
Lightning Source LLC
Chambersburg PA
CBHW030357230426
43664CB00007BB/625